Rational fears

Rational fears

American horror in the 1950s

Mark Jancovich

Manchester University Press

Manchester and New York

distributed exclusively in the USA and Canada by St. Martin's Press

Copyright © Mark Jancovich 1996

Published by Manchester University Press
Oxford Road, Manchester M13 9NR, UK
and Room 400, 175 Fifth Avenue, New York, NY10010, USA

Distributed exclusively in the USA and Canada
by St. Martin's Press, Inc., 175 Fifth Avenue, New York, NY 10010, USA

British Library Cataloguing-in-Publication Data
A catalogue record for this book is available from the British Library

Library of Congress Cataloging-in-Publication Data
Jancovich, Mark.
  Rational fears : American horror in the 1950s / Mark Jancovich.
    p.   cm.
  Includes bibliographical references.
  ISBN 0–7190–3623–2 (hardback). — ISBN 0–7190–3624–0 (pbk.)
  1. Horror films—History and criticism.   I. Title.
PN1995.9.H6J37   1996
791.43'616—dc20   95–26494
                                                                            CIP

ISBN 0 7190 3623 2 *hardback*
     0 7190 3624 0 *paperback*

First published 1996

00 99 98 97 96   10 9 8 7 6 5 4 3 2 1

Typeset in Great Britain
by Northern Phototypesetting Co Ltd, Bolton

Printed in Great Britain
by Bell & Bain Ltd, Glasgow

Contents

Illustrations

Preface

W hen I began this book, I intended to write a study of American horror from the 1950s to the present. The material on the 1950s itself was only meant to provide an introduction to later developments. However, as I began writing, I realised that the material on the 1950s was not merely an introduction, but a book in itself. While most critics have written it off as trashy and sensationalist, I soon realised that it was these very features which made 1950s horror such a rich and fascinating field.

However, assumptions about the nature of 1950s horror are central to discussions of horror. While most studies of horror ignore any detailed analysis of the 1950s in favour of other, more legitimate, periods – the silent, expressionist classics, the 1930s productions of Universal pictures, the films of Val Lewton, Hammer horror, and, more recently, contemporary horror – in most of these accounts, 1950s horror is central as a way of legitimating these other periods. The 1950s, it is assumed, constitutes a period of conservatism within horror, whether this conservatism is conceived of in aesthetic or political terms, and critics usually establish their own areas as worthy of study by defining them as different from the horror of the 1950s.

For example, Robin Wood has claimed that the horror film's radical potential lies in the fact that 'the true subject of the horror genre is the struggle for recognition of all that our civilization represses or oppresses'.[1] The monster is therefore seen as a profoundly ambiguous figure which challenges social norms and so reveals society's repressive monstrosity. 1950s horror films, however, are generally dismissed by Wood, or excluded from this general, radical tendency. The horror film, it is suggested, realised its radical potential in other periods, but the 1950s films represent the genre's 'reactionary wing', a wing that is also resurrected in the 1980s through the Reaganite attempt to reverse the liberalism of the 1960s and 1970s and return to the values of 1950s America. As Wood puts it, one of the ke_____ wing is the

presen. ation of the monster as totally nonhuman. The progressive-
ness of the horror film depends partly on the monster's capacity to
arouse sympathy; one can feel little for a mass of viscous black slime.
The political (McCarthyite) level of 50s science fiction films – the
myth of Communism as total dehumanization – accounts for the
prevalence of this kind of monster in that period.[2]

In short, Wood dismisses the 1950s as an essentially reactionary
period in horror.

One of the problems in this account is the concentration on the
1950s invasion narratives as representative of American horror in
the period. Not only does this concentration exclude a great many
films which simply do not fit with this subgenre, but an examination of the 1950s invasion narratives within the context of these
other films (to say nothing of the forms of horror found in the literature and comics of the period) can radically change one's understanding of the 1950s invasion narratives themselves.

Indeed, like many other critics, Wood's references to 1950s
horror tends to revolve around a very limited group of texts (usually *The Thing from Another World*, *Them*, and *Invasion of the Body
Snatchers*), and it is often assumed that other films are merely inferior copies of these 'originals'. However, far from being 'all the
same', even the 1950s invasion narratives are often markedly different from one another. They may share particular patterns and
features, but they deploy them in very different ways.

Indeed, if there is a common feature to the majority of horror
texts within the 1950s, it is not a conservative, Cold War politics,
but rather a shift in emphasis away from a reliance upon gothic
horror and towards a preoccupation with the modern world. Again
and again, the threats which distinguish 1950s horror do not come
from the past or even from the actions of a lone individual, but are
associated with the processes of social development and modernisation. In this period, it is the process of rationalisation which is the
threat, and in this way, horror texts were at least as concerned with
developments within American society as they were with threats
from without.

Here rationalisation is understood as the process through which
scientific-technical rationality is applied to the management of
social, economic and cultural life, a process in which rational pro-

cedures are used to examine and reorganise social, economic and cultural practices in an attempt to produce order and efficiency. However, as will be illustrated in the first part of this book, this process caused considerable anxieties within the 1950s and provoked considerable debate. This system relied on the authority of an elite of experts whose task it was to govern social, economic and cultural activities, and this new system of organisation was seen by many as an inherently totalitarian system which both created conformity and repressed dissent.

As a means of examining these preoccupations within 1950s horror, I have divided this book into three parts which will discuss different, but overlapping, areas of horror within the period: the 1950s invasion narratives; the outsider narratives; and the narratives concerned with 'crises of identity'.

The first part sets out the major debates over the 1950s invasion narratives. It not only examines the claims that they are conservative, Cold War narratives, but also their awkward status as horror/science fiction hybrids. In the process, it is argued that the taken for granted assumptions about these texts need to be challenged, and that these texts can be seen as complex responses to the condition of post-war America, responses which were at least as concerned with internal changes within American life as they were with fears of Soviet aggression. However, it will be argued that these general features are dealt with in very different ways within individual texts and the section will also examine both the various subgroupings within this subgenre, and the ways in which it developed from 1951 to the late 1950s.

The next part will then concern the outsider narratives of the 1950s. In these texts, the outsider is not presented negatively, but is rather presented as an alternative to existing norms. In the fiction of Ray Bradbury and Richard Matheson, the films of Jack Arnold, and many of the films produced by AIP and its rivals, there is a recurring preoccupation with alienation, isolation and estrangement. In these texts, it is the norms of American life which become strange and alien, while the outsiders are presented as victims who are as much threatened by these norms as they are threatening to them. In this way, these texts examine the dilemmas of those who are unable or unwilling to 'fit in' and so challenges the notions of 'normality' associated with the 1950s.

Finally, the last section examines the claims about generic changes in the late 1950s, especially the supposed transformation of the genre after the release of Hitchcock's *Psycho*. Rather than seeing this moment as a break from the concerns of the 1950s, this part not only traces the numerous texts which prefigured *Psycho* from the late 1940s onwards, but also argues that these texts are less concerned with the American nuclear family than they are with a 'crisis of identity' within the period, a crisis which is attributed to the process of rationalisation. It is argued that while many 1950s invasion narratives and outsider narratives opposed 'rationality' and saw the 'irrational' features of emotion, intuition and spontaneity as potential sites of opposition to rationalisation, there was a growing concern that rationality was increasingly organising and controlling the 'irrational' (or the unconscious), particularly through techniques such as advertising. As a result, this tendency caused considerable anxiety because it seemed to remove any sense of a stable and reliable point of resistance to rationality. Unable to rely on either rational thought or irrational feelings, there seemed to be no way of confidently resisting the powers of rationalisation.

In the process, it will be argued that post-1960s horror should not be seen as the product of a break from 1950s horror, but simply as a development from its central features and concerns. Indeed, the 1950s needs to be understood not as a static period, but as a process during which the central features of post-1960s horror developed and established themselves.

This situation also helps to account for the fact that many 1950s horror texts have not only acquired the status of classics for horror fans, but have also been so important to contemporary popular culture. 1950s horror not only lives on as vital points of reference within popular culture, but many of the key practitioners of contemporary horror (and indeed popular culture in general) often refer to 1950s horror texts as the most significant and formative texts within their appreciation of horror in particular, and popular culture in general.

Indeed, not only have many of the 1950s horror films been remade in the 'New' Hollywood, the 'New' Hollywood itself can be seen as a development of tendencies which were established in the 1950s. The 1950s horror texts were often made as a result of changes within the nature of both the industry and the audience in the years after the Supreme Court decision of 1948. This decision forced the studios to sell off their theatres and so enabled the growth of independent producers such as AIP. However, the success of independents such as AIP also depended on the emergence of specialist audiences – in AIP's case, it was teenage audiences which proved significant. As a result, as has often been pointed out, the products of the 'New' Hollywood often look like examples of the 1950s exploitation cinema (of which horror was a vital and central component).

As a result, this reappraisal of 1950s horror is not only intended as a re-examination of 1950s popular culture and its relation to contemporary popular culture, but also a reappraisal of the 1950s as a period and its relationship to subsequent periods of American history.

Many people have helped in the writing of this book. Many ideas were developed or refined through class discussions with students. Without their comments and contributions, this book could not have been written. I am also indebted to many others who have offered ideas and support over the years. Most particularly I would like to thank the following for their enthusiasm and encouragement: Martin Barker, Steve Cohan, Ian Conrich, Ina Rae Hark, Kevin Hetherington, Peter Hutchings, Henry Jenkins, Adam Knee, Peter Kramer, Frank Krutnik, Anna Powell, Eric Schaefer, Lisa Taylor, Duncan Webster and Andy Willis. However, the one person who has really had to put up with the worst job of all is Joanne Hollows. She has not only read most of this book in its various stages and given me the most vital and detailed responses – few people could want a better editor – she has also had to put up with me wittering on about books, movies and critics when she has certainly had much better things to do herself. She has none the less remained a source of continual inspiration and encouragement without whom many of the best ideas in this book would never have been developed. It is for all these reasons, and for many more, that this book is dedicated to her.

Notes

1 Robin Wood, *Hollywood from Vietnam to Reagan* (New York: Columbia University Press, 1986), p. 75.
2 *Ibid.*, p. 192.

Part one

Creatures from beyond: rationalisation and resistance in the invasion narratives

Friend or foe: 'Out of space ... a warning and an ultimatum' in *The Day the Earth Stood Still* (1951).

Chapter 1

Alien forms:
horror and science fiction
in the 1950s

Problems in genre criticism

One of the central problems with genre criticism has been the tendency to view genres as coherent and hermetically sealed objects. Indeed, in film studies, the initial impetus behind genre criticism was an attempt to view genres as 'structures' with specific underlying myths.[1] This attempt, which Andrew Tudor has referred to as the search for an elusive 'X-factor' has been hotly debated and criticised.[2] Essentially, however, it creates two main problems. The first is a tendency to conflate very different forms in a manner which can ignore or minimise both historical change across periods, and differences or struggles within any particular period. The second problem, which is a consequence of the first, is that genre critics have usually felt compelled to define specific genres in ways that will mark them off as distinct and different from one another – the attempt, for example, to distinguish the specific structure of horror from that of science fiction. This compulsion not only leads critics to ignore the fact that different audiences may classify films in very different ways, but also the fact that genre hybridity is not simply a feature of the 'New' Hollywood,[3] but rather something which has always been an important feature of American popular cinema, and one of the central ways in which genres are used and developed.

Indeed, probably no area of horror has created more problems for those who search for distinct genre classifications than the invasion narratives of the 1950s with their overt hybridisation of horror and science fiction. In this group of texts, the human world is threatened by a destructive force from some previously uncharted region, usually outer space, the depths of the sea, or the desert, and many have felt the need to classify and resolve the specific nature of their generic identity.

However, such attempts are always bound up with the conflicts between different social groups and their attempt to defend or increase the cultural value of their specific forms of cultural capital.[4] It is for this reason that genres are such loose and indefinite categories which is not to say they are therefore unimportant. Indeed, their very sense of looseness and indefiniteness is a result of the struggles over them and the stakes which are involved in such struggles.

Indeed, the differential distribution of cultural competences and dispositions means that different audiences have very different senses of how genres are defined and where the boundaries between them lie. As a result, the genre distinctions which usually dominate within film studies seem almost irrelevant when one enters most video stores, where films are rarely divided into the various categories discussed in the academy – melodrama, westerns, romantic comedy, science fiction, horror, film noir, etc. – but are often classified under completely different categories such as romance, drama, action, martial arts, etc. Even then it is quite common for films to shift location from one rack to another, and not just as a result of mis-filing. Indeed, in the case of the 1950s invasion narratives, the question of whether they were *really* horror or science fiction was irrelevant during the period within which they were produced, and they were more usually simply referred to as 'monster movies'. None the less, there are still considerable struggles over their classification within genres.

For some of the champions of the science fiction genre, for example, these films are an embarrassment. It is often claimed that they lack any serious concern with scientific possibilities, and are therefore dismissed as *merely* 'monster movies' in which phoney scientific explanations are only used to justify the introduction of the monster. In this way, these films are distinguished from science fiction and merely identified as horror movies with technological or futuristic trappings.

Not only are these films distinguished from science fiction due to the supposed inaccuracy or implausibility of their action or locations, they are often distinguished from science fiction for being anti-scientific in their attitude. For many writers on science fiction, the genre is founded upon a respect for scientific activities and an attitude of hope and wonder at the possibilities which they offer. In contrast, the 1950s invasion narratives are often criticised for displaying a fear of science. However, any definition of science fiction which limits it to positive accounts of scientific progress is highly questionable. Brian Aldiss even introduces the reader to his collection, *The Penguin Omnibus of Science Fiction*, with the claim that 'the most powerful and compelling theme in science fiction is the fate which overcomes man when he attempts to outdo nature, when he is faced with menaces of his own making. Throughout the genre since its beginning, nemesis has clobbered hubris.'[5]

Even if this were not the case, there are many critics who see these films quite differently. They claim that these films are not really horror at all, but science fiction. For example, Lucanio claims that the difference between horror and science fiction is that while the former is concerned with 'inner worlds', the latter is concerned with 'outer worlds'.[6] Horror, he claims, is concerned with an isolated, exotic and alternative world which is different from that of the society in which it is produced, and which does not obey its accepted social or physical laws. Science fiction, on the other hand, is said to concern a world which is historical and scientifically continuous with the society within which it was produced. If the world of science fiction seems different, it is only because it portrays a future which is one possible result of development from the present.

According to Lucanio, this distinction between the worlds of horror and science fiction is also related to a distinction between the monsters which distinguish these genres. Horror uses an alternative world because it is concerned with the internal, subjective world of its characters, whereas science fiction is supposedly concerned with the external social world. In horror, the monster is therefore seen as a relatively sympathetic and complex being, while in science fiction, the monster is supposed to lack these qualities.

Vivian Sobchack makes a very similar case in her distinction between horror and science fiction.[7] She argues that while horror concerns the conflict between the individual and society, science fiction concerns the conflict between social institutions or between different social groups. In horror, it is claimed, humanity is not in control of its own destiny. Individuals are thwarted by their own limitations. Horror presumes a natural order which must not be disrupted or transgressed. Science fiction, on the other hand, is supposedly unconcerned with the internal struggles of individuals. It concerns the objective social and physical world, not subjective worlds, and it portrays humanity as being in fundamental control of its own destiny. It concerns the possibilities of human action, not their limitations.

In this way, both Lucanio and Sobchack make a distinction between horror and science fiction which shares many of the assumptions of critics mentioned earlier. Science fiction is associated with a fundamental faith in scientific activities and progress. It relies upon, and encourages, a sense of wonder and hope. This position also leads them to claim that while horror is essentially conservative and posits the existence of a closed, natural order, science fiction is essentially liberal or left-wing because it presents an open view of the world and of the possibilities of transformation and change within it.

As a result, both Lucanio and Sobchack argue that the 1950s invasion narratives differ from horror narratives because they lack an interest in the internal world of their monsters. Like other distinctions between horror and science fiction, this position tends to overemphasise the optimistic attitude to science in science fiction, and to ignore the negative accounts stressed by Aldiss. This may partly be due to their emphasis on film. One of the problems with the analysis of film genres has been that while the emphasis on 'film form' has been important and positive, it has also led many critics to ignore the fact that most people's understanding of a genre is developed through their awareness of a number of different cultural forms: film, literature, television, comics, etc. Their image of the genre is drawn from a sense of the continuity between these forms – even if they do not actually consume them. Even if it were true that the science fiction film tends to portray science in a positive manner, it would still be the case that many, if not most, people would have some awareness of a vast range of science fiction which was far from positive about scientific activities, and their understanding of the films of the genre would also be shaped by this broader awareness.

Another problem arises from the definition of horror upon which critics such as Lucanio and Sobchack rely. In fact, they are not discussing the horror genre as a whole, but only one subgenre of horror: Gothic horror. This subgenre may well have been dominant within the horror film prior to the 1950s, but this has not been the case since then. As a result, their distinctions seem highly dubious when one looks at most contemporary horror and science fiction films. In these texts, horror is often placed within the setting of the modern, everyday world; the monsters are often distinguished by their lack of any sense of internality (see, for example, slasher and zombie movies);[8] and even in contemporary science fiction films, there is usually a profound lack of faith in scientific progress. As a result, Lucanio and Sobchack's distinctions fail to recognise that the 1950s invasion narratives represent a distinctive transformation not only in the horror genre, but also in science fiction.

However, perhaps the most central problem with their work is

that their analytical distinctions do not help classify particular films
or even groups of films. For example, Sobchack finds that the 1950s
invasion narratives fit neither her definition of horror, nor her definition of science fiction. She therefore defines these films as
'hybrids'. But such a solution is ultimately unconvincing: it allows
her to eat her cake and still have .; to hold on to a notion of fixed
genre distinctions and yet isolate problematic cases 'as something
other than SF or horror films – as having a fascination and aesthetic
value of their own'.[9] This position offers no real solution. It threatens to dissolve the very distinctions which it seeks to maintain. As
Lucanio notes, this scheme 'allows far too many variables to enter;
in the long run, we have no distinction at all. Placing the alien invasion film in the middle of a spectrum is not the answer'.[10]

Unfortunately, Lucanio's alternative is no more convincing. He
simply asserts that these films are not a hybrid of horror and science
fiction at all, but purely and simply science fiction. The problem
with this alternative is that Lucanio's definition of science fiction
becomes so all-encompassing that it ends up including most of the
classic Gothic horror films. 'William K. Everson's *Classic Horror
Films*', he argues, 'includes discussions of James Whale's *Frankenstein*, Rouben Mamoulian's *Dr Jekyll and Mr Hyde*, and Ernest B.
Schoedsack's *Dr Cyclops* – all of which are best seen as alien invasion films'.[11]

Lucanio does not stop with these individual films though, but
argues that 'the many films which constitute the prometheus varia-
tion, notably the myriad Frankenstein films, have been and continue to be misread and misinterpreted as horror films'.[12] Even the
Frankenstein films made by Hammer are defined as science fiction
rather than horror, although most of these films actually seem to be
examples of the very category of horror from which Lucanio has
just distinguished science fiction! They are set in alternative worlds
and regard science with, at the very least, some sense of suspicion.
But even if one was to accept these films as science fiction, it is difficult to see why they should be classified as alien invasion narratives, especially given that Lucanio's book clearly associates the
alien invasion narratives with a particular period, the 1950s.

The 1950s invasion narratives and Cold War America

Indeed, most critics of the 1950s invasion narratives bypass the question of genre almost entirely, and concentrate instead on the relationship between these texts and the period in which they were made. The most common claim is that these texts are examples of Cold War ideology in which the fear of alien invasion is seen as merely a code for fears of Soviet aggression. More particularly, it is argued that these texts work not only to demonise the Soviet Union, but all potential opposition to the central institutions and authorities of American society. For example, Peter Biskind claims that these texts 'presented America in the grip of an emergency, and ... these emergencies dramatised the need of consensus, of pulling together'.[13] They portrayed a world of stark choices, a Cold War world in which there was no room for neutrality: one either swore allegiance to American institutions and authorities or was seen to be aiding and abetting the enemy. In this world, there was a clear distinction between right and wrong, order and chaos, the self and the other.

For this reason, these films have been seen as not only deeply xenophobic, but also as engendering a passivity in the population who were taught to defer unquestionably to authority. As Andrew Tudor puts it:

> In this xenophobic universe we can do nothing but rely on the state, in the form of military, scientific and governmental elites. Only they have the recourse to the technical knowledge and coercive resources necessary for our defense. In this respect, then, fifties SF/horror movies teach us not so much 'to stop worrying and love the bomb' as 'to keep worrying and love the state', an admonition which accords perfectly with the nuclear conscious cold war culture of the period.[14]

This position is echoed in a whole series of different studies, although different critics have come to different conclusions as to which system of authority these texts actually endorse. If, as Tudor argues, these films endorse the state, it is still necessary to determine how the state is defined within them, and also in what ways it is presented as legitimate. For example, it is worth noting that the state is rarely associated with politicians or political activities. They may occasionally act as its emblems, but they are almost entirely absent from these films, and totally absent from the action. Instead, as Brian Murphy has claimed, the state and its authorities are usually associated with 'military-scientific types' or more precisely, 'scientists working in "full co-operation" (such an important word, that "co-operation") with the military'.[15]

Murphy is right to emphasise the importance of the word 'co-operation'. He is implying that it disguises issues of power and dominance. If science works in 'co-operation' with the military, he encourages the reader to ask which group is presented as dominant in this relationship, and why? Murphy suggests that the military is dominant and that these texts are a celebration of militarism in which science is subordinated to the military as a mere aid or support. Biskind, on the other hand, suggests that science is dominant. He claims that, during the late 1940s and early 1950s, there was a fundamental change in the organisation and legitimation of authority. The old style professional, he contends, was replaced by the technical expert who used his specialised knowledge to administer society.

As a result, in a discussion of *Panic in the Streets* (1950), he argues that the film represents a displacement of authority away from the police or cops and on to the medical experts or docs. In this film, the police must learn to defer to the medical expert who has the specialised knowledge necessary to protect and defend society. As Biskind puts it:

> *Panic* substitutes illness for crime, and cure for punishment. It prefers the needle to the gun, Bufferin to bullets. It was one of the first films of the 'therapeutic society'.[16]

This argument is alluded to later in his book when Biskind discusses the 1950s invasion narratives. In these films, he claims, 'Science replaced therapy as the guiding light of corporate-liberal sci-fi, in which the coalition of the centre was managed by scientists and soldiers, not cops and docs.'[17] The implication is clear: science is dominant and the military is presented as a mere functionary to be ordered and controlled by the technical expertise of scientists.

For this reason, Biskind challenges critics such as Susan Sontag who have seen these films as the product of anxieties about nuclear weapons.[18] He argues that these films 'are not primarily worried about the Bomb; they loved the Bomb, or at least the technology that made it possible'.[19] The 1950s invasion narratives which are often used as evidence of anxieties about nuclear weapons are not those which concern an invasion from outer space, but films such as *The Beast from 20,000 Fathoms* (1953), *Them!* (1954) and *It Came from Beneath the Sea* (1955). In these films, society is menaced by creatures who are either the product of radiation, or are unleashed by atomic explosions. In *Them!*, society is threatened by ants which have been mutated by radiation so that they have become giants, while in *It Came from Beneath the Sea*, a huge, radioactive squid is forced to leave the ocean depths and feed upon humans when its food supply is destroyed by atom bomb tests. For Biskind, however, science is not the problem in these films. He claims that science and the existing social order are presented as good. In certain cases, science may initiate the problem, but the problem is really 'nature run amok'.[20] In these films, he claims, nature is defined as the Other: 'it is all that threatens to disrupt and destroy culture'.[21] Nature is that which science exists to order and control, and if it resists that control, nature becomes monstrous. In this way, he claims, science was reinstated to a position of power, dominance and authority within these films.

Biskind also relates these claims to issues of gender and sexuality. It is not only nature which is presented as the Other, but also, by association, women and in particular female sexuality. As he argues, these films 'feared the eruption of nature within culture and were therefore afraid of sex and mistrusted women, particularly sexual women'.[22] For Biskind, these films are patriarchal in their ideology and define science and culture as male. Women, it is therefore claimed, are associated with nature within these films, and hence identified with the forces which need to be ordered and controlled. Biskind also notes that in films such as *Them!*, the monster is identified as female, and that, like many 1950s monsters, it is her profligate breeding practices which threaten to overwhelm humanity.[23]

These claims about the 1950s invasion narratives have virtually achieved the status of an orthodoxy, but there are considerable grounds for challenging, or at least qualifying, them. For example, as Biskind himself enables one to argue, the alien's association with the Soviet Union did not necessarily imply an affirmation of American society. Indeed, the concerns with the Soviet Union were often merely a displacement or a code which different sections of American society used in order to criticise those aspects of American life which they feared or opposed. As Biskind puts it, 'the soviet threat was as much a function of squabbles between Democrats and Republicans as it was a reality', and he quotes I. F. Stone: 'The Republicans fought Russia in order to prevent a New Deal, while the Democrats fought Russia as a rearguard action against Republicans.'[24] Nor were such squabbles limited to the centre of American politics. Sections of the radical left attacked the Soviet Union in order to associate it with the centre and right, while the radical right attacked the Soviet Union in order to associate it with the centre and left. The Soviet Union was used to highlight and challenge aspects of American society itself. It was not simply an 'external Other' which was used to legitimate American society completely. If the Soviet Union was seen as 'unAmerican', it is necessary to examine how different sections of American society used it to develop and defend their concepts of 'Americanness' against other sections of American society. For these reasons, it is useful to re-examine the context of American life in the 1950s.

Fordism and the critique of conformity

The social organisation of American society in the 1950s was significantly different from that of earlier periods in American history. The period around World War II had seen the dramatic consolidation of corporate or 'Fordist' systems of regulation. This use of the term 'Fordist' is not limited to the labour processes usually associated with Henry Ford, but refers to a whole series of arrangements which were designed to regulate social, political, economic, and even cultural activities.[25] During the depression of the 1930s, it was often claimed that the capitalist market was incapable of regulating itself as a system, and that a more organised response was necessary to ensure the smooth running of social life. In the development of Fordism, new laws were passed which gave labour considerable new powers and freedoms, but only on the condition that it accepted the authority of, and collaborated with, corporate capital. Capital, on the other hand, had become increasingly centralised and had adopted a bureaucratic rationality in which the techniques of scientific management were applied to an expanded range of corporate activities. For example, corporations not only took greater control in managing the process of production, but also took greater control of personal relations, training, product design, pricing policies, and planned the obsolescence of both equipment and products. They also became more concerned to extend the sphere of their control into the processes of consumption, and used a series of techniques such as advertising in order to manage and control these processes rationally. The state also took on new roles and powers. In contrast to the period of *laissez-faire* capitalism, the

'Fordist' state sought to control the economy through a series of fiscal and monetary policies, as well as taking greater responsibility for social welfare.

As a result, Fordism was a system of centrally ordered administration which relied on an elite of experts. It was their task to regulate social, political, economic and cultural life, and they did so through the use of scientific-technical rationality.

This system ushered in a period of unprecedented economic prosperity in American society which seemed to many people to have rendered the political left redundant. As Richard Pells has claimed, it became commonplace for people to claim that 'the problems of modern America were no longer ideological but technical and administrative, and that these could be solved by knowledgable experts rather than mass movements'.[26] Many recognised the persistence of class distinctions, but argued that class relations need no longer be based on conflict. This situation led many later commentators to claim that American culture in the 1950s was essentially uncritical of itself, that intellectuals and others became mere apologists for the system of scientific-technical rationality. However, Richard Pells also points out that while it was more usual for people to emphasise the strengths of the system rather than its weaknesses, this situation was less the result of a 'failure of nerve'[27] than of fundamental faith in prosperity. In fact, many left critics also accepted the same assumptions. The writers of the Frankfurt School and left intellectuals such as C. Wright Mills all tended to accept that the capitalist economic system had overcome its economic contradictions, and that the proletariat were no longer presented as an oppositional potential but had now fully integrated into the system.[28] As a result, it became common for people to emphasise the value of gradualism over the dangers of millennial utopianism, particularly after the horrors of Nazi germany and the Stalinist Soviet Union.

But this faith in prosperity did not necessarily mean that people were uncritical of American society. On the contrary, there were numerous signs that people were worried about the effects of the new 'Fordist' system. It was frequently claimed that people had little control over their lives, and that their existence was becoming increasingly routinised and devoid of differentiation. As Pells argues, the faith in prosperity which distinguished the 1950s did not lead people simply to become champions of American society. It merely half-concealed and altered the nature of their dissatisfac-

tions. For example, there was a shift in social criticism from a concern with economic injustice to ideology in which people talked
less about the disadvantaged and more about the psychological
effects of contemporary society. Many complained about the
impersonality of social systems, rather than about economic injustice. In this situation, Pells argues, mass culture often came to
replace the bourgeoisie as the main object of criticism.

In the work of Dwight MacDonald, for example, mass culture is
associated with certain totalitarian tendencies within American
society, although these tendencies are seen as the product of specific
forms of social and economic organisation, forms of organisation
which were internal to America itself. For MacDonald, popular culture had become, within the capitalist United States, just another
commodity alongside cars and toothpaste, and this situation had
damaging ideological and aesthetic effects. First, he claimed that
unlike the popular culture of earlier periods, mass culture was no
longer produced and consumed by communities, but 'comes from
above. It is fabricated by technicians hired by business men.'[29]

Second, and more significantly, he claimed that the industrial
process of mass cultural production resulted in an attempt to dominate and control the process of consumption. The producers of
culture had to guarantee a regular market for their products. Unlike
food and other commodities, cultural goods were not essential to
people's material existence, and hence the audience had to be
trained into habitual cultural consumption. Drawing on the writings of T. W. Adorno[30] and Clement Greenberg,[31] MacDonald
claimed that this attempt to rationalise and control consumption
produced a culture which was distinguished by 'the Built-In Reaction'. Unlike high culture, he maintained, mass culture 'includes the
spectator's reactions in the work itself instead of forcing him to
make his own responses'.[32]

As a result, MacDonald argues that mass culture comes to dominate the consciousness of the population. It breaks down folk cultures and communities (which he describes as 'a group of
individuals linked to each other by concrete interests'[33]) and reor-
ganises social relations 'so as to bind each atomised individual
directly to the centre of power'.[34] This form of culture, he claims,
pacifies the population and makes them uncritical and compliant. It
trains them not to think for themselves, and leads them to believe
that if they simply identify with the figure of the mass and defer to

experts, the system will do everything for them and fulfil all their desires.

MacDonald does not claim that mass culture produces large amounts of dross. He is quite willing to admit that much of high culture is of a poor standard. Instead he argues that

> Masscult is bad in a new way: it doesn't even have the theoretical possibility of being good. Up to the eighteenth century, bad art was of the same nature as good art, produced for the same audience, accepting the same standards. The difference was simply one of individual talent. But masscult is something else. It is not just unsuccessful art. It is non-art. It is even anti-art.[35]

The result, for MacDonald, is a vast system which subordinates the population to its impersonality and remains resistant to human consciousness or agency.

These kind of claims were common within American culture in the 1950s. David Reisman, for example, claimed that modern American society was increasingly organised as 'a lonely crowd' in which the individual was psychologically dependent on the judgement of others and incapable of opposing such judgements. Individuals were no longer 'inner-directed' as they had been in the period of nineteenth-century capitalist accumulation, but were becoming increasingly 'other-directed'.[36] Even writers such as John Kenneth Galbraith, who is often seen as a champion of American liberal economics, 'objected strenuously to the process by which businesses manipulated consumer tastes and behaviour in order to create a steady demand for their goods and services'.[37] The expansion of American production, Galbraith claimed, meant that the satisfaction of individual needs was less and less the goal of the economic system, but rather individuals were increasingly being reorganised so that they would satisfy the economic system's need to increase its output and profits.[38]

In this situation, critics such as Daniel Boorstin claimed that the individual became submerged in a world of unreality.[39] People were flooded with images of the world through television, newspapers, magazines, adverts, etc. But, he claimed, rather than increasing their awareness of the world, these media simply placed people in a position of passivity in which they viewed the world from a distance. They experienced it vicariously. For Boorstin, not only were these experiences second-hand, but they were also usually contrived. Politics, for example, had merely become a series of staged events, or 'pseudo-events', in which the techniques of presentation became more important than the issues. In this situation, it was claimed, the population was not only placed in the position of passive spectators in relation to their world, but also lost the ability to distinguish reality from unreality. Indeed, he argued, unreality often became more important to them than reality.

Mass culture was not seen as the only force responsible for these developments. Similar claims were also made about the organisation of people's working lives. For example, William Whyte, in his influential study, *The Organisation Man*, argued that while in previous stages of American history employers had primarily demanded only the workers' labour, the corporate organisations of 'Fordism' demanded 'one's soul'.[40] According to Whyte, this goal was not achieved through coercion, but through the techniques of personal management which presented corporations as benevolent and so made it difficult for individuals to justify *to themselves* any deviations from the norm. Individuals came to identify their own interests with those of the corporation, and submitted themselves to its authority.

These arguments suggest that people were not as complacent in the 1950s as it is often suggested. There was a deep-seated anxiety about social, political, economic and cultural developments which led many to argue that America was becoming an increasingly homogeneous, conformist and totalitarian society; that the basis of individualism was being eroded; and that the possibility of resistance was disappearing. The weakness of many of these arguments was less a result of the depth of their concern than of the solutions which were offered. While many identified structural explanations for these developments, few offered structural solutions. All too often, it was argued that the only solution was for individuals to extricate themselves from the systems of power within which they were ensnared. But such solutions rarely explained how individuals were to do so. Their faith in the ability of individuals to resist these systems seems out of character with the very analyses of American society which these critics were themselves proposing. Dwight MacDonald, for example, had little hope for the majority of the population, but sought to protect and encourage a small elite of avant-garde artists and critics who would somehow hold out against mass culture. In the complexity of high culture, he believed, individual artists could not only express their own personal vision – rather than produce the impersonal, standardised product of mass culture – but in the process, would also require their audiences to think for themselves and develop their own responses.

In a similar manner, David Reisman called for the individual to acquire 'autonomy'. Rather than becoming a revolutionary who was opposed to society, individuals had to resist the compulsion to accept the opinions of others. They simply had to learn how to make rational decisions of their own through an acknowledgement of, and an investigation into, the various possible options available. Boorstin also saw the solution as primarily one of personal action. Somehow, he argued, individuals had to free themselves of the world of 'unreality' created by modern society, and rediscover reality. Even Whyte, whose analysis focused on the world of economic activity, proposed a solution which was ultimately individualistic. Individuals, he argued, must learn to avoid continually deferring to the organisation. They must learn how to distinguish between co-operation and conformity, and acquire the strength to champion the unpopular view if necessary. People had to learn to work inside the system, but without relinquishing their own capacity for judgement. Indeed, like many others, Whyte argued that in doing so individuals would provide a greater contribution both to the corporation and to society in general. They would not only remind others of ideals which the majority of the population had lost or forgotten, but also challenge others and so force them to question their own assumptions. In this way, it was claimed, individuals could reintroduce the dynamism and creativity necessary for economic development and growth.

However, the limitations of these critics' solutions are hardly surprising given the distrust of mass movements which followed the revelations about Nazism and Stalinism, a distrust which underpins most of their criticisms of American society. These writers were trying to resolve the almost impossible dilemma of how one can combat potentially totalitarian structures without reproducing their problems in a different form.

Ironically, it was Daniel Bell who not only offered one of the most incisive criticisms of American life in the 1950s, but also proposed one of the most challenging solutions. Bell is usually seen as an ardent 'advocate of pragmatism, negotiation and compromise'.[41] He even challenged critics of mass society, and argued that the concept of mass society was inappropriate to American life. For Bell, the concept was drawn from an analysis of European culture, and did not fit the liberal political and cultural structures of American society.[42] However, Bell did see problems with the nature of work in America. In this sphere, he claimed, rationalisation concentrated power in the hands of a small elite of industrial planners who reduced the labour process to a series of repetitive routines. In this situation, workers lost a sense of the process of production as a whole, and were condemned to a meaningless, humiliating and dehumanising existence. Bell traced these problems back to the needs of the market which required technological efficiency to create greater productivity, and he argued that these conditions led to psychological manipulation and the suppression of industrial conflict, both of which adversely affected society and culture in general.[43]

This attack on the 'capitalist industrial order' in America did not lead him to support the socialist solutions on offer elsewhere. For Bell, the abolition of private property could not, in itself, redress the consequences of rationalisation. In socialist countries, such as the Soviet Union, it was claimed, the labour process was still run by experts in the interests of efficiency, and workers still did not control the economy. Instead, Bell argued that the only solution was to reject the goal of efficiency in favour of the needs of the work-force. Labour had to be reinvested with a sense of 'spontaneity and freedom'. Unlike many of his contemporaries, he did not see the solution as being purely an individual matter, but as a social one. Indeed, it sounds far closer to Marx's own conception of socialism than the system which Bell opposed in the Soviet Union. As a result, Bell's claim that he was 'a conservative in culture, a liberal in politics and a socialist in economics'[44] might not be as inaccurate as is often implied. His problem is that, like Marx himself, he gave little indication of how such a dramatic transformation might be accomplished. His disillusionment with the communist movements of the 1930s and 1940s had led him to defend political liberalism and gradualism, but it is difficult to see how such a dramatic transformation could be accomplished without considerable conflict and opposition.

However, such problems were not restricted to the right and centre of American politics. Both the Frankfurt School and C. Wright Mills, who was to become the hero of the 1960s New Left, showed a basic faith in prosperity. They too accepted that the American economy had overcome the contradictions of capitalist production, and focused instead on the effects of mass culture and society. They argued that the structures of social and cultural life treated people as mere objects of power, a situation which created conformity and passivity in the population. Mills, for example, claimed that society was governed by the elites of the military, government and industry which interlocked with one another and made it increasingly difficult for most people to affect the decisions which influenced their own lives. Cultural institutions placed them in positions of passivity in which the flow of information was controlled and managed in order to manipulate opinion. The media organised the population into a position of powerlessness and conformity. American society, Mills argued, was organised by centres of information and power to which most people were peripheral, except as objects to be ordered and controlled by the centre. Like other critics of the period, Mills was therefore most worried about the impersonality of the system. It did not seem to be geared to the interests of the people which it governed, and resisted their attempts to influence it. This position is best seen in his account of American militarism.[45] For Mills, the development of nuclear weapons systems, and the preparations for nuclear war, seemed to be inexorable processes which followed their own logic and could not be affected by ordinary people. This situation was also associated with the impersonal violence of totalitarian societies such as the Stalinist Soviet Union and Nazi Germany, and it was used to challenge the effectiveness of both liberal politics and traditional Marxism.

Like many of his contemporaries, Mills also denied that class politics was relevant to American political life. Indeed, the working class was no longer seen as the agent of social transformation. Instead it was the 'new class' of students and professors which was seen as the best agency of historical change.[46] If he criticised other intellectuals of the period,[47] it was only because they did not live up to the high expectations which he had set for them. His criticisms and his solutions were therefore much closer to those of his contemporaries than is often implied. He called for intellectuals to resist developments in American society. Intellectual resistance was also the solution offered by the Frankfurt School.

Re-examining the 1950s invasion narratives

If the 1950s invasion narratives are considered within this context, it can be seen that rather than legitimating Fordism and its application of scientific-technical rationality to the management of American life, these texts often criticised this system by directly associating the alien with it. It has often been pointed out that the qualities which identify the aliens with the Soviet Union is their lack of feelings and the absence of individual characteristics. It was certainly the case that during the 1950s, many American critics claimed that in the Soviet Union people were all the same; that they were forced to deny personal feeling and characteristics, and to become mere functionaries of the social whole. It should also be noted, however, that, as has been illustrated, it was common in the 1950s for Americans to claim that the effects of scientific-technical rationality upon their own society was producing the same features within America itself.

If the alien was at times identified with Soviet communism, it was also implied that this was only the logical conclusion of certain developments within American society itself. The system of scientific-technical rationality was impersonal, and it oppressed human feelings and emotions. It did not value individual qualities, but attempted to convert people into undifferentiated functionaries of the social whole, functionaries who did not think or act for themselves but were ordered and controlled from without by experts. It is for this reason that even in the most pro-scientific of the 1950s invasion narratives, the scientists often display a respect for, and a fascination with, the aliens which, it is stressed, represent their 'ideal' of a society ordered by scientific-technical rationality. Indeed, the aliens are often directly associated with technology. They either threaten the earth with it, or are produced by it. Science may at times be necessary to destroy the aliens, but these texts often highlight the uselessness of scientific experts in favour of spontaneity, practicality and even domestic knowledge. As a result, even the most positive accounts of science within these texts suggest a sense of ambivalence with regard to technology.

The aliens are also often represented as the 'ideal' image of a scientifically-ordered military. Lucanio challenges Murphy and others by claiming that these films are not celebrations of militarism, but that the military simply offers an image of community.[48] Such a claim is ultimately unconvincing in itself, but it is significant that in those cases where military personnel are presented positively, they are usually distinguished from the scientific-rationality of the military high command. They are usually acting on their own and often directly disobeying orders from above. Co-operation may be necessary within these films, but it is not the co-operation required by the Fordist system. It is the co-operation of an interactive community threatened by Fordist rationalisation and domination.

For these reasons, it is difficult to argue that nature itself is the problem within these films. As Biskind himself claims in the case of *The Thing from Another World* (1951): 'Despite the fact that it is part of the natural world, more vegetable than mineral, the Thing is a robot.'[49] If the invaders are presented as natural, they are carefully distinguished from associations with 'human nature'. They are vegetables, insects or reptiles. They are cold-blooded beings which lack what are generally understood to be human feelings or thought processes. They resist anthropomorphism, and are usually presented as little more than biological machines.

As a result, the fact that many of these monsters are the products of science is significant. These texts often display an anxiety about humanity's role within the cosmos. The familiar world becomes unstable and potentially dangerous. Science may save us at times, but it also creates a world which we can no longer recognise, a world in which giant ants or man-eating plants threaten to overwhelm us. As Clarens claims, these texts represent a world in which 'humanity has slipped from its position at the centre of the cosmos'[50] and is now under threat from monsters which are often of its own making. In the case of the 1950s alien invasion narratives, this situation could be associated with the end of American isolationism and the nation's growing awareness of its place within a complex and often hostile world order. But even this context can only be seen as the result of more general anxieties about whether one can trust one's world, or whether one's life is subject to forces over which one has less and less control. In a world where people have faith in the rightness of their way of life, involvement in the international sphere would not provoke the anxieties which one finds in the 1950s invasion narratives.

It is also difficult to argue that these texts are patriarchal in the way that critics such as Biskind claim. The monsters' association with rationality and science usually means that they are associated

with masculinity and not femininity. Furthermore, those qualities
which are usually associated with femininity are highly valued
within these texts. It is not rationality, but those qualities such as
emotion, feeling, intuition, interaction and imagination – qualities
that are usually defined as feminine and 'irrational' – that are identified as distinctly 'human'. Indeed, within these texts, women
often occupy central positions within the action, as subjects rather
than objects of the narrative. Lucanio argues that this is simply a
ploy used by the texts in order to get women near the action where
they can then be saved by the male hero,[51] but it is usually a key
index of the ideological problems with which these texts are
engaged. Rather than being merely a ploy, these texts often present
women's active involvement in the struggle as absolutely essential
to the victory over the menace, and it is the men who fail to appreciate their contribution who are usually portrayed as a 'problem'. It
is these men who must learn to acknowledge the error of their
ways, or else be punished for their failure to do so.[52]

Biskind himself acknowledges the active role which Pat Medford
assumes in *Them!*, but he argues that the film's message is simple:
'Better to give them [women] an inch than lose a mile, better to let
Pat Medford assert herself, or face a more serious challenge to male
power in the future.'[53] To some extent, this may actually be the way
in which gender issues operate within these films, but, even if this
is the case, it seriously challenges many of the claims about the
sexual politics of 1950s culture, including those of Biskind himself.

Many critics, drawing on Betty Friedan's *The Feminine Mystique*,
argue that the message of 1950s popular culture was that women
who assumed or even desired positions of power had failed to
adjust to their rightful role within the family, and that the only roles
within which women can be truly fulfilled were those of wife and
mother.[54] As a result, 1950s popular culture is often accused of
having actively directed women away from public activities and
towards the privacy of the domestic sphere. Even if Biskind is right
about the way in which Pat Medford is used within *Them!*, the film
is therefore not functioning in the way in which it is generally
assumed that films of the period operated. Indeed, rather than confining women to the domestic sphere, many if not most of these
texts actually challenge the separation of the public and the private,
the masculine and the feminine, the rational and the irrational. It is
only when these distinctions are rejected, these texts suggest, that

the problems which threaten humanity can be overcome.

Nor is it the case that sexuality is the problem within these texts as Biskind and others have argued. Instead sexuality is usually defined as the ultimate expression of human feelings, emotions and interaction, and it is therefore opposed to the monstrousness of the aliens' *asexual* reproductive activities. Asexuality rather than sexuality is the problem, and this is related to a long history in horror fiction that dates back at least as far as Mary Shelley's *Frankenstein* (1818).[55] Furthermore, asexuality is a problem exactly because of its association with masculinity and science. As in *Frankenstein*, asexual reproduction is associated with the male fantasy of producing life without recourse to women, and it is this fantasy which is defined as monstrous specifically because it is founded on a male fear of female sexuality in particular, and sexuality in general.[56]

If these films do emphasise the need to 'pull together', they do not endorse the kinds of conformist consensus which Biskind, Tudor and others suggest. They are actually deeply critical of conformity, and clearly distinguish their positive groups from the centrally-organised systems of Fordism. Rather than a rational structure of domination and control, these groups are interactive communities which are trying to defend themselves against rationally-organised hierarchies.[57] Their 'xenophobia' is therefore less problematic than is often implied. It is not just a fear of strangers, but an altogether more admirable attempt to defend the human against the inhuman; to privilege certain communal values in opposition to the 'dehumanising' domination of scientific-technical rationality.

Indeed, it is worth noting that most critics of these texts attack them for being non-intellectual or even anti-intellectual. They are often accused of provoking anti-communist 'hysteria', and exploiting 'irrational' or 'primitive' emotions such as xenophobia. But these criticisms actually reproduce the very values and positions which these texts challenge and reject. These criticisms accept a clear distinction between the rational and the irrational in which the former is privileged over the latter. They fail to acknowledge the legitimacy of the 'irrational', and ultimately share the same values as the systems of power which these texts attack.

As a result, not only do these texts contradict the claims of most mass culture theories, they are also frequently more sophisticated and complex than those theories. First, they indicate that mass culture critics, such as Dwight MacDonald, were simply wrong when they claimed that mass culture is incapable of producing critical texts, and that it ultimately endorses an elite of experts and adherence to conformity. Second, these texts actually offer an advance over mass culture theory to the extent that they present the solution to mass culture as being social rather than individual. They emphasise not only the need for group interaction, activity and resistance, but also that the simple opposition between society and the individual is a myth. In many texts, the individual not only needs the support of a communal group, but also needs stable social patterns. The conflict in these texts is between different social orders, not simply between society and the individual. This situation also enables these texts to give a more satisfying account of the seductions of conformity and routine than is available in most mass culture theory. They are able to give some sense of why people might be willing to surrender to such systems and pressures.

Finally, these texts also raise an issue which is absent from mass culture theory, at least until *The Feminine Mystique* nearly ten years later,[58] and that is the relationship of mass culture and society to the construction of gender relations. While much mass culture theory was based on the implicit and even explicit concern that mass culture 'feminised' men by encouraging conformity and passivity,[59] the 1950s invasion narratives often challenged not only the ways in which masculinity was constructed within 1950s America, but also the ways in which femininity was constructed.

It is also worth noting that those critics who discuss these films in relation to the context of Cold War America often fail to examine their relationship to the science fiction literature of the period. In science fiction literature, the alien invader (or Bug-Eyed Monster (BEM) as it is often described) was not a product of the Cold War, but had been popular in the 1930s and 1940s. John Campbell's 'Who Goes There?', on which *The Thing from Another World* was based, was originally published in 1938.[60] Indeed, by the late 1940s, the subgenre had become so familiar that it was already the object of parodies such as Ray Bradbury's 'The Concrete Mixer' (1949).[61] By the 1950s, much science fiction literature was desperately trying to distance itself from an association with this subgenre. This is partly responsible for the derision with which 1950s science fiction/horror is often regarded by those with an investment in contemporary science fiction. They were seen as 'out of date' in relation to the science fiction literature of their period. On the other hand, not all advocates of science fiction have been negative about them. Indeed, Arthur C. Clarke and Michael Crichton, both of whom write more legitimate or 'serious' science fiction, claim that *The Thing from Another World* is one of the best science fiction films of all time. As a result, the relationship between this subgenre and the period of the 1950s is much more complex than is often implied. The alien invader predates the Cold War.

It is also dangerous to see the subgenre as a unitary object. Many texts use elements of this subgenre while remaining very different types of texts, and even the films which can easily be discussed as part of the subgenre use its elements in very different ways, and develop the subgenre in very different directions. They may deal with a common series of issues and problems, but they deal with them in different ways and frequently take different ideological positions. The subgenre not only develops historically, but within any particular stage of development, different films may contradict or conflict with one another.

1951: the year the aliens arrived!

One of the clearest examples of the ideological differences between films within this subgenre can be found in comparisons between *The Thing from Another World*, the first significant example of the 1950s invasion narratives, and *The Day the Earth Stood Still*, which was released in the same year, 1951. These two films are frequently compared because they share common themes and issues, but while *The Thing from Another World* is usually seen as an authoritarian text, *The Day the Earth Stood Still* is often praised as liberal or even left-wing in its politics. This distinction can be seen in Bruce Kawin's discussion of the two films. Like Lucanio and Sobchack, Kawin is attempting to identify the features which distinguish science fiction and horror, but he argues that genre distinctions 'are determined not by plot-elements so much as by attitudes towards plot-elements'.[62] Indeed he shares Lucanio and Sobchack's claim that the difference lies in the two genres' respective attitudes towards science. If, as Kawin claims, these two genres are 'comparable in that both tend to organise themselves around some confrontation between an unknown and a would-be knower',[63] horror is claimed to present the unknown as threatening and works to defend and re-establish the *status quo*, while science fiction is not supposed to present the confrontation with the unknown as dangerous, but as potentially liberating. It allows for the possibility of change and development. If these differences are discussed in terms of genre distinctions, Kawin also implies a political judgement. Horror is identified as implicitly conservative, while science fiction is presented as implicitly progressive (as either liberal or radical).

Kawin's comparison of *The Thing from Another World* and *The Day the Earth Stood Still* is meant to draw out these distinctions. Both films, he points out, share similar issues and plot-elements. They both concern an alien being which comes to earth, and they revolve around a similar series of distinctions. But he argues that they take very different positions in relation to these distinctions. For example, he notes that while the alien provokes a conflict between science and the military in both these films, *The Thing from Another World* presents the military as right to regard the alien as a threat which must be destroyed, while in *The Day the Earth Stood Still*, the scientists are presented as right to regard 'the alien as a visitor with superior knowledge, to be learned from, and if possible, joined'.[64] As a result, it is argued that these films have different ways of presenting the distinction between the human and the inhuman. In *The Day the Earth Stood Still*, the inhuman has value, while the inhuman is simply destructive in *The Thing from Another World*. The central opposition in these films is therefore claimed to be one between violence and intelligence. *The Thing from Another World* is supposed to value violence, while *The Day the Earth Stood Still* is supposed to value intellect. In the former, the creature is simply a threat and can only be dealt with through violence, while in the latter, the alien is highly intelligent and violence is an inappropriate response to it. Communication is the way of dealing with the alien in *The Day the Earth Stood Still*. A meeting of minds is possible, and rational discussion is the positive value.

Biskind comes to similar conclusions. He claims that *The Thing from Another World* associates the alien with Soviet aggression and so stresses the necessity of supporting the American state. But he also acknowledges that the alien's presence provokes a conflict between the military and the scientists. The former recognise the alien as a threat and want to destroy it, while the latter, led by Professor Carrington, want to communicate with it and learn from it. This latter goal is clearly presented as absurd within the film but, for Biskind, the film suggests that the scientists' real problem is not their use of reason, or even their attempt to consort with the enemy, but rather their refusal to accept the authority of the military, and by extension, the state. Biskind does acknowledge that the film presents rational, bureaucratic procedures as inadequate, and that the alien is presented as 'reason run amok',[65] but he still argues that the soldiers are 'employed by government, [and are] working ultimately in its interests'.[66] Indeed, Biskind claims that the film also associates the alien with the military leader's id (his irrational sexual desire), a force which must be 'symbolically subdued' in order to clear the way for socially sanctioned heterosexual behaviour (marriage). As a result, the film is read as a conservative one in which force is used to destroy anything that threatens or challenges the *status quo*. It is a film which cannot accept the validity of anything which departs from its limited notions of 'normality'.

In contrast, *The Day the Earth Stood Still* is seen as a radical critique of American society. Biskind argues that it uses the figure of the lone alien to challenge society for its inability to accept him, or the wisdom which he offers. In this film, the alien is good, and society is 'dystopian'.[67] Like *The Thing from Another World*, the alien is associated with science, and threatened by the military, but in this case, science is not only presented positively, but also as justifiably subversive in relation to the dystopian order. For example, Professor Barnhardt, the brilliant scientist who is able to recognise the alien's wisdom, is claimed to bear 'a striking resemblance to Albert Einstein'.[68] According to Biskind, 'Einstein was never a favourite of the authorities', and in 'making an Einstein figure the hero of sorts, *The Day the Earth Stood Still* was crawling far out on a very thin limb'.[69] Barnhardt also calls a meeting of scientists from all over the world to come and hear the alien's wisdom, and for Biskind, the meeting 'bears a passing resemblance to the Cultural and Scientific Conference for World Peace held at the Waldorf-Astoria Hotel in New York amid a storm of protest in 1949'.[70] This conference was picketed and people who attended it were criticised for being either naive or subversive, but in *The Day the Earth Stood Still*, it is presented as the only hope for humanity.

Biskind does recognise that by making 'heroes of professors and aliens', the film 'creates a top-down hierarchy' in which ordinary people 'are not rational enough' and need to be controlled by experts.[71] But this situation does not seem to trouble him unduly. Nor does he seem particularly worried by the alien's mission.

Klattu, the alien, has been sent to earth to inform humanity that its
'irrationality' threatens the universal order and that it must accept
the rule of a robot police force or else face annihilation. Gort, the
robot which Klattu brings with him, has the power to destroy the
earth if it does not put its 'irrational' squabbles and petty interests
aside. But again Biskind does not seem particularly alarmed by this
solution, which is presented as entirely just and benevolent – even
utopian. Instead he argues that

> where Klattu comes from, the robot cop is trusted. It is only on earth
> (and here, Earth stands for society, as society stands for centre) that
> Gort is dangerous, only on Earth, the world of disharmony and intol-
> erance, that Gort would menace Helen Benson, that technology and
> humanity, head and heart, are at odds. Where Klattu comes from,
> Gort is either an obedient servant or benevolent master ...[72]

As a result, Biskind interprets *The Day the Earth Stood Still* as a
positive, enlightened and even radical film, and claims that as a critique 'of the witch-hunt and the cold war, [it] skated close to the
edge of permissible dissent'.[73]

The Thing from Another World

However, these films can be seen quite differently. Indeed, Biskind's
interpretation of them contradicts his own claims about the dominance of scientific and therapeutic forms of control. Both he and
Kawin also end up ultimately defending the very values of rationality and conformity on which the dominance of scientific-technical rationality is supposed to depend. In the process, they ignore or
distort aspects of these films. For example, in *The Thing from
Another World*, it is not the military personnel who are associated
with the authority of the state, but the scientist. While he is associated with the highest levels of state authority and is given the full
support of the military hierarchy, the military heroes have little
authority and even have to disobey orders to defeat the alien. They
are not the representatives of state authority, but its subjects.

The scientist, Carrington, is clearly presented as one of the
experts of the new Fordist order. He has been involved in the Bikini
atom-bomb tests, and both the government and the military elites
look to him for advice. Indeed, so established is his authority that
even the military superiors back at base camp complain that they

are told nothing about what he is doing at the North pole. The military heroes, on the other hand, are far from experts. They are not only required to refer back to their superiors at every available opportunity, but do not even understand the principles of scientific-technical rationality. Hendry, the hero, is constantly telling the scientists that they have 'lost' him as they try to explain scientific details and procedures, and the orders from his superiors are forever telling him to defer to Carrington.

As a result, the conflict is not simply between the military and the scientists, as Biskind suggests, but one between ordinary working people and the authority of experts. The military itself is not presented positively, but only the soldiers on the ground. The military authorities, and particularly the high command, are presented as not only inadequate, but as an actual problem. They are presented as cumbersome and out of touch. They install doorways which are inappropriate to the arctic environment and send pith helmets to the North pole. They publish bulletins in *Stars and Stripes* which contradict the evidence, and lay down standard operating procedures which do not take account of the context of their use and so have destructive results. When the soldiers use these standard operating procedures to uncover the alien space ship which they have found buried in the ice, they only succeed in blowing it up. Indeed, whenever orders do come from above, they are either too late or else completely misguided. As the battle against the alien intensifies, the soldiers keep getting messages which tell them to protect the creature at all costs.

In this context, Carrington's interest in the thing is significant. After one confrontation with the alien, it is attacked by the camp dogs which tear off one of its arms. As the scientists inspect this arm, they find that the alien is a vegetable and that it has seed pods under its skin. From this information, Carrington deduces that the alien's reproductive system is asexual, and he proceeds to give a speech which indicates not only why he considers this discovery so important, but also the values which the creature embodies for him:

> Yes, the neat and unconfused reproductive technique of vegetation. No pain or pleasure as we know it. No emotions. No heart. Our superior in every way. Gentlemen, do you realize what we've found? A being from another world, as different from us as one pole from the other. If we can only communicate with it, we could learn secrets that have hidden from man since the beginning.

For Carrington, the alien is the 'ideal' of the system of scientific-technical rationality. It is a creature which has no personal or irrational features. As Lukacs argues in relation to the labour process, scientific-technical rationality is not concerned with the individual qualities of its workers' labour, but only with the quantity of their labour, their output. Indeed, he claims that as scientific-technical rationality is used by management to create greater efficiency, the individual qualities of a worker's labour are redefined 'as mere sources of error when contrasted with those special laws functioning according to rational principles'.[74] In this process of production, and by extension, in a society ordered according to the principles of scientific-technical rationality, individuals must deny their individual qualities in order to become interchangeable components within a system which is ordered and controlled by experts.

Carrington admires the alien because it lacks the very features which he defines as an impediment to efficiency. The alien race is not made up of individuals with individual features or qualities. Each is a replica of its parent and is produced through a system of reproduction which is not only seen as more efficient by Carrington, but is also associated with the standardisation of mass production. Not only does this system of reproduction define the alien race as little more than biological machines, it also means that they lack the features which Carrington sees as the ultimate form of 'irrationality', sexual desire. It is sexual desire which is seen as the ultimate expression of all human emotions and feelings, but it is this very feature which Carrington's scientific-technical rationality seeks to control or erase. It is not only seen as an impediment to the efficient performance of social roles, but it also requires interaction. Carrington's ideal model of society must seek to eradicate interaction in favour of a centrally-ordered system of control, and it is the struggle between interaction and domination which preoccupies this film.

Just as MacDonald and Mills argued that the new system of domination broke down interactive communities in order to bind individuals directly to the centres of power, so *The Thing from Another World* dramatises the conflict between these two modes of social organisation. It suggests that in the latter system, people are merely objects to be used, and this situation is dramatised through the film's presentation of the alien as a kind of modernist vampire. It feeds on human blood which it also needs to reproduce itself as a species. Marx had used the image of the vampire to describe the workings of capitalism, and argued that 'Capitalism is dead labour which, vampire-like, lives only by sucking living labour, and lives the more, the more it sucks.'[75] In a similar way, as Carlos Clarens puts it, *The Thing from Another World* suggests that 'superior science ... will bleed us to death'.[76] Even Carrington is worried by this situation. If the alien only sees humans as a means of sustaining and reproducing itself, why should it want to communicate with them? As Carrington puts it: 'He regards us as important only for his nourishment. He has the same attitude towards us as we have towards a field of cabbages. That is our battle.' Unfortunately Carrington is as unable to influence the actions of the alien as ordinary people are able to influence the elites of mass society. He is as unsuccessful in persuading the alien to communicate with him as the soldiers are in trying to persuade him to interact with them.

The issue of communication is therefore central to the film, and it is partly dealt with through the different styles of speech which distinguish the film. While Carrington tends to give speeches or monologues, the soldiers tend to speak in overlapping dialogue, a feature common to those films associated with the director Howard Hawks who produced *The Thing from Another World*. The soldiers talk fast, bouncing ideas off one another, finishing each others' sentences as they add ideas and comments. In this kind of dialogue, meaning and ideas do not originate in the authority of any one individual, but develop out of communal interaction. Hendry may act as the leader, but instead of dictating to the group as Carrington does, he mainly acts to facilitate dialogue. Indeed, he is often given ideas and even orders by his subordinates, and in the final battle, he actually loses track of what is being planned. He becomes displaced from the centre of the group, which now no longer needs him to co-ordinate it, and moves to a place on the sidelines from which he keeps asking what is going on. However, this situation is not presented negatively, and Hendry does not resent it. In fact, the reverse is true: Hendry turns it into a joke because he is able to accept that his men know what they are doing, and may even be better equipped in certain areas than himself. Indeed, the group even involve themselves in his 'private life', and finally succeed in pushing Hendry and Nicky, his girlfriend, together. As she tells him, 'they know what's best for you'.

In contrast, Carrington gives monologues and speeches in which he sets himself up as an authority who hands down information and orders to others. Indeed, rather than interacting with others, he frequently withholds information in an attempt to control situations, and he shows little concern when this often endangers people. When he discovers that the alien is using the camp's greenhouse to reproduce itself, he refuses to tell Hendry and the others. Instead he leaves a couple of his fellow scientists to keep watch and so causes their deaths. He even begins secretly to breed the alien's seeds himself. Indeed, the more he tries to understand the alien and to communicate with it, the more he finds himself unable to communicate with other humans. His powers of speech start to deteriorate, and he frequently resorts to passing his notes over to Nicky, his secretary, who reads them for him. This technique is similar to the way in which experts often use press conferences to control and manage the flow of information to the rest of the population. He even finds it increasingly difficult to interpret the responses of others. When he explains to the other scientists that he has been breeding the alien seed pods, he mistakes their looks of horror and disapproval for disbelief. This situation is unsurprising given that their lives are unimportant to him, except as an aid to the further development of scientific knowledge. As Carrington puts it, 'knowledge is more important than life'.

The film's concerns with issues of interaction and communication are also dealt with through the figure of Scotty, the newspaper man who comes to the base with Hendry. In this film, the news media are not presented as a form of mass cultural manipulation, but as a democratic force. It is their role to disseminate information to the public. But when the soldiers find the alien space ship, a conflict develops between Hendry and Scotty. Hendry will not let Scotty release the story of the discovery. He claims that the army radio cannot be used for 'private information', but when Scotty retorts that this information is not private, but belongs to the whole world, Hendry replies that he is not working for the whole world, but for the US army. This exchange is given a darker dimension later in the film when Scotty comments on the destruction of the space ship and claims that the military will probably make Hendry a general for destroying embarrassing information. The implication of these comments should be clear. The film raises the issue of the military hierarchy's control and manipulation of information. If Scotty represents the democratic flow of information, the military, like Carrington, seek to dominate and control information for their own ends, rather than in the interests of the wider population.

However, Hendry is largely dissociated from this problem. He is clearly seen to be acting under orders, and he makes great efforts to get permission from his superiors for Scotty to release his story. Indeed, Hendry has been responsible for persuading his superior to allow Scotty to go to the North pole in the first place. As the film progresses, Hendry also becomes distanced from the hierarchy and learns the importance of disobeying orders. Scotty seems to acknowledge this situation, and though he still complains, he is spontaneously included within the group. The group even makes him their spokesperson after the conflict. Scotty is given the radio and not only addresses the world, but also talks for the group. His speech even includes Carrington within the group under the assumption that he has probably learned his lesson and will now respect the interactive community.

If the film concerns a conflict between the interactive community and the authority of scientific-technical rationality which seeks to dominate and reconstruct this community, these issues are also dealt with in relation to sexuality and gender. Not only is the alien's mode of asexual reproduction that which is ultimately defined as monstrous, but in American culture, as linguistic theorists such as Deborah Tannen have claimed, overlapping dialogue and interaction are usually associated with the feminine, while monologue and rationality are usually associated with the masculine.[77] As a result, while it could be argued that the alien's association with reproduction defines it as feminine, its physical appearance and its association with rationality define it as male. Indeed, there is a long history of horror texts, dating back to the early Gothic novels, concerned with the patriarchal fantasy of producing life without interaction with women and define the attempt to realise this fantasy as that which is ultimately monstrous. Mary Shelley's *Frankenstein* is a particularly clear example, and like *The Thing from Another World*, this novel relates this fantasy to the logic of scientific rationality. Not only is it this asexual method of reproduction which leads Carrington to associate the alien with technology and rationality, both of which are usually defined as masculine, but this method also leads him to distinguish it from those very qualities which are usually defined as feminine, qualities such as interaction and emotion.

Indeed, the film is highly critical not only of the distinction between rationality and irrationality, but also of the distinction between masculinity and femininity to which it is related. As a result, it not only contains a strong central female character, but also presents its male characters as emotionally weak. Not only does Nicky wear trousers throughout the film, she is often at least as capable as the men in traditionally masculine activities. She has been able to out-drink Hendry, and knows enough about science to understand Carrington's work and its implications. Indeed, the military team accept her as an equal within their group without question. At one point, she does turn up with coffee for the men, but this scene is particularly telling with regard to the film's self-conscious handling of gender roles. As the men are discussing how to combat the alien, Nicky arrives at the door with coffee and asks if anyone wants a cup. Recognising that this is an excuse, they say that they don't want any coffee, but that she can join them anyhow. Having already been accepted, she admits that she had only brought the coffee so that she could join them. Only at this point, once the men have made it clear that she has been welcomed into the group as an equal, and not in order to perform traditionally female roles, do they then agree to drink the coffee.

But if Nicky is skilled in traditionally masculine activities, she is not a surrogate male.[76] She does not distance herself from traditionally feminine qualities in order to achieve male approval. Indeed, her strength is that she embodies both masculine and feminine virtues, but is not confined to either one. If she does trouble and disturb the male characters, it is due to their own inadequacies. Hendry, for example, is quite capable in traditionally masculine activities, but he is unable to deal with his emotions and so finds it difficult to relate to women. In the film's terms, he is not only presented as immature, but this immaturity is also associated with the rationality of the scientists and the alien. These latter figures either lack or despise emotion, and the scientists are frequently claimed to be 'like kids with a new toy'. If, as Biskind argues, this situation implies that the alien is not just associated with rationality but also with Hendry's sexuality, it is not because it is associated with his id, or his sexual desire. After all, the alien has no sexual desire. Instead, the alien is associated with Hendry's masculinity, and his inability to deal with women as anything more than objects for sexual conquest. In the film's terms, he must grow up, but this does not mean that he must repress his sexuality. Quite the reverse, he must acknowledge his feelings, including his sexual feelings, and learn how to interact with women as equals. In short he must acquire traditionally feminine qualities.

Not only does Nicky call into question traditional gender roles, and gender distinctions, she is also for this very reason absolutely essential to the destruction of the alien. Indeed, she is the one who comes up with the comment from which the final plan is developed. As the group tries to work out how to kill a vegetable, she jokingly suggests cooking it. It is by combining her domestic knowledge with practical science that the group is finally able to destroy the alien by burning it to death with electricity. It is only when the distinctions between the masculine and the feminine, the rational and the irrational, the domestic and the scientific, are dispensed with that the threat represented by the alien can be finally eliminated.

The Day the Earth Stood Still

The Day the Earth Stood Still, on the other hand, is a far more authoritarian film. Its criticism of American society is simply that it is not rational enough, and it calls for the repression of individual feelings, interests and desires, all of which are simply defined as both irrational and destructive. This repression is necessary in order to ensure the efficient running of a state which is not merely national or even international, but a fully 'universal' order. Nor is this film any less violent in its values than The *Thing from Another World*. It is just more impersonal. Violence, or at least the threat of violence, is essential to the smooth running of the rational state. It has to be used to keep irrational elements repressed. Violence may be denied to individuals or nations, but only because it is given over to the rule of technology and science embodied in the robot police force of which Gort is a member.

Klattu has been sent to earth to inform us that the earth's internal conflicts threaten the peace of the universe, but the language which he uses to describe humans and human society clearly defines these conflicts as simply the products of irrationality. He criticises humans for their 'unreasoning attitudes' and when he is asked by an interviewer (who does not know his identity) if he fears the alien's arrival, Klattu answers that he is only 'fearful when [he] sees people substituting fear for reason'. For Klattu, human emotions have no foundation or validity, and it is only rational thought which has any positive value. The problems of human societies and their conflicts are simply dismissed as the product of these irrational emotions. When the nations of the earth refuse to meet one another in order to hear Klattu's message, he is angered by their 'childish jealousies and superstitions'. They are not based on a reasonable foundation and are merely described as 'petty squabbles'. For Klattu, and for the film, individual and national interests must be put aside in favour of the Universal, but the Universal is not an interactive community based on shared interests. It is an abstract, rational and totalising order to which individuals and nations must surrender themselves. It is vertical, rather than horizontal, in its organisation.

Indeed, rather than criticising the scientific-technical rationality of the American state, the film continually defends and even champions it. For example, the film is careful to emphasise that it is not the American state which is responsible for the conflicts between the nations of earth. Henley, the diplomat who tries to organise the meeting of national representatives which Klattu demands, is presented as honest and sincere. He genuinely wants to help Klattu, but it is the other nations which cause problems. The American president has even tried to appease the Soviet Union by agreeing to their demand that the meeting should be held in Moscow, and it is the British government who complicates matters by refusing to attend the meeting if it is held there. If there are problems with American institutions, it is that they are not rational enough in their organisation.

Neither is the American military presented negatively as is often claimed. It is presented as a problem only in so far as it functions to defend the interests of an individual nation, rather than universal interests. Indeed, Klattu does not even disapprove of war itself, but only wars fought for supposedly 'petty interests'. Strangely, when Klattu is taken on a tour of Washington by the young Billy Benson, a young boy whom he befriends during the course of the film, he is awestruck by both the Lincoln Memorial and Arlington cemetery. Indeed Billy's father, who has given his life in World War II, is not presented as a fool who died in a meaningless war. Instead, both the American Civil War and World War II are implied to have been heroic struggles for grand universal values. Lincoln in particular is seen as a 'great man'. The Gettysburg address is not seen as a piece of propaganda designed to encourage men to fight in one of the bloodiest wars of American history, but rather as a heroic testament to the values of 'Union' over sectionalism, of universal over particularistic interests. Unfortunately for Biskind, and others who defend this film as a critic of Cold War ideology, it was this rhetoric of universalism over particularism which America used to justify its Cold War politics. America, it was claimed, was defending universal human values over the particularism of the Soviet Union. Indeed, at the beginning of the film, the military is not even presented as having been responsible for the shooting of Klattu. The shooting is the fault of an individual soldier who panics when his emotions get the better of him. It is a lack of military discipline which is the problem, not military discipline itself.

As a result, in *The Day the Earth Stood Still*, it is ordinary people who are the problem, and they are presented as needing the authority of experts in order to keep them in line. Throughout the film, people are presented as prone to irrational panic and in need of discipline. When the space ship lands, they run in terror. Later they form crowds around the vessel and need to be controlled by the military and police. When Gort appears they react in horror, and flee once more. Indeed, while Klattu claims that his message is too important to be entrusted to any one individual or nation, he does not seek to address the ordinary people, but only their leaders. If he has the power to make the world stand still for half an hour, it is difficult to accept that the film cannot find a way for him to address all the peoples of the earth (as the aliens do in *Earth Vs the Flying Saucers* (1956)). Indeed, while he does go amongst the ordinary people, he explicitly states that he is doing so in order to discover the basis of the irrationalities which divide the world. It is the irrationality of ordinary people which causes problems at the higher levels of government, not vice versa. Furthermore, the film does not contradict Klattu's view of people. When he goes amongst the people, he takes a room in a boarding house in which everyone except a young woman, Helen Benson, and her son, Billy, display irrationality and panic. They either suspect the alien of being a Russian, or are just plain 'jittery'.

If Helen Benson and her son do not display these negative features, it is not because the film values the feminine qualities of interaction or emotion. Instead, Helen displays the traditionally maternal qualities of self-denial and self-sacrifice. She represses her own interests and defers to authority. This feature is particularly clear in her relationship with her boyfriend, David. When he finds out that Klattu is the alien, David decides to inform the Pentagon. However, Klattu has spoken to Helen and has persuaded her of the universal importance of his mission. She accepts his authority and tries to persuade David not to inform. Unfortunately, he is filled with dreams of individual power and heroism. He says that by informing he will become a 'big man' and that he will 'be able to write [his] own ticket'. In response, Helen asks him to consider the broader implications of his actions, but he only responds, 'I don't care about the rest of the world'. In this film, individualism is merely irrational selfishness, but all the film has to offer in its place is self-denial. It hardly offers the image of a society in which humans can live more fulfilling lives, and simply calls for the repression of individual desires before an authoritarian state.

Helen's son operates in much the same way as his mother. Children are seen as open to the wonders of the world, but in the film, the reason for their openness is that they look up to others. Indeed, their sense of wonder is almost entirely presented in relation to scientific achievements. While adults are terrified by the space ship, the children are presented as being excited by, and in awe of, the vessel. Billy is also fascinated by Klattu's stories about the scientific wonders of his civilisation.

Indeed, science in general is presented as wondrous and benevolent. Not only does the film emphasise that the science of Klattu's society is more advanced than that of humans, it often associates it with medicine. It is claimed that due to their advanced medicine, the life expectancy on Klattu's planet is twice that on earth. At another point, a doctor comments on the miraculous properties of an ointment which Klattu has brought with him, an ointment which has healed a bullet wound on Klattu's arm within one day. But the greatest display of the healing powers of science occurs at the end of the film when Gort uses technology to bring Klattu back from the dead after he has been shot by the army for the second time. Indeed, this sequence also gives science religious overtones. The film has a clear parallel with the New Testament, in which Klattu takes the role of Christ. He comes to earth to save it from its follies; goes amongst the common people; is killed by human ignorance and intolerance; and eventually rises again before delivering a message to the world and ascending to the heavens. He even takes the name Carpenter while on earth. Klattu does tell Helen that his resurrection is only temporary and that only God can give back life once it has been taken, but this only further associates technology and science with the powers of God. They become powers to be worshipped and adored.

The film also goes to great lengths to allay fears about science. For example, at one point, Klattu tells Billy that his space ship is powered by atomic energy. Billy is surprised and claims that he thought atomic energy was only useful in the making of bombs. In response, Klattu explains that atomic energy is useful for a great many other things, too. The implication should be clear: science in general and atomic energy in particular are not bad in themselves, but only when used in an irrational and irresponsible manner.

Indeed, science is presented as the only potential saviour of humanity. When Klattu finds that the world's leaders will not meet with him, he tries to find an alternative way of delivering his message, and asks Billy who is the greatest person in America. Billy seems a bit confused, and well he might. Klattu really means: who is the most intellectually brilliant, or as Billy puts it, the 'smartest' person. There are many different ways of defining 'greatness', but for Klattu, as for the film, greatness means scientific genius. Billy decides that the answer is Professor Barnhardt, and Klattu decides that instead of addressing the world's political leaders, he will address its scientists. His preference for science over politics is again related to issues of rationality. Politicians are associated with the defence of particular interests, while scientists are presented as objective and rational. They are supposedly above the 'petty squabbles' of politics and address universal truths in a logical and rational manner. For this reason, they can overcome the irrationality which divides the world and come together for the good of all.

Not only are scientists the best way of spreading the message, the message itself is that humanity must put aside its irrational behaviour and accept the rule of science in the form of a robot police force. These robots are the embodiment of super-rationality and Klattu informs the scientists that the peoples of the universe have given them 'absolute power over us'. They have incredible destructive powers and have been programmed to destroy any planet which behaves aggressively. Klattu claims that this solution to war does not involve any loss of freedom, except the freedom to behave 'irresponsibly'. But there is a problem with the word 'irresponsible': it is not as easy to define as Klattu implies. What may be irresponsible to one person may not be to another. It is also worth noting that instead of a solution to aggression, the justification for this scheme sounds very similar to the Mutually Assured Destruction (MAD) philosophy which was later used to justify the arms race. According to this philosophy, the stockpiling of nuclear weapons was an aid to world peace, not a threat. The combined destructive strength of these weapons, it was argued, would be so great that no nation would dare to act aggressively for fear of starting an atomic war which would destroy the planet. It would assure the mutual destruction of both sides. Klattu's proposal does not reject violence, but places it firmly within the hands of the state. Nor is it presented as an option. He informs the scientists that there is no alternative. Earth must either accept the rule of robots such as Gort, or be destroyed. Instead of respecting difference, the film demands rigid conformity to the universal order, an order from which there can be no valid dissent.

Notes

1 For a good introduction to genre theory and its problems see Peter Hutchings, 'Genre Theory and Criticism', in Joanne Hollows and Mark Jancovich, eds, *Approaches to Popular Film* (Manchester: Manchester University Press, 1995), pp. 59–78. For a collection of many of the central articles in genre criticism, see also Barry K. Grant, ed., *The Film Genre Reader* (Austin: University of Texas Press, 1986).

2 Andrew Tudor, 'Genre', in B. K. Grant, ed., *The Film Genre Reader* (Austin: University of Texas Press, 1986).

3 For a discussion of genre hybridity in the 'New' Hollywood, see, for example, Jim Collins, 'Genercity in the Nineties: Electic Irony and the New Sincerity', in Jim Collins *et al.*, eds, *Film Theory Goes to the Movies* (New York: Routledge, 1993); and Yvonne Tasker, *Spectacular Bodies: Gender, Genre and the Action Cinema* (London: Routledge, 1993).

4 This term is drawn for the work of Pierre Bourdieu. See, for example, Pierre Bourdieu, *Distinction: A Social Critique of the Judgement of Taste* (London: Routledge, 1984).

5 Brian Aldiss, *The Penguin Omnibus of Science Fiction* (Harmondsworth: Penguin, 1973), p. 11.

6 Patrick Lucanio, *Them or Us: Archetypal Interpretations of Fifties Alien Invasion Films* (Bloomington: Indiana University Press, 1987).

7 Vivian Sobchack, *Screening Space: The American Science Fiction Film* (New York: Ungar, 1987).

8 For a longer discussion of these developments, see Mark Jancovich,

Horror (London: Batsford, 1992).

9 Sobchack, *Screening Space*, p. 45.

10 Lucanio, *Them or Us*, pp. 18–20.

11 *Ibid.*, p. 2.

12 *Ibid.*, pp. 46–7.

13 Peter Biskind, *Seeing is Believing: How Hollywood Taught Us to Stop Worrying and Love the Fifties* (London: Pluto, 1983), p. 103.

14 Andrew Tudor, *Monsters and Mad Scientists: A Cultural History of the Horror Movie* (Oxford: Blackwell, 1987), p. 220.

15 Quoted in Sobchack, *Screening Space*, p. 45.

16 Biskind, *Seeing is Believing*, p. 21.

17 *Ibid.*, p. 103.

18 Susan Sontag, 'The Imagination of Disaster', in *Commentary*, (October 1965), pp. 42–8.

19 Biskind, *Seeing is Believing*, p. 107.

20 *Ibid.*, p. 107.

21 *Ibid.*

22 *Ibid.*, p. 133.

23 Similar claims have been made about the horror genre as a whole. Most particularly, Barbara Creed claims that horror is based on a fear of the female body in general, and the figure of the mother in particular. See, Barbara Creed, *The Monstrous-Feminine: Film, Feminism, Psychoanalysis* (London: Routledge, 1993).

24 Biskind, *Seeing is Believing*, p. 111.

25 For a more detailed discussion of the concept of Fordism, see, for example, David Harvey, *The Condition of Postmodernity* (Oxford: Blackwell, 1989).

26 Richard Pells, *The Liberal Mind in a Conservative Age: American Intellectuals in the 1940s and 1950s* (Middletown: Wesleyan University Press, 1989), p. 130.

27 This phrase was first used by Phillip Rahv to describe the intellectual climate of the 1950s, but has become more widely used. See, for example, Phillip Rahv, *Literature and the Sixth Sense* (Boston: Houghton Mifflin, 1970).

28 See, for example, C. Wright Mills, *The Power Elite* (New York: Oxford University Press, 1956); C. Wright Mills, 'On the New Left', in Paul Jacobs and Saul Landau, eds, *The New Radicals* (Harmondsworth: Penguin, 1966), pp. 107–20; and T. W. Adorno and Max Horkheimer, *The Dialectic of Enlightenment* (London: Verso, 1979).

29 Dwight MacDonald, 'Masscult and Midcult', in *Against the American Grain* (London: Victor Gollancz, 1963), p. 14.

30 Adorno and Horkheimer, *The Dialectic of Enlightenment*.

31 Clement Greenberg, 'Avant-garde and Kitsche', in B. Rosenberg and D.

Manning White, eds, *Mass Culture: The Popular Arts in America* (New York: Free Press, 1957).

32 MacDonald, 'Masscult and Midcult', p. 29.

33 *Ibid.*, p. 8.

34 *Ibid.*, p. 9.

35 *Ibid.*, p. 4.

36 David Reisman, *The Lonely Crowd: A Study of the Changing American Character* (New Haven: Yale University Press, revised edition, 1970).

37 Pells, *The Liberal Mind in a Conservative Age*, p. 168.

38 John Kenneth Galbraith, *The Affluent Society* (Boston: Houghton Mifflin, 1958).

39 Daniel Boorstin, *The Image: or What Happened to the American Dream* (Harmondsworth: Penguin, 1963).

40 William Whyte, *The Organization Man* (New York: Simon Schuster, 1956), p. 397.

41 Pells, *The Liberal Mind in a Conservative Age*, p. 193.

42 Daniel Bell, 'America as a Mass Society: A Critique', in Bell, *The End of Ideology: On the Exhaustion of Political Ideas in the Fifties* (Cambridge, Mass.: Harvard University Press, revised edition, 1988).

43 Daniel Bell, 'Work and its Discontents: The Cult of Efficiency in America', in Bell, *The End of Ideology*.

44 Daniel Bell, *The Cultural Contradictions of Capitalism* (London: Heinemann, 1979), p. xi.

45 C. Wright Mills, *The Causes of World War III* (New York: Simon & Schuster, 1958).

46 Mills, 'On the New Left'.

47 Mills, *The Power Elite*.

48 Lucanio, *Them or Us*.

49 Biskind, *Seeing is Believing*, p. 134.

50 Carlos Clarens, *Horror Movies: An Illustrated Survey* (London: Secker and Warburg, 1967), p. 147.

51 Lucanio, *Them or Us*.

52 Even in texts such as *War of the Worlds* where the woman's role is far more peripheral to the action except as an object to be protected, the male scientist-hero eventually occupies the very same position which the woman has occupied throughout the film. He learns the futility of his science in the face of the alien invaders, and the world is only saved when he is finally stripped of his technology and dominance, and embraces the woman's Christian faith.

53 Biskind, *Seeing is Believing*, p. 133.

54 Betty Friedan, *The Feminine Mystique* (New York: Dell, 1963).

55 Mary Shelley, *Frankenstein: or the Modern Prometheus* (1818) (Oxford: Oxford University Press, 1969).

56 See my analysis of *Frankenstein* in Jancovich, *Horror*.

57 While there are considerable problems with the concept of 'interactive communities', what is important is that these films operated around very similar oppositions to those which can be found in the mass culture critics of their period, critics who were at best dismissive of these films. Indeed, even within contemporary criticism, the opposition between 'interaction' and 'domination' is often present, even if it assumes very different guises.

58 Friedan, *The Feminine Mystique*.

59 For a discussion of these issues, see Barbara Ehrenreich, *The Hearts of Men: American Dreams and the Flight from Commitment* (London: Pluto, 1983).

60 John Campbell, 'Who Goes There?' (1938), republished in *The Mammoth Book of Classic Science Fiction* (New York: Carroll and Graf, 1988).

61 Ray Bradbury, 'The Concrete Mixer' (1949), in *The Illustrated Man* (1951) (London: Corgi, 1955).

62 Bruce Kawin, 'The Mummy's Pool', in Barry K. Grant, ed., *Planks of Reason: Essays on the Horror Film* (Metuchan: Scarecrow, 1984), p. 5.

63 Kawin, 'The Mummy's Pool', p. 5.

64 *Ibid.*, p. 7.

65 Biskind, *Seeing is Believing*, p. 134.

66 *Ibid.*, p. 132.

67 *Ibid.*, p. 157.

68 *Ibid.*, p. 153.

69 *Ibid.*

70 *Ibid.*

71 *Ibid.*, p. 154.

72 *Ibid.*, p. 158.

73 *Ibid.*

74 Georg Lukacs, 'Reification and the Consciousness of the Proletariat', in Lukacs, *History and Class Consciousness* (London: Merlin, 1971), p. 89.

75 Karl Marx, *Capital Vol. I* (Harmondsworth: Penguin, 1976), p. 342.

76 Clarens, *Horror Movies*, p. 182.

77 Deborah Tannen, 'Relative Focus on Involvement in Oral and Written Discourse', in David R. Olsen *et al.*, eds, *Literacy, Language and Learning: The Nature and Consequences of Reading and Writing* (Cambridge: Cambridge University Press, 1985).

78 There is considerable debate over the representation of women within the films of Howard Hawks. For an alternative view to the one presented here, see Peter Wollen, *Signs and Meanings in the Cinema* (London: Secker and Warburg, 1972).

Machines of mass destruction: the martian war machines from *The War of the Worlds* (1953).

Chapter 2

The end of civilisation as we know it?:
from mass destruction to depersonalisation

Introduction

The success of these two films established the subgenre, and in 1953 three more films were released which were to become the virtual prototypes for later developments. These films were *The Beast from 20,000 Fathoms*, *The War of the Worlds* and *Invaders from Mars*. The first two focus on the spectacle of mass destruction, while the last focuses on the threat of dehumanisation in which ordinary people are 'taken over' or 'brainwashed' by the alien enemy. However, while both *The Beast from 20,000 Fathoms* and *The War of the Worlds* are concerned with mass destruction, they present the threat in different ways. In the first, it is a natural creature from the earth's own prehistory which is unleashed from its icy tomb by a nuclear test, while in the second film, it is an all-out invasion of the earth by Martians. In both films, the threat grows as the action moves from an isolated locality to a major metropolitan area which is virtually demolished in a spectacle of carnage. However, they also present the solution in very different ways.

In *The Beast from 20,000 Fathoms*, science may unleash the problem, but also eventually provides the solution. The creature not only threatens to destroy New York City with its strength, it is also the carrier of a virulent and ancient disease to which humanity has no immunity. As a result, Nesbitt, the scientist-hero, points out that any ordinary use of military force will only run the risk of spreading the disease, even if it succeeds in killing the creature. Instead, he proposes to use a radioactive isotope which can be fired into the creature by a skilled marksman. The isotope will not only kill the creature, but also destroy the plague which it carries. Atomic science not only causes the threat of the creature, but also provides the only way of protecting society from it.

However, the film has a much more ambivalent attitude towards science than this description might suggest. Certainly the hero, Nesbitt, is a scientist who runs into the prehistoric monster while he is conducting nuclear tests, but none the less, the film displays anxieties about his activities, anxieties which the hero himself voices. At one point, a colleague (who is soon to die in the first encounter with the creature) speaks a little too over-enthusiastically about the test and claims that he feels as though they were starting a new book of Genesis, a statement which Nesbitt undercuts when he responds that he hopes that they are not simply writing the end of the original.

Indeed, after Nesbitt's encounter with the beast, he does not assume a position of scientific authority, but is rather dismissed and ridiculed for his claims. He himself acknowledges that his story sounds 'fantastic', and it is routinely repressed as impossible. It confounds the believable limits of the possible and is interpreted as a hallucination. A psychiatrist is even introduced to explain away rationally Nesbitt's experience as the result of a psychological trauma, an unreasonable and irrational response which has no validity whatsoever.

In this way, Nesbitt becomes alienated and isolated from others, unable to square his experiences with the official version of the experts and unable to attribute any authority to his claims. It is only with the introduction of the female lead, Leigh, that he is able to form some sense of community and acceptance. She offers him emotional support and enables him to find others who share his perceptions, a strategy which eventually wins over the authorities who have ridiculed him.

Indeed, Leigh is an interesting figure to the extent that she exists as a transitional case between Nicky in *The Thing from Another World* and figures such as Pat Medford in *Them!*. She is neither as sharp nor as independent as Nicky or her successors, but like many later female leads, she is not simply presented as the secretarial aid to a male figure of scientific authority, but as a scientist herself. Her motives for helping Nesbitt may seem to lack a strictly scientific basis – she seems to be doing so more out of a romantic interest in him than in the cause of science – but none the less, even this stresses the importance of emotional, rather than simply rational, criteria as a response to the situation. She may be largely relegated to the role of a nurturing and supportive female who exists to care for the male characters, but even so, the film has no problem with her role as a scientist who exists outside of the domestic sphere and follows her own initiative when it counts. The film even pointedly raises the issue of gender roles at one point in which Nesbitt comments that he is surprised that 'a girl like you' could be a palaeontologist, a comment which she quickly deflects as irrelevant. 'What's wrong with palaeontology?' she asks, deliberately misreading the remark.

However, the relationship between Nesbitt and Leigh also raises other issues. As scientists, they have different interests. His work is preoccupied with the future, while hers is concerned with the past.

As Leigh remarks in a defence of palaeontology, knowledge of the past is essential for an understanding of the future. But this remark is given a darker inflection by her next comment in which she notes that Professor Elson, her fatherly, scientific mentor, often says that 'the future is simply a reflection of the past'. This comment focuses certain aspects of the creature's role within the film, and it implies that the scientific pursuit of progress is actually in danger of simply destroying the world rather than improving it. It is in danger of hurtling humanity back into prehistory rather than forward into a brave new world. Indeed, Nesbitt's response only succeeds in unwittingly emphasising this point when he claims that the future could be 'bright', a response which unconsciously raises the spectre of nuclear destruction. Indeed, the film is preoccupied with reversals and returns. Not only is the monster's destructive path and its invasion of New York City a result of its desire to return to what had been its natural habitat and breeding grounds, but the film opens with the image of a whirlpool, a spiralling vortex in which everything is sucked in towards the absence at its centre. In this way, the film continually emphasises its own ambivalence to science as both the cause of, and solution to, the threat.

However, if science does offer the possibility of resolving matters in *The Beast from 20,000 Fathoms*, the solution proposed by *War of the Worlds* is quite different. In this film, science is quite futile as a way of combating the aliens who represent not merely the threat of science, but of 'superscience'. Indeed the film opens with an account of the developing relationship between science and warfare in the twentieth century, and portrays the use of science in World Wars I and II as resulting, almost inevitably, in the terrifying use of 'superscience' in the 'war of the worlds'. The aliens are also described as creatures of 'intelligence greater than ours', but this intelligence is only presented as making them 'cool and unsympathetic'. Not only are the aliens portrayed as highly organised and efficient, they are directly associated with technology. It is their war-machines which are the film's most dramatic image, and it is these machines on which the film concentrates in its presentation of the aliens. The aliens themselves are rarely glimpsed, and when they are, they are either shown only in part or else obscured by shadows. There is even the suggestion that the aliens and their machines share an almost symbiotic relationship. The aliens are not only presented as physically weak and hence as dependent on their machines, but when the hero manages to cut off one of the mechanical eyes which the machines use like a periscope, he later finds blood on the cloth in which he has wrapped it. Not only are the aliens presented as virtually machine-like, but their machines bleed as though they were mere extensions of the aliens' bodies.

As a result, it is hardly surprising that while the hero is a scientist, science remains a distinctly ambiguous force within the film. At first, it seems to lend the hero authority, but as the film continues, the value of this authority is progressively undermined. Indeed, at the moment when the aliens first attack, all the technology in the local town breaks down. The electricity and phones go dead, and all the watches stop. Even the eventual use of the atomic bomb fails to make any impact on the invaders. Human science is entirely redundant in contrast to the 'superscience' of the aliens.

But if scientific authority fails, ordinary people are also ambiguous within the film. When the first attack occurs, the hero is enjoying an ordinary Saturday night with the local townspeople. He recognises their virtues, and even states: 'if you could gather all the energy expended at just one square dance, we could send that meteor [the martians' space ship] back where it came from'. The energy and vitality of the common people, it would seem, is no match for science. But actually people are no match for the aliens. As the invasion gets under way, they put their faith in the authorities, and gather in the hills in the hope of seeing the aliens defeated by the combined might of science and the military in the form of an atomic explosion. But when this attempt fails, they either become a destructive mob, or else huddle helplessly in churches where they wait and pray for deliverance.

In *War of the Worlds*, humanity is helpless against the alien invasion, and it is only divine wisdom that saves the day. The aliens are eventually destroyed by the Earth's germs against which they have no resistance. As the omniscient narrator of the film puts it, 'after all that men could do had failed, the aliens were defeated, and the Earth saved, by the littlest things which God in His wisdom had placed upon the Earth'. This solution is also related to issues of science. As they study the aliens, the scientists discover that while the invaders are scientifically and intellectually advanced, they are physically primitive and undeveloped. It is this physical lack of development which makes them prone to the Earth's diseases. The Martians are all mind, and this condition leaves them vulnerable. For this reason, the film clearly contradicts the priest at the beginning of the film who argues that 'they are more advanced than we are and therefore nearer to the creator'. Scientific advance, within this film, is no guarantee of superiority. Indeed, it is science, not nature, which is the problem. The aliens' weakness is their association with the former rather than the latter. They have advanced intellectually, but only at the expense of their natural and physical selves.

This position also accounts for the rather ambiguous role of women within the film. While the heroine is not developed as a character and seems to exist only as a love interest for the male hero to protect, she is actually much more important than she at first appears. She embodies the Christian values which the film promotes, and which the hero must eventually learn to embrace. His superiority and heroism is progressively stripped from him until he eventually finds himself in the same position of helplessness as the heroine. They cower in a church as they hold each other and pray for deliverance. It is only at this moment that the threat is finally ended. If this deferral to religious authority sounds similar to the values of *The Day the Earth Stood Still*, the difference is actually quite significant. *War of the Worlds* does not attempt to deify science and scientific authorities in the manner of *The Day the Earth Stood Still*. Indeed, its values are opposed to the values of science. Instead it challenges centralised scientific authority as hubris, and offers a rather too cosy image of an interactive community in the form of the family. The heroine spends most of the film looking and feeling lost, but she also spends much of it extolling the virtues of being a member of a large family in which one feels that one is loved and that one belongs. It is the warmth of small, local groups which is positive within the film and is distinguished from the large, abstract structures of Fordist America. Indeed, it is only once the film's action reaches the large urban areas of Los Angeles that people are presented as a destructive mass. In small towns and in nature, they are presented as warm and supportive to one another.

If these two films focus on the spectacle of mass destruction, the third film of 1953, *Invaders from Mars*, focuses on the process of depersonalisation in which people are 'taken over' by the alien invaders. The story involves a young boy, David, who witnesses an alien space ship land near his home, and comes to realise that the aliens are controlling people through special devices which are implanted in the back of the victims' necks. This process turns people into little more than robots who exist to carry out the will of the invaders. Their expressions become blank and impersonal, and they become unable to show warmth and compassion for those people for whom they previously cared. Indeed, when David's father returns after being taken over, he is not only dictatorial, but ends up hitting his son to the ground. In this film, the threat is once again from 'dangerously higher forms' with superior intelligence.

The aliens themselves fall into two categories. The first of these is the 'supreme intelligence' which is little more than a head in a glass jar, and it is described as 'mankind developed to its ultimate intelligence'. Like the aliens in *War of the Worlds*, it is an intelligence which has advanced itself at the expense of its own physical body. This 'supreme intelligence' controls the second category of aliens, the 'synthetic humans' or 'mutants'. These are large, physical beings, whose heads seem disproportionately small in relation to their bodies. They have no will of their own, and are described as merely 'slaves which exist to do [the supreme intelligence's] will'. The threat which the aliens present to human beings is that they will turn humans into little more than the 'mutants'. Humans will have no will of their own, but merely exist to be controlled by the 'supreme intelligence'. In this way, the film plays on the fear of a centrally-organised society which is ordered and controlled by experts.

Unfortunately, it does not follow through the implications of these central features. While the film starts out by concentrating on David's feelings of alienation and isolation, it almost immediately drops this feature, the very feature which would become central to later films of this type. At the start, it is those people whom David would normally expect to trust and rely upon who are taken over first: his father and mother; the police; and a close friend. In this situation, he finds that there is no one to whom he can talk or get to believe his story. In this way, the familiar world becomes strange and impersonal. As Vivian Sobchack puts it, when he goes to the police, the 'small town police station becomes a setting as visually jolting and alien as any other-worldly planet'.[1] But the film only keeps this up for a very short while before it introduces Dr Blake, a young and kindly female educational psychologist who listens to David and believes him. She not only offers him moral support and saves him from his mother, who has now been taken over by the aliens, she also helps him to contact scientific and military experts. Another weakness of the film is that the distinction between the 'depersonalised' and the 'normal' humans is all too clear. The film does not require the audience to question the appearance of 'normality' as do later films. As a result, it relieves the very sense of uncertainty and paranoia which it could have exploited.

The ease with which experts accept David's story also undermines the film's critique of science and centrally-organised societies. The scientific and military experts, Dr Kelson, Dr Blake and Colonel Fielding, even form a kind of surrogate family for David. They are distanced from the aliens, but only because they are presented as a benevolent form of authority which is willing to listen to rational individuals. Dr Blake even associates science with religion by telling David that 'doctors are like ministers: you can tell them anything'. In this way, science and authority are ultimately distinguished from their more terrifying manifestation as represented by the aliens, and ultimately presented positively. Indeed, not only is it David's own fascination with science which allows him to detect the menace, but the film describes him as a 'little scientist'. The scientific expert, Dr Kelson, is even willing to believe David because he believes him to be a 'cold, scientific type'. The very coldness which distinguishes the aliens as bad is used to identify David as trustworthy and good.

Mass destruction

In critical writing, those films concerned with depersonalisation are usually given higher value. Not only do critics tend to regard them as more 'subtle' than those films which concentrate on the spectacle or threat of mass destruction, but they also tend to see them as more radical. These distinctions rest upon a critical preference for the rational over the emotional. These critics assume that the films concentrating on mass destruction are too 'sensational' or even 'hysterical', while those concerned with depersonalisation are more thoughtful and considered. As a result, they assume that the former is less critical than the latter. But this is not necessarily the case. As has already been argued, the former may be just as critical of scientific-technical rationality, and this feature can be seen in the numerous films that drew upon and developed the invasion narratives throughout the rest of the 1950s.

For example, *Them!* combined the terrestrial threat with mass invasion. It concerns a race of ants which, as the result of atom-bomb tests, have mutated and grown to enormous size. The plot involves the discovery of their existence and the attempt to stop them from taking over the world. In this film, the ant society is not only associated with scientific-technical rationality, it is also associated with the military. As Professor Medford puts it,

Ants are ruthless, savage and courageous fighters ... Ants are the only other creatures on earth, other than man, who make war. They campaign. They are chronically aggressive. And they make slaves of the captives they don't kill ... They have an instinct and a talent for industry, social organization and savagery which makes man look feeble by comparison.

Ant society is almost the 'ideal' image of Fordist rationality and its application to the military.

In response, the film takes a very complex position in relation to human authority. It presents American society as a social order made up of a variety of different types of experts, all of whom have specialist knowledge in their own area and must learn to work with one another in order to achieve success. At the start, each field of expertise annoys the others. A local cop finds the first signs of the ants' existence when he discovers a trailer which has been torn apart and a man who has been killed. He does not know that the ants are responsible, but it does become clear that the dead man was an FBI agent. The death of the agent involves the FBI in the investigation, but the local cop is annoyed by their way of doing things and complains that he is being kept in the dark. Later, when two scientists turn up, Professor Medford and his daughter, Pat, there are complaints from the FBI who claim that if the scientists would only talk English, there would be some basis for understanding between the scientists and the law enforcers. Not only do the scientists talk strangely, but the FBI and the local police also complain that they don't listen either. Even the scientists get annoyed by others' rules and procedures. At one point, Professor Medford tries to send a radio message, but is confounded by the radio codes which he is forced to use. As he comments: 'This is ridiculous. A lot of good your rules are going to do us'.

But all these groups eventually learn to work together, each relying on the others' expertise. All groups are included in a balance which allows the film to present the collection of experts as a kind of interactive community. As a result, the film also tries to resolve conflicts between local and national interests. Professor Medford tells the local cop that while the latter is trying to solve a local crime, the former is trying to prevent a nationwide panic. However, local interests are not defined as irrelevant, and the local cop remains an active member of the group even once the action has switched from his local area to the national and even international scene. His skills and values are still important and necessary to the investigation. Indeed, when the final ants' nest is discovered in the storm drains under Los Angeles, the machinery of the state bends to the needs of individuals. The mission is reorganised so as to ensure the safety of two boys who have been trapped by the ants. The final sequence keeps switching between the military manoeuvres of the state and shots of the boys' mother as she waits to see if her children will be saved. The interests of individuals are not simply subordinated to the interests of the state, but each must take account of the other.

However, as Biskind points out, not only are almost all of the ants' victims male, but the figure of centralised authority within their society is a female: the Queen. The human group's mission is to prevent the profligate breeding practices of the three Queens (which have escaped from the first nest) because these breeding practices threaten to overwhelm humanity. For this reason, Biskind suggests that the film displays a patriarchal fear of female sexuality and its reproductive powers. He also argues that the female scientist within the group, Pat Medford, operates to convey the message that men must make some concessions to women or else 'face a far more serious challenge to male power in the future'.[2] But even if this is the film's position, the issues of sexuality and gender are more interesting than he implies. Not only do the concessions made to Pat Medford contradict claims about the role of women in 1950s American film, but also claims about the role of women in popular culture in general. Biskind also ignores the extent to which this film's concern with reproduction is related to that of films such as *The Thing from Another World*. The ants themselves are used because they appear to be virtually biological machines, and this is part of the reason why the use of other types of animals, such as the giant rabbits in *The Night of the Lepus* (1972), seem so ridiculously inappropriate. As a result, the ant Queens, like the alien in *The Thing from Another World*, act as images of mass reproduction in which standardised drones are turned out which exist simply to do their will. The ants' reproductive methods are used as a metaphor for a social order in which the populace are little more than standardised, conformist and interchangeable subjects who simply exist to fulfil the needs of the state. It is this feature, not the issue of the Queens' gender, on which the film concentrates.

Indeed, little or no connection is made between Pat's authority and that of the ant Queens. Instead, it is the men's response to her which is presented as a problem. It is the men who must learn to accept her as an equal. Pat actually lacks any negative associations within the film. She is not presented as 'too pushy' or 'too masculine' as one might expect. Nor is there any sense that a contradiction exists between her femininity and her position of authority. Even romance is not presented as inappropriate, so long as the men can get over their prejudices and learn to recognise her worth. As a result, even if the film is attempting to make concessions to women, it makes much greater concessions than are normally claimed of films in the 1950s or indeed of Hollywood films in general. For example, she does not conform to claims about women's relationship to the 'investigating gaze' in Hollywood film.[3] She is frequently allowed to control the gaze. Even at the end of the film, it is she who must check the Queens' chamber and decide at which point it should be destroyed. But her control of the gaze does not result in her punishment, but rather the safety of the world depends upon it. She is not only able to combine the traditionally masculine and feminine virtues, but is actually presented as a positive figure as a result.

However, Pat Medford was not unique to the 1950s invasion narratives though, and a year later in 1955, It Came from Beneath the Sea also featured this 'new breed of woman'. The film is very similar to The Beast from 20,000 Fathoms, but it replaces the prehistoric monster from the arctic with a giant squid from the depths of the sea. The film's special effects were even created by the same man, Ray Harrihausen, as the earlier film. In It Came from Beneath the Sea, the creature comes to threaten humanity when its feeding grounds are destroyed by nuclear tests. At the opening, a nuclear submarine is attacked and damaged by some unknown force. When the vessel is examined a strange substance is found attached to it, and scientists are called in to identify the substance. Of the two scientists who arrive, one is female and the submarine commander finds himself attracted to her. Unfortunately, he is intimidated by her authority and by her relationship with her male colleague. But in this film the problem is all his. He must learn to accept women in positions of authority, and reject his received ideas about the roles appropriate to women. The victory over the squid depends on her scientific knowledge and skills. Indeed, even at the end of the film, she resists his attempts to make her marry him and settle down to a domestic life, and instead, she eventually persuades him to collaborate with her on a book. If science produces both the problem and the solution in this film, it is male authority and its assumptions about women on which the film concentrates and which it criticises.

Not all 1950s invasion narratives represented women in this way, though. At the opening of *Earth Vs the Flying Saucers*, the hero's wife does claim that she has contributed as much to her husband's research as has he, but her contribution is clearly presented as that of a caring and supportive wife, rather than as an active participant. She may act as his secretary, but she is never shown to contribute ideas of her own. She merely exists to accept and maintain his authority over her. In many ways, the film is a reworking of elements from *War of the Worlds*, in which alien war-machines threaten human society in an attempt to conquer the world. The aliens are the survivors of a disintegrated solar system, just as the Martians in *War of the Worlds* were the survivors of a dying planet. But in *Earth Vs the Flying Saucers*, science provides the solution, rather than divine intervention. The film does associate the aliens with science and technology by concentrating on their war-machines – the flying saucers – and though the aliens do appear independent of these machines, they are presented as robotic figures. Like the aliens in *War of the Worlds*, their bodies are undeveloped and they have to rely on technology in the form of a special suit which covers them entirely. It is this suit which not only makes them look and move like robots, but also takes the place of their skin and muscle, neither of which they possess. The suits also act to enhance their inadequate sight and hearing.

The film even includes elements from the depersonalisation films. The aliens have a device which enables them to drain the memory of humans for their own use, and this process converts their victims into brainless husks with no sense of identity or will. Despite the film's use of these features, science and the military are presented positively. Though the start of the film suggests that it is uncertain whether science and the military would be effective against an alien invasion, this sense of insecurity is dispelled by the end of the film.

The various elements of these films were combined and reworked in numerous different ways in an incredible proliferation of films throughout the 1950s. However, by the late 1950s, the distinction between the alien invader and the natural creature had either blurred or disappeared. The latter was the case in *The Blob* (1959). In this film, the creature is from outer space, but it is not the vanguard of an invading alien culture. It is a natural force which has come to earth in a meteor. But if it is a natural force, it lacks many of the characteristics usually associated with life. It is even more impersonal than the traditional alien or natural creation. It not only lacks any sense of feeling or emotion, but also any sense of consciousness. It just exists, and feeds upon humans in order to enlarge itself. Self-expansion seems to be its only motivation, and in this way, it is similar to the vampiristic aspects of *The Thing from Another World*, although it does not reproduce itself. Instead it engulfs people and expands as its digests them. In this way, the film operates in relation to fears about the loss of identity through engulfment by, and absorption into, some larger mass.

As a result, the film is not preoccupied with centrally-organised societies, but with conformity. The action takes place entirely within a small American town, and the struggle is as much between the conformist community and its various outsider figures as it is between the humans and the blob. In this particular case, the outsider figures are teenagers. They know of the blob's existence and try to tell the community, but the community is hostile towards them. They exist outside its notions of 'normality' and are not taken seriously because their perceptions are seen as having no validity. Parents and police see them as irresponsible and troublesome, but the film suggests that these figures of authority and conformity must learn to take the perceptions of outsiders into account and to listen to them. This situation is made particularly clear in the conflict between two police officers, one of whom distrusts and dislikes the teenagers, while the other claims that they need understanding. Indeed, the community's survival not only depends on the perceptions of the teenage outsiders, but at the end of the film, one of the parents actually has to break the law in order to support them. It is the teenagers' inability to remain within the confines of the law which makes them dangerous and suspect within the view of the conformist community. By breaking the law himself, the father not only associates himself with the teenage outsiders, but actually calls into question the forms of conformity upon which the community depends.

Depersonalisation

It is this conflict between outsiders and organised conformity which preoccupies most of the invasion narratives concerned with depersonalisation. As Biskind claims of these texts, they

> focused on the struggle of the outsider, the kook, the end-of-the-worlder, to force the community to acknowledge the validity of the self's private vision, even if it violated the norms of credibility that govern the expectations of experts and professionals. Far worse than invasion, what these films anxiously imagined was the loss of community, the estrangement of the one-who-knows from those who don't, Us from Them.[4]

Biskind makes this claim in relation to the most famous of these texts, Don Siegel's film, *Invasion of the Body Snatchers* (1956). This film was based on Jack Finney's *The Body Snatchers* which was serialised in *Collier's* magazine during 1954 and published in book form in 1955. Both Finney's novel and Siegel's film have been the subject of much debate. They have been read both as endorsements of the anti-communist witch-hunts associated with McCarthyism, and as presenting a critique of those witch-hunts.

In the case of the first argument, it is claimed that the aliens represent a kind of Soviet 'fifth column' which is infiltrating the fabric of American society and need to be rooted out. The aliens are the 'reds under the beds'. The alternative claim is that these texts criticise the pressures towards conformity and the repression of dissent which McCarthyism entailed. Jack Finney himself has claimed that he is amused by such interpretations, and argues that he never intended any overt political subtext to his novel. Siegel, on the other hand, has maintained that he considers *Invasion of the Body Snatchers* to be his most important film because of its political message. Unfortunately, he has never stated what he considers that message to have been. But even if the novel lacks any overt and self-conscious subtext, it clearly works in relation to fears of conformity and standardisation, and as is the case with the film, these threats are not solely identified as the product of the alien invasion. These texts do not suggest that the threat is purely external, but that it is only the inevitable outcome of developments within American society and culture. It is not just communists and fellow-travellers who are the problem, as the McCarthyite witch-hunters suggested, but the structure of government, the media and technology within America itself; that is the very structure of modern American society. The pod invasion may have exacerbated and highlighted certain features, but they were already there before the pods arrived and will remain after they are conquered. As Miles comments in the film, people tend to let their humanity slip away, and it is only when they are forced to fight and protect it that they realise how precious it is.

Indeed, the narrator of Finney's novel, Miles, often nostalgically compares the Santa Mira of his own time with that of his father's day in order to emphasise the problems of his present. In one of the most telling passages, for example, he comments upon changes in the telephone system after he has received an anonymous call. In his 'father's day', he claims

> a night operator, whose name he'd have known, could have told him who'd called. It would probably have been the only light on her board at that time of night, and she'd have remembered which one it was, because they were calling the doctor. But now we have dial phones, marvellously efficient, saving you a full second or more everytime you call, inhumanly perfect, and utterly brainless; and none of them will ever remember where the doctor is at night, when a child is sick and needs him. Sometimes I think we're refining all the humanity out of our lives.[5]

This passage clearly comments on the destructive implications of the rationalisation of contemporary communications systems, but it also clearly associates these implications with the aliens themselves.

Not only is efficiency referred to as 'inhuman' and 'brainless', it is these very features which the aliens themselves represent. They appear to be human in every way except one: they lack emotion. Like most alien invaders, they are not themselves individuals with personal features, but mere components within a larger order. As a result, in this novel, humanity is not associated with rationality, but with the irrational, with feelings and emotions. It is these features which Miles learns to value, and which he fights to protect throughout the course of the narrative. Towards the end of the novel, the pods try to persuade him to become one of them. They tell him that there is little significant difference between the humans and their pod replicas. The pod replacements still share the same memories. But Miles points out that there is a difference. Human personality, he suggests, is not based on a fixed identity, but upon activity. It is not presence which is important, but absence. It is creativity, hope and most especially desire which are essentially human. It is desire which motivates action, and requires interaction with others. For Miles, the greatest proof that the pods are different from humans is that the former lack a sexuality and sexual desire.

Indeed, rationality is a problem within the novel. It cannot be used to identify the threat, but only to disguise it. It is not the aliens' difference from normal Americans which is the greatest horror, but their similarity. They are difficult to detect, and there is no rational way to identify them. As Becky's Aunt Wilma explains to Miles at the start of the novel, 'there is no difference you can actually see' (p. 15). There is nothing tangible to detect, no definitive proof. Everything about the pod replacements is the same, 'but not the feeling' (p. 19). The difference can only be detected emotionally through personal intuition, and only by those who have a close personal relationship with the victim.

Rational procedures are not only useless, but can actually hinder things. Miles will not believe Wilma because her story sounds too fantastic, and Becky will not trust her own feelings. The humans in the novel are so under the thrall of rationality that they have learned to regard emotional responses as 'irrational' and of little validity. Instead they have come to defer to experts for an explanation of both themselves and their world. As a consequence, Miles turns to Mannie Kaufmann, a psychologist, for answers, but the novel suggests that such actions are dangerous. Mannie uses psychology to explain problems away, and despite the fact that throughout the majority of the novel, he does so because he is a pod replica, it is suggested that this fact itself makes little difference. The original Mannie would have given the same responses, even if he wasn't trying to cover up the alien invasion. As a psychologist, he regards people's emotional responses as psychological problems to be managed. For Mannie, problems do not exist in the world itself, but only in people's minds, and these people must be taught to adjust and fit into the world as it is. As a result, Biskind claims that in this context, 'therapy is brainwashing'.[6] Rationality and science are dehumanising and dangerous.

It is therefore unsurprising that it is Jack, Miles's friend, who becomes Mannie's main opponent throughout the early parts of the novel. He is a writer, and therefore associated with imagination and intuition, rather than rationality; and it is he who provides the central critique of rationality. Jack is uncomfortable with Mannie's attempt to explain things away and at one point, he produces a collection of news-clippings which describe strange and unexplained incidents. For Jack, the clippings

> prove at least this; that strange things happen, really do happen, every now and then, here and there throughout the world. Things that simply don't fit in with the great body of knowledge that the human race has gradually acquired over thousands of years. Things in direct contradiction to what we know to be true. Something falls up, instead of down. (p. 74)

For Jack, it is dangerous simply to try and explain things away: it is both a refusal to admit a challenge to our ways of seeing and understanding the world, and a refusal to admit that there are limits to rational explanations. However, Jack also argues against the theoretical claims of science: 'Science claims to be objective ... To consider all phenomena impartially and without prejudice. But of course it does no such thing. This kind of occurrence ... it dismisses with automatic habitual contempt' (p. 74). Indeed, Jack's use of the terms 'automatic' and 'habitual' directly associate science with the unthinking conformity which the novel presents as a threat. Jack even describes science in a manner which is similar to the work of Kuhn and Feyerabend,[7] and claims that it took 'Hundreds of years to accept the fact that the world is round. A century resisting the knowledge that the earth revolves around the sun.' For Jack, humanity hates 'facing new facts or evidence, because we might have to revise our conceptions of what's possible and that's always uncomfortable' (p. 74).

Experts are not only dangerous and dehumanising in the novel because they stifle intuition, imagination and individuality, they are also often the first to be taken over by the pods. Indeed, those people who do detect the menace are usually from those sections of society who have little authority and are associated with the irrational, groups such as children, women and dreamers like the writer, Jack.

As a result, the novel does not encourage a reliance on experts, but rather emphasises how dangerous such a reliance can be. Even those authorities which have not been taken over by the pods are entirely useless, or worse. At one point, for example, Miles contacts an old war buddy, Ben, who is now working in the Pentagon. But this attempt to get help from the authorities is a complete failure. Ben even has to ask Miles what to do. As Ben implies, the chain of command is designed to control subordinates, and subordinates can do little to initiate or even influence the actions by those at the higher levels. As Ben argues:

> I'll do what I can, do all I can. If it's what you really want, I'll give this whole story to my colonel within the hour ... And I'll add my own report that I know you well, that you're a sane, sober and intelligent citizen, and that I am personally certain you're speaking the truth, or believe that you are. But that's all I can do. Miles, absolutely all, even if it means the end of the world before noon ... And, Miles, it won't do one bit of good. Because what do you expect him to do with the story? He's not imaginative, to put it mildly. And even if he were, the colonel's no man to stick his neck out ... But even if the impossible happened, even if my colonel took this to the brigadier, who took it to the major-general, who carried it on up to three- or four-star level, what the hell are *they* going to do with this? By that time it'll be a weird fourth- or fifth-hand story started by some fool of a lieutenant colonel they've never heard of or seen. And *he* got the story in a phone call from some crackpot friend, a civilian, out in California somewhere. Do you see? Can you actually imagine this reaching a level where something could be done; and then having it actually done? My God, you know the Army! (pp. 96–7)

Finally Miles and his friends are forced to realise that they can expect no help from the authorities, and that they can only rely on one another.

Indeed, they are also forced to realise that even escape is useless. When they try to flee the town, they eventually are forced to return and to recognise that there is no place of sanctuary outside:

> We'd had our running away, and it had done us good; me, anyway. But we belonged at home, not some vague, unknown, mythical new place. And now it was time to go back, to the place we belonged,

which belonged to us, and fight against whatever was happening, as best we could, and however we could. (p. 104)

It is not just that the pods are spreading beyond Santa Mira, it is also that the only resistance to them is on a personal level. If a pod replica can only be detected by someone with a close relationship to their victim, any escape into the world of strangers beyond the town will probably prove unproductive, and create the very sense of isolation and insecurity to which it was supposed to provide a solution.

However, if the pods threaten Miles and his friends, the novel frequently emphasises that they have already been depersonalised and that they frequently perform in ways that are unthinking, automatic and the product of habit and routine. When Miles first describes himself he does so as if filling in a census form:

> Just to get the record straight: my full name is Miles Boise Bennell, I'm twenty-eight years old, and I've been practising medicine in Santa Mira, California, for just over a year. Before that I interned, and before that, Stanford Medical College. I was born and raised in Santa Mira, and my father was a doctor here before me, and a good one, so I haven't had too much trouble snaring customers.
>
> I'm five feet eight inches tall, weigh one-sixty-five, have blue eyes, and black, kind of wavy hair, pretty thick, though already there's the faintest beginning of a bald spot on the crown ... I play golf and swim whenever I can, so I'm always pretty tanned. Five months earlier I'd been divorced, and now I lived alone in a big old fashioned frame house ... That's about all. I drive a '52 Ford convertible, one of those fancy green ones, because I don't know any law absolutely requiring a doctor to drive a small black coupe. (p. 12)

Furthermore, he frequently suggests that in his dealings with people, he relies on the media as a guide to appropriate behaviour.

For example, when Becky finally admits to herself that she thinks her father has been replaced by an imposter and breaks down in tears, Miles states:

> I don't claim a lot of experience with crying women, but in stories I read, the man always holds the girl close and lets her cry. And it always turns out to have been the wise, understanding thing to do; I've never heard of a single authenticated case where the wise understanding thing was to distract her with card tricks or tickling her feet. So I was wise and understanding: I held Becky close and let her cry, because I didn't know what else to do or say. (p. 42)

Even when Miles later saves Becky from this imposter, he realises that he is behaving like a caveman from a movie as he carries her down the street in his arms.

However, the most sinister sequence follows the next day when Miles, Becky, Jack and his wife, Theodora, meet in the morning. Unable to face the shock of their discovery about the pods, they lapse into behaviour which is not only clearly presented as mechanistic through the rhythm of the language, but seems almost 'pavlovian': 'Then, almost as if a signal had been given, we all began chattering, laughing a lot, making jokes' (p. 20). Indeed this behaviour is also shown to be gendered:

> the two women began turning on gas jets, getting out skillets and pans, opening cupboards and the refrigerator, while the three men sat down at the kitchen table. Becky poured us some coffee. ... Sausage began spluttering on the stove, Theodora turning it with a fork, and Becky began beating up eggs in a bowl, the metal spoon tapping rhythmically against the china, a nice sound. (pp. 70–1)

If the pods represent a mindless and impersonal conformity, the novel continually emphasises that even its human heroes are not free from such associations. Indeed, the pod threat is clearly shown to be only the logical extension of processes already well established within America.

In the process, the novel also suggests the reasons such conformist behaviour might be so appealing. As Miles' comments about his relationships with crying women illustrates, the problem is not simply between the individual and society, or between pure individual spontaneity and impersonal conformity. Playing card tricks and tickling Becky's feet would not be an appropriate response to her tears. Humans need predictable and fairly stable patterns in order to communicate with one another. They cannot communicate with, or relate to, one another through pure spontaneity. Indeed, as both Jack and the pods suggest in different ways, conformity is appealing and even at times necessary because it helps to order and repress the painful uncertainties of social existence. Indeed again and again, the novel emphasises that the appearances of the normal and conventional world are themselves founded upon the repression of that which is painful and disruptive.

This is probably most clearly seen in Miles's account of Billy, a black shoe-cleaner whom he had known while attending college.

Miles uses this account to describe the shock of seeing the pods as they really are, or rather when they have let down their guard and think that they are not being watched by humans. The story of Billy is a story of a black man who is popular with whites. He is known as a 'character', and has many customers. His genial servility is enjoyed by whites such as Miles who recognise that it is 'flattery', but 'liked it just the same'. However, Miles describes how, one night, he overheard Billy talking with a friend in another part of town. But, in this context, Billy was not the same as he was at his stand. He parodies his public persona and performs 'a vicious, jeering imitation of his familiar patter' (p. 120). For Miles, this experience is a shock: 'never before in my life had I heard such ugly, bitter, and vicious contempt in a voice, contempt for the people taken in by his daily antics, but even more for himself, the man who supplied the servility they brought from him' (p. 120). However, this experience does little to alter Miles's behaviour. He recognises that it reveals the racial and class oppression on which his previous pleasure in Billy's performance had depended, but it does not lead him to challenge such oppression. Instead, his sense of shame only makes him avoid Billy's stand in an attempt to repress this knowledge and allow him to continue his normal life.

Indeed, the novel also emphasises that Miles and the other characters are all playing roles, roles which disguise and repress particular desires and motivations. When Miles comforts Becky using the conventions learned from books, it is also emphasised that he is not only playing the role of a caring partner, he is also doing so to satisfy quite different aims. While Becky cries in his arms, Miles is taking the opportunity to satisfy his own desires:

> Anyway, I liked holding Becky. She wasn't a big girl, exactly, but she wasn't small, and nothing in her construction had been skimped or neglected. There in my car, on the silent street in front of her home, Becky fitted into my arms very nicely, her cheek on my lapel. I was worried and scared, even panicky, but there was still room for enjoying the warm, alive feel of Becky pressed close. (p. 42)

It is not just the pods who are engaged in a masquerade of deception.

However, if the maintenance of Miles's normal everyday life requires forms of repression and masquerade, the defeat of the pods depends upon the recognition and the rejection of these forms. In particular, Miles is forced to recognise that gendered behaviour is the product of a conformity which is learned from the mass media. In the final crisis of the narrative, Becky and Miles find themselves trapped by the pods and Miles desperately tries to devise a plan of escape. However, as Becky points out, his difficulty in devising a plan is based on his assumptions about gender:

> Miles, I know there's no reason why anything we can think of has to work out at all. But now *you're* thinking like a movie. Most people do – sometimes, anyway. Miles, there are certain activities most people never actually encounter all their lives, so they picture them in terms of movie-like scenes. It's the only source most people have for visualizing things they've had no actual experience of. And that's how you're thinking now: a scene in which you're struggling with two or three men, and – Miles, what am I doing in that scene in your mind? You're seeing me cowering against the wall, eyes wide and frightened, my hands raised to my face in horror, aren't you? (p. 171)

What is more, Becky points out that not only will the pods share these assumptions, which they have taken from the minds of their human victims, but that she can behave differently; that it is not a natural female response, but a form of conventional and conformist feminine behaviour.

It is only on the basis of this realisation that they manage to escape. They exploit conformist assumptions about gender and reject them. Becky performs the masquerade of the passive and helpless female until the pods have discounted her and concentrated their efforts on Miles. Then, once they have turned their attention away from her, she rejects this role and comes to Miles's rescue.

Indeed, this concentration on gender as conformity is of crucial significance. Not only does it challenge traditional accounts of 1950s American popular culture, but it also marks a distinct advance upon the forms of mass culture criticism current at the time of the book's publication. As has often been pointed out, to the extent that 1950s mass cultural criticism did concentrate on issues of gender, it was usually out of a conservative nostalgia for a lost masculinity. As Barbara Ehrenreich and others emphasise, mass culture criticism did not tend to challenge definitions of femininity, but rather objected to the supposed feminisation of males within mass culture. As Ehrenreich argues, for most intellectuals in the period, conformity meant emasculation.[8] What is more, if Friedan's *The Feminine Mystique*[9] did use the basic assumptions and rhetoric of mass culture criticism to develop its feminist attack on the situation of women in America, this book was not published until nine years after Finney's novel. As a result, this illustrates that the 1950s invasion narratives were in many ways more sophisticated than the intellectual positions usually used to dismiss them.

Indeed, not only is this the case with its handling of gender politics, but the novel also refuses complete narrative closure and even foregrounds its narrative features in ways that are usually associated with the avant-garde, or at least with the impact of structuralism and semiotics from the mid-1970s onwards. For example, as the novel states at its opening:

> I warn you that what you are starting to read is full of loose ends and unanswered questions. It will not be neatly tied up at the end, everything resolved and satisfactorily explained. Not by me it won't, anyway. Because I can't say I really know exactly what happened, or why, or just how it began, how it ended, or if it has ended; and I've been right in the thick of it. Now if you don't like that kind of story, I'm sorry, and you'd better not read it. All I can do is tell what I know. (p. 7)

However, the novel goes even further in its refusal of narrative closure. The pods may give up their invasion of the earth (or at least seem to do so) but afterwards the community does not eliminate the replicas which remain in town. On the contrary, their presence seems to be fully accepted.

Indeed even the defeat of the pods does not end the gradual depersonalisation of the town. The continual migration of the American population soon fills up the homes of those who have died so that many of the people in town are no longer long-term neighbours whom Miles has known all his life, but rather strangers who come from elsewhere and whose names he does not even know. As a result, as Miles states rather ominously: 'In a year, maybe two, or three, Mill Valley will seem no different to the eye from any other small town. In five years, perhaps less, it will be no different' (p. 190). This comment is ultimately double-edged. On one hand, it suggests that the impact of the pods is disappearing but, on the other, it suggests that the town is not returning to what it had once been. Instead, it hints at a creeping conformity and a lack of identity in which Santa Mira is becoming indistinguishable from any other small town, in which American communities lose their identity and become mere replicas of one another.

Even Miles's emphasis on the awkward status of his narrative is undercut in a similar way. While Miles emphasises his own unreliability as a narrator, it is also suggested that his questioning of the story may actually be the result of his own loss of individuality – his own return to conformist assumptions – as the events 'have faded into final unbelievability'. In short, the suggestion is that 'there are times, and they come more and more frequently' (p. 190) when Miles no longer trusts his own experiences and comes to accept conformist notions of what is possible.

But still the novel does end with a final statement in which Miles manages to hold on, however tentatively, to his sense that it is neither possible nor desirable to rationalise everything, that finally there are things which do not conform to rational and conformist interpretations, and which cannot not, and should not, be ultimately repressed by them.

Despite these features, Finney's novel is often dismissed as 'pulp' fiction, and discussions of the story almost exclusively concentrate on Don Siegel's film version, *Invasion of the Body Snatchers*. Film studies, unlike literary studies, has a strong history of celebrating popular directors, even if it does so by seeking to identify their rejection of the conventional nature of popular film in general. Indeed, this approach was probably *the* founding approach in the development of film studies as a distinct and coherent discipline within the academy.[10] But such a strategy would be inappropriate in relation to Finney's novel in any case. The novel does not work against the materials of 1950s SF/horror, but merely contradicts the frequent claims which are made about the workings of these texts. Certainly, Finney does rework and transform elements of earlier texts, but he does not 'subvert' them in the sense that an *auteur* is supposed to 'subvert' their material. If Finney's novel shows a concern with conformity, so do others; and if his novel popularised narratives of depersonalisation, duplication and substitution, there were others which also contained aliens who could imitate and replace humans. Probably the most famous of these is John W. Campbell's 'Who Goes There?' which was published in 1938 and formed the basis for *The Thing from Another World*.

However, if the concentration on Siegel's film is due to his established status as an *auteur* who is supposed to subvert his materials and transforms them, it is interesting that his film remains faithful to Finney's novel up until the point in the novel at which Becky points out that gender roles are conventional and conformist in character. Indeed, the film does not include this observation and it is from this point on that the narratives of the novel and the film begin to diverge dramatically. If, in Finney's novel, Becky's realisation enables her and Miles to defeat the aliens, the absence of such a realisation in the film prevents any effective solution to the crisis. In fact, rather than rejecting conformity to gender roles, Becky eventually embraces conformity altogether and is transformed into an alien. While in the novel she rejects the passivity and weakness associated with femininity, in the film she proves unable to resist sleep and so allows herself to be duplicated. In reworking its supposedly 'pulp' materials, Siegel's film does not necessarily subvert an essentially formulaic text and challenge accepted perceptions, but actually replaces its most original and incisive features with more standard and conventional materials.

None the less, isolated, alone and unable to find a way of defeating the pods, Miles finally escapes to the human world outside Santa Mira, but finds that it is as unthinking and conformist as the alien society from which he has just escaped, at least until the studio insisted on a new ending. The point at which Siegel had ended the film was with Miles alone on a busy highway as he tries to warn humanity of the alien menace, but is unable to make anyone listen. In fact, there are no other humans visible in the scene. All that can be seen is Miles as he calls out to the cars and lorries which swarm along the highway, machines within which the humans remain hidden and obscured.

The studio, however, insisted on a new beginning and end in which the main narrative is presented as a flashback. In these sequences, Miles is brought into a hospital where his wild behaviour is interpreted as madness by everyone else. Desperately, Miles tries to explain himself to a psychologist, and so begins to narrate the main body of the film. Finally, at the end, the film returns to the encounter between Miles and the psychologist, but it is clear that Miles has not been believed. Indeed, he only seems to have confirmed the experts' assumptions. Suddenly, however, everything changes in a rather unconvincing manner as the victim of a car-crash is brought into the hospital and it is revealed that one of the vehicles involved in the crash was a lorry which had been carrying a cargo of strange-looking pods. This information causes the doctor to reassess his opinion of Miles's story and to call the FBI, an action which it was hoped would soothe the audience's fears. Ignoring the content of the novel and the film, the studio assumed that the call would produce effective intervention by the FBI. However, this end never really convinces. It cannot finally erase the distrust of experts which the film has encouraged up to this point.

However, if the film ignores the novel's concern with gender roles, the focus on gender was also a central feature of another depersonalisation narrative, *I Married a Monster from Outer Space* (1958), although it is handled very differently. In this film, a dying alien race lands near a small American town and begins to replace the young males in the hope of finding ways to use human females to repopulate their race. Under this slightly ludicrous premise, however, lies a touching and tragic account of the dysfunctional lack of communication between husbands and wives. Indeed, while the film uses an alien invasion to explore these relationships, and while the lead female, Marge, and her lover, Bill, are finally reunited at the end, the story really focuses on the estrangement of married couples who find themselves intimately attached to someone whom they do not really know and cannot ultimately satisfy.

Initially, the story starts as Bill is replaced the night before his marriage to Marge, and it focuses, at least in the early section of the film, on Marge's sense that her husband is not the man with whom she fell in love. On her wedding night, Bill seems cold, awkward and distant. However, as she gradually realises that Bill literally is not the man with whom she fell in love, the focus shifts towards Bill's duplicate as Marge herself becomes increasingly cold, awkward and distant and the alien male finds that the human body which he is inhabiting has an unconscious of its own. His race is cold and rational, without feelings or emotions, but the longer he inhabits his human body, the more he begins to understand and feel the force of human emotions. As Marge retreats from him, he begins to love and long for her. At one point he enters her bedroom, and is moved to remark, 'You're beautiful, aren't you?' But Marge knows he is an alien by this point, and regards him as a monster. What is more, he realises that, despite his desire for her, she will not accept him, and as a result, he offers to sleep in the guest room before commenting that the idea of 'making guests comfortable' is a 'nice' one, in principle.

If the film uses the conflict between the human woman and the alien man to highlight the difficulties of marriage, it also emphasises that these problems are rather more general. When Bill is late for his marriage to Marge, his friends excuse his previous night's drinking by claiming that it was, after all, his last night of 'freedom', a remark which Marge finds insulting. As she recognises, it highlights the men's fear of commitment. These problems are also emphasised in other points in the film. In one sequence, Bill's two friends are shown in a bar where they spend much of their time in an attempt to escape from their partners. Indeed, one of the friends even has to persuade the other to go home to his wife and calls the bartender a 'home-wrecker'. These problems are also emphasised later in the film when the alien males despondently congregate in the bar in a similar way, though at this point it is because their wives have rejected them rather than the other way around.

However, in other parts of the film, it is also made clear that the women are not entirely blameless victims of masculinity. One female friend continually talks about her attempts to 'land' herself a husband, and ignores any warnings against marriage, so great is her desire to legitimate herself through marriage, an institution which seems to have less importance to her as an emotional bond than as a sign of status and conformity. Even Marge is presented as a callous conformist who enters her marriage without thought, and fears anything which differs from her conventional terms of reference.

As a result, the 'happy ending' in which Marge and the real Bill are finally reunited is a token, rather than a convincing, conclusion to the narrative. Indeed, the film provides little sense of Bill as a character. He is not involved in the main part of the narrative, but remains unconscious throughout the majority of the film. On the contrary, it is Marge and her alien husband who are the two characters on whom the film concentrates, and it is they who develop as characters throughout the narrative; it is they who have suffered the rigours of a failed marriage. There is even reason to wonder whether Marge's experiences over the previous year and more will have made her so different from the person Bill remembers that they will suffer the same sense of distance and alienation that she had shared with her alien husband.

In the process, the film also draws upon elements of the 'outsider narratives' which will be the topic of the next section. In its concentration on the feelings of isolation and alienation, particularly those of the alien husband, the film actually examines the situation of the outsider and the values through which they are rejected. When Bill's replica finally confronts Marge at the end, he says to her, 'Your people have won – that makes you happy, doesn't it?', a remark which works on many levels. It emphasises that the humans' victory also means defeat for the aliens, and the film ends with the image of the space ships which belong to his desperate race as they move on in their hopeless search. But it also suggests a sense of his empathy with her, an empathy which the humans seem incapable of showing to the aliens. He not only seems resigned to his own death, but also gains pleasure from the joy which the humans' victory brings to her, even through it is a joy which can only be obtained at the expense of his own life. As a result, the film uses the aliens to examine the forms of normality and conformity which predominated in 1950s America while also suggesting that the alien outsider may be, by the end of the film, in many ways more sympathetic than the society which sees him as monstrous.

Notes

1 Vivian Sobchack, *Screening Space: The American Science Fiction Film* (New York: Ungar, 1987), p. 87.
2 Peter Biskind, *Seeing is Believing: How Hollywood Taught Us to Stop Worrying and Love the Fifties* (London: Pluto, 1983), p. 133.
3 See, for example, Laura Mulvey, 'Visual Pleasure and Narrative Cinema', in Bill Nichols, ed., *Movies and Methods Vol. II* (Berkeley: University of California Press, 1985); and Constance Penley, ed., *Feminism and Film Theory* (London: Routledge, 1988).
4 Biskind, *Seeing is Believing*, p. 139.
5 Jack Finney, *The Body Snatchers* (New York: Dell, 1955), p. 39.
6 Biskind, *Seeing is Believing*, p. 140.
7 Thomas Kuhn, *The Structure of Scientific Revolutions* (Chicago: Chicago University Press, 1962); P. Feyerabend, *Against Method* (London: New Left Books, 1976) and *Science in a Free Society* (London: New Left Books, 1978).
8 Barbara Ehrenreich, *The Hearts of Men: American Dreams and the Flight from Commitment* (London: Pluto, 1983), p. 30.
9 Betty Friedan, *The Feminine Mystique* (New York: Dell, 1963).

10 For discussions of *auteur* criticism, see Christopher Brookeman, 'Coming to Terms with Hollywood', in *American Culture and Society since the 1930s* (London: Macmillan, 1984); John Caughie, ed., *Theories of Authorship* (London: Routledge, 1981); Pam Cook, 'Authorship and Cinema', in *The Cinema Book* (London: BFI, 1985); Robert Lapsley and Mike Westlake, 'Authorship', in *Film Theory: An Introduction* (Manchester: Manchester University Press, 1988); and Helen Stoddart, 'Auteurism and Film Authorship' in Joanne Hollows and Mark Jancovich, eds, *Approaches to Popular Film* (Manchester: Manchester University Press, 1995).

Part two

The outsider narratives

Introduction

I f the aliens which distinguished the 1950s invasion narratives tended to be totally unsympathetic, in other texts of the period aliens were not presented as threateningly monstrous. While the 1950s invasion narratives used the alien invaders as an image of rationalisation and conformity, other horror texts of the period used aliens as an image of difference through which they investigated, problematised and even rejected the notions of 'normality' prevalent in 1950s America. In this latter group of texts, the figure of the alien was used to criticise rationality and conformity, and the intolerance and lack of empathy which they produced. Indeed, these narratives were part of a larger group of texts, many of which did not feature aliens, but are related to one another through a pre-occupation with the figure of the outsider, and their experience of alienation, estrangement and powerlessness.

These outsider narratives are a fairly eclectic group of texts which include films, television programmes, literature and comics. None the less, this section will concentrate on three main areas. The first of these areas is composed of the writings of two close friends: Ray Bradbury and Richard Matheson. Despite significant differences, these two writers formed an informal group (along with their friend Charles Beaumont) which was based upon personal friendship and influence. Although Bradbury had been publishing for some time before Matheson, his most influential works were those which followed the success of his book, *The Martian Chronicles* (1950). In this work, Bradbury created the space within which Matheson could publish, and, regardless of the extent to which Matheson differed from Bradbury, the younger writer continued to regard Bradbury as a mentor.

The second area is composed of the films which Jack Arnold directed at Universal Pictures, a group of films which are none the less related to the previous area. Arnold's first major success in science fiction/horror, *It Came from Outer Space* (1953), was based on a short story by Ray Bradbury, and the script for Arnold's last major success in the field, *The Incredible Shrinking Man* (1957), was written by Matheson and based upon his novel, *The Shrinking Man* (1956). Not only have Arnold's films become cult classics, but they have also received a degree of critical praise which is unusual for 1950s horror films.

The final group of texts to be discussed in this section is much less coherently organised that the previous two, but like Matheson's novel, *The Shrinking Man*, and Arnold's film version of this novel, the texts which compose this final group are usually concerned with transformations. In some cases, they even overtly reverse Matheson's original premise: *The Amazing Colossal Man* (1957), its sequel, *The War of the Colossal Beast* (1958), and *Attack of the Fifty Foot Woman* (1958), all concern massive enlargement rather than shrinking. This group also includes a series of teenage monster movies which starts with a lone teenager transforming into a beast in *I was a Teenage Werewolf* (1957), but later gave rise to somewhat different attempts to address teenage concerns in films such as *I was a Teenage Frankenstein* (1958) and *How to Make a Monster* (1958).

Despite the significance of their particular formal properties as films, television programmes, literature or comics, these outsider narratives need to be related to one another. They were not consumed in isolation from one another, but were part of a broader 'cultural repertoire'. The teenagers who consumed one form usually consumed the others, and their understanding of one form was shaped with reference to other forms. In fact, even many of the producers of these texts were fans who may have worked in one area, but were also deeply influenced by developments in other forms. For example, Ray Bradbury was not only a fan of literature, films and comics, but was also responsible for producing literary fiction, film and television scripts and stories for comics.

In fact, these texts were not only the focus of fan cultures within the 1950s, but have acquired the status of 'trash classics'. Critical attention may have focused on other areas of horror which have been taken more seriously, but it is these texts which despite, or more accurately because of, their 'trashiness' are often the most fondly remembered. *Creature from the Black Lagoon* (1954), for example, has been referred to by Leonard Wolf as 'a darling of horror film aficionados',[1] while David Skal goes somewhat further. He argues that films such as *Creature from the Black Lagoon* along with EC comics, *The Twilight Zone* and *Shock Theatre* are the 'most vivid formative memories of a large section of the [American] population'; and that for many these texts have operated as 'mass cultural rituals'.[2] Indeed, many contemporary figures, including Stephen King, John Carpenter, Stephen Spielberg and others, often refer to these texts as the formative moments not only in their experience of horror, but of childhood and popular culture. And as such, these texts remain the epitome of everything to which these figures aspire as writers and directors.

None the less, such affection does not lead fans to deny that these texts are 'trashy'. Instead, it is their very 'trashiness' which operates as a sign of their value. As a result, this section will explore how the trashiness of these texts became a sign of value for their teenage fans in the 1950s, and how these texts actually deployed their trashiness as a formal strategy which had specific critical implications.

That these texts are concerned with alienated outsiders and notions of normality should be no surprise. As was suggested in the previous section, while the 1950s is often described as a decade of conformity, it was just as much a period which was deeply critical of conformity. As Daniel Bell claimed: 'The curious fact, perhaps, is that no one in the United States defends conformity. Everyone is against it'.[3] As a result, the 1950s is probably better understood as a decade undergoing transitions in styles of dissent and resistance. While many, even those on the left, felt that traditional class politics was redundant, there were many in the decade who were searching for new agents of social change and new sites of political contestation. While intellectuals called for people to resist conformity and searched for a 'unassimilated other' who might act as a challenge to prevailing social and cultural norms, new social and cultural movements were emerging which set the stage for developments in the 1960s, 1970s and 1980s.

These social and cultural movements can be grouped around three main issues: race; youth; and sexuality and/or gender. In the case of youth, juvenile delinquency became one of the major issues of the decade; and while this issue provoked a widespread moral panic among certain sections of society, others claimed that youth cultures were in search of something different to the conformity of middle-class culture, however incoherently; and that youths were attempting to find a different set of values and aspirations. As a result, while the new youth cultures were condemned by some, they were also praised or, at the very least, defended by others. Harvey Swados, for example, claimed that a 'tormenting discontent' was experienced by youth for whom 'everything is being done, to whom everything is being given ... except a reason for living and building a socially useful life'.[4] Nor was Swados alone in arguing that youth cultures and juvenile delinquency were responses to the modern American way of life. Paul Goodman also described youth culture as a response to the rationalisation and conformity of American life,[5] as did Mailer in 'The White Negro'.[6] C. Wright Mills also looked to youth as the new agent of social change.[7] In fact, as Pells puts it, 1950s youth 'stood as an authentic outsider, a personification of the youthful attraction to maladjustment and non-conformity, an inarticulate but vivid reproach to the comfortable reign of the middle-class organisation man'.[8]

While many intellectuals identified with youth cultures, youth cultures usually rejected the culture of white middle-class America through an identification with other outsider figures, and this can be seen most clearly in the ways in which white youth became preoccupied with African-American culture. For both white intellectuals and white youth cultures, this identification also involved an identification with supposedly 'alternative' notions of gender and sexuality. As Barbara Ehrenreich has pointed out, 'in the Fifties conformity became a code word for male discontent – the masculine equivalent of what Betty Friedan would call the problem with no name'. She claims that in Fordist America, the traditionally masculine values of independence and heroism had little place, and that many critics of conformity implied that 'conformity meant emasculation'.[9] As a result, Ehrenreich argues that attacks on conformity were part of a 'male revolt' against the family, and an attempt to reassert traditional masculine values. Certainly such claims may be relevant to figures such as Paul Goodman and Norman Mailer, but the critique of conformity also enabled a far broader reassessment of gender and sexual politics.

For example, the debates over conformity gave women a language of resistance. In her classic feminist text, *The Feminine Mystique*, Betty Friedan drew upon the mass culture debate and its concerns with conformity to discuss the condition of women, or as she referred to it, 'The problem with no name'. Indeed, in her introduction to the book, she sought to identify this problem: 'There was a strange discrepancy between the reality of our lives as women and the image to which we are trying to conform, the image which I call the feminine mystique.'[10] And for Friedan, this image was one created by mass culture in the form of magazines, films, books and on TV.

As a result, the critique of conformity was not simply a defence of traditional forms of masculinity, but part of a broader reaction again the concept of 'maturity'. This concept regulated many of the social codes of 1950s behaviour and, as Ehrenreich puts it, maturity 'required the predictable, sober ingredients of wisdom, responsibility, empathy, (mature) heterosexuality and "a sense of function," or, as a sociologist would have put it, acceptance of adult sex roles'.[11] These adult sex roles were embodied in the domestic roles of the male breadwinner and the housewife. However, if maturity meant acceptance of these roles, any deviance from them was defined as invalid, a mere failure to mature: immaturity. However, it should also be emphasised that maturity was more identified with men than with women. Even the mature woman who accepted the role of housewife was accepting a role which was largely seen as one of infantile and almost child-like dependence. They still remained other to the definitions of mature adulthood which were hence defined as implicitly masculine.

As a result, in rejecting the concept of maturity, youth cultures were not solely part of a 'male revolt' against the family. It is important to remember that youth does not simply equate with young men.[12] The young women and men who made up these youth cultures were not simply defending traditional notions of masculine independence and sexuality. They not only questioned the model of development which 1950s America defined as natural, but often questioned whether development of any sort was either desirable or necessary. As a result, one of the main attractions of 1950s horror films was that the outsiders who populated them were usually distinguished from traditional constructions of gender and sexuality. In *The Creature from the Black Lagoon*, for example, the creature remains tied to the 'warm depths' of the water in which, it is stated, 'life was born'. The creature remains tied to the 'feminine', and enjoys a diffuse and non-genital sexuality; qualities usually associated with female sexuality. If the creature refuses to grow up and become a 'man', the incredible shrinking man learns the uselessness of his conformist notions of masculinity, and finally merges in a blissful union with 'creation'.

In rejecting the values of maturity, white youth also came to identify with cultural forms which were different from those valued by their elders. They rejected the culture of white middle-class America in favour of 'disreputable' forms such as Afro-American music, rock'n'roll, and horror. Unlike earlier generations of youth, the youth of the 1950s had an unprecedented amount of money available for the consumption of cultural goods, and they were able to spend this money on the acquisition of alternative forms of cultural capital, forms which could be used to exclude and reject adults.

This strategy was much more complex than is often supposed. By using certain forms of popular culture to distinguish themselves from the supposed conformity of adult life, youth cultures had to resist the suggestion that they themselves were conformist consumers of mindless 'trash'. One way of understanding this strategy is through Andrew Ross's discussion of 'hip' in the 1950s. Ross describes 'hip' as 'a mobile taste formation that clearly registers shifts in respect/disrespect towards popular taste'.[13] The hipster must define him- or herself against popular taste, but there are two ways of doing so. On the one hand, 'the middle class, hip intellectual, whether Beat or, later, countercultural … assumes the appearance of being ill-informed or *underinformed* [about popular taste] – he doesn't want to appear to know anything about it'.[14] The 'lower class, hipster', on the other hand, is '*overinformed* about popular taste – he knows all about it, even as he keeps his distance from it'.[15] The identity of both groups depends on their relationship to the popular, though. Both may, for example, champion 'authentic popular forms' in a reaction against the 'debased, popular' forms of 'mass culture': hence the Beats' appropriation of 'bebop' rather than forms such as 'swing'. However, such strategies are never stable, given the tendency of supposedly 'authentic popular' forms to become more broadly and commercially successful. In such a situation, the hip becomes unhip, and hipsters must change their allegiances in order to maintain a sense of distinction from popular taste.

Some of these observations are applicable to the consumption of 1950s horror texts. While 1950s intellectuals opposed mass culture through a rejection of popular texts and so took the strategy of the underinformed, many producers and consumers of horror texts took a route which was closer to that to that of the 'lower class hipster'. Rather than rejecting popular culture they became overinformed, able to detect and exclude the underinformed while never simply being naive consumers. They knew the forms of horror so well that they could recognise their artificiality and preposterousness, and this allowed them to celebrate these texts without being cultural dupes.

But there was an important difference between these horror fans and the overinformed hipster, and it is to be found in the precise nature of their distance from popular taste. While the overinformed hipster affected an air of 'cool' detachment, many of the overinformed fans of 1950s horror were anything but 'cool' and detached. They were 'hotly' enthusiastic. For example, Ray Bradbury's advice to young writers reads like a virtual manifesto for the overinformed fan:

> Love comic strips. I have collected them all my life ... know all the books in your local library better than the librarian. Go there every night. Live there. Educate yourself. Know all the stock in your local bookstore. I do. There is no day in my life I do not go to at least one bookstore. Go to art galleries. Look. Fill up. See every film ever made. Fill up on the medium. Know everything that is bad. Only by knowing what is bad can you avoid badness. The snob who refuses knowledge in mediocrities remains always second rate himself. I have collected PRINCE VALLIANT for 30 years. Listen to bad music and good music and great music. Study architecture. Read science fiction, because it is the one fiction which is curious about ALL of the above, all and everything on every level. In sum: run, shout, search, be puzzled, go on, from day to day, with high enthusiasm.[16]

This passage perfectly combines the complex sense of 'hot' enthusiasm with the sense of knowing overinformed distance. The writer is a fan who, none the less, knows too much about popular culture to be a naive dupe. In fact, it actually reverses the implications of the mass culture critique, and uses popular culture to accuse the culture of the underinformed of an unthinking conformity, a strategy which is common to the 1950s horror texts.

Bradbury's status as both a fan and producer of 1950s outsider narratives – who could both recognise the artificiality and preposterousness of these texts while still being able enthusiastically to celebrate his love for them – should also indicate that such a strategy was often encouraged by the formal features of the texts themselves.

As a type of fantasy fiction, 1950s horror was not only at odds with the aesthetics of realism, but also incompatible with the aesthetics of 1950s modernism. It even seemed to cultivate a 'disreputable' image with its lurid marketing campaigns. It refused the standards of maturity and as the decade moved on, it was more and more directed at teenagers. The 'trashiness' of these texts was also a feature of their relationship to genre. Martin Barker claims that the horror comics, for example, encouraged 'an inbuilt unease in our relationship to the genre',[17] a feature which was also important to other outsider narratives. According to Barker, these texts worked 'by distancing us and throwing us into uncertainty'.[18] The term distancing may be misleading. Certainly audiences were involved and often scared by the texts, but these texts 'play[ed] on the very boundary between horror and parody'.[19]

It is for this reason that audiences were able to appreciate even the trashiest of texts. Many texts were not meant to be taken straight, and for audiences which were used to these texts, even a 'really bad' film could be read as parody rather than as horror. In fact, it was usually difficult to tell a 'really bad' film from a parodic one, given the particular strategies used to create parody. Arkoff has complained, for example, that Corman often spent far less on his films for AIP than the studio had provided; that he actually chose to make his films look cheap and artificial. But as Barker argues in relation to the comics, the best texts did not simply play *upon* the line between horror and parody, but *with* that line. As Barker puts it:

> Being self parodying, such strips would make no sense unless we see them as acknowledging where they stand, on a fine line between horror and a parody of horror, and as playing with the fact that they are on the line.[20]

They were self-conscious about the formal features of their genre, and play with these features in order to keep their audiences in a state of uncertainty. They work with generic conventions, but always emphasise that they are conventions.

These formal features are also related to other ways in which these texts kept their audiences in a state of uncertainty. For example, it is difficult to find a stable point of identification within these texts. In some cases, particularly in the comics and short stories, this feature was achieved through shock-endings in which revelations were used to undermine or question the identifications previously encouraged by the narrative.

Even in the case of film narratives, such as *The Incredible Shrinking Man*, which bind the audience to a single character's point of view, the audience is constantly encouraged to question the protagonists' responses, and the narratives frequently concern the gradual erosion of these characters' assumptions about the world. As a result, these narratives require audiences to question their own assumptions and perceptions, and so illustrate that the notions of normality on which conformity depends are relative rather than absolute. For example, through their sympathetic handling of the monstrous outsider, they frequently question what it means to be human, and so establish the right to be different. For this reason, they are often preoccupied with other cultures and other life-forms, but they also raise questions about sexuality and gender. Films such as *Creature from the Black Lagoon* and *The Incredible Shrinking Man*, for example, not only question conventional notions of sexuality and gender, but also suggest that alternatives can exist which may be more desirable. As a result, in the 1950s outsider narratives, the familiar becomes alien whether the narrative point of view concentrates on the perceptions of the representatives of normality, the alienated outsider, or the transformation of the former into the latter.

As a result, while the analysis of more 'reputable' forms of culture usually legitimates them through a concentration on the formal features of individual texts or groups of texts, this analysis of a particular group of 'disreputable' cultural forms suggests that analysis must not concentrate on the texts alone, but also on the distribution of cultural capital and the ways in which these shape the interaction between producers, texts and audiences.

Notes

1 Leonard Wolf, *Horror: A Connoisseur's Guide to Literature and Film* (New York: Facts On File, 1989), p. 49.
2 David J. Skal, *The Monster Show: A Cultural History of Horror* (New York: Norton, 1993), p. 364.
3 Ehrenreich, *The Hearts of Men: American Dreams and the Flight from Comitment* (London: Pluto, 1983), p. 30.
4 Harvey Swados, 'Popular Taste and the Agonies of the Young', Dissent, V (Spring 1958), pp. 176–7.
5 Paul Goodman, *Growing-Up Absurd: Problems of Youth in the Organized Society* (New York: Vintage, 1956).
6 Norman Mailer, 'The White Negro', in *Advertisements for Myself* (New York: G. P. Putnam's, 1959).
7 C. Wright Mills, 'On the New Left', in Paul Jacobs and Saul Landau, eds, *The New Radicals* (Harmondsworth: Penguin, 1966).
8 Richard Pells, *The Liberal Mind in a Conservative Age: American Intel-*

lectuals in the 1940s and 1950s (Middletown: Wesleyan University Press, 1989), p. 206.

9 Ehrenreich, *The Hearts of Men*, p. 32.

10 Betty Friedan, *The Feminine Mystique* (New York: Dell, 1963), p. 7.

11 Ehrenreich, *The Hearts of Men*, p. 17.

12 This point has been made forcefully by Angela McRobbie in her critique of subcultural approaches to youth. Angela McRobbie, 'Settling Accounts with Subcultures: A Feminist Critique', in Tony Bennett *et al.*, eds, *Culture, Ideology and Social Process: A Reader* (London: Batsford, 1981). Indeed, it is worth emphasising because so many of the writings on 1950s youth concentrate almost exclusively on male youth. For example, while Mailer implicitly associates youth with certain constructions of masculinity, Goodman explicitly states that the problems which he associates with 'youth' 'belong primarily, in our society, to boys'. (Paul Goodman, *Growing Up Absurd: Problems of Youth in the Organized Society* (New York: Vintage, 1956), p. 13.) However, this acknowledgement only leads him to disregard the problems of young women, and to continually associate 'human nature' with *man*kind.

13 Andrew Ross, *No Respect: Intellectuals and Popular Culture* (London: Routledge, 1989), p. 83.

14 Ross, *No Respect*, p. 83.

15 *Ibid.*

16 Ray Bradbury quoted by Gary K. Wolfe, 'Ray Bradbury', in Noelle Watson and Paul E. Schellinger, eds, *Twentieth Century Science-Fiction Writers* (Chicago: St James Press, 1991), p. 71.

17 Martin Barker, *A Haunt of Fears: The Strange History of the British Horror Comics Campaign* (London: Pluto, 1984), p. 131.

18 *Ibid.*

19 *Ibid.*

20 *Ibid.*

Don't be fooled by appearances! Difference is a viable alternative in *It Came from Outer Space* (1953) based on a story by Ray Bradbury.

Chapter 3

Fantasies of mass culture:
the fiction of Ray Bradbury

The mixture of celebration and parody with regard to popular forms can be seen in the work of Ray Bradbury and Richard Matheson. These two writers shared a friendship based on mutual admiration and a similarity of interests, and one feature which links them is their particular type of cross-genre writing. Neither of them fit clearly into any category of SF, horror or fantasy. Often the science is less than convincing and the future worlds, particularly in Bradbury, are little more than allegorical settings which are neither socially or materially credible. Furthermore, not all their writing can clearly be categorised as horror. Some is clearly gothic or horrific, but other stories lack any horror elements. Even the term fantasy seems unconvincing, for while their writing often contains fantastic aspects, these are usually set within an imagined version of everyday life. In fact, for many commentators, such as Stephen King, Matheson's importance was that he (along with Jack Finney) 'made the break from the Lovecraftian fantasy that held sway over serious writers of horror for over two decades or more.[1] As Keith Neilson puts it, Matheson 'moved the horrific away from the ornate bizarre and self-consciously mythic worlds of H. P. Lovecraft and the *Weird Tales* tradition to the everyday world of ordinary people'.[2] This quality is even true of Bradbury, despite the fact that he began in the Lovecraftian tradition; published his earliest stories in *Weird Tales*; and has a rather too romanticised and mythic sense of 'the everyday world of common people'.

This kind of cross-genre writing is significant for a number of reasons. It is a product of a deep involvement with popular genres, but a refusal to be limited by them. It also often creates a similar type of unease to that which Martin Barker discusses in relation to the horror comics.[3] A story such as Matheson's 'Death Ship' (1953),[4] for example, starts out as what appears to be a science fiction tale only to transform itself into a ghost story. In others such as Bradbury's 'The Concrete Mixer' (1949)[5] and Matheson's 'The Creeping Terror' (1959),[6] genre narratives are parodied to produce social and cultural satire. The similarities between these writers' work and the horror comics is hardly surprising, though. Bradbury, for example, was a fan of comic strips as is clear from his advice to young writers which was discussed in the introduction to this section.

It is also significant that both of these writers did their best work in the short story form, and that it was this type of fiction which formed the majority of their output. Bradbury does present *The Illustrated Man* (1951) and *The Martian Chronicles* (1950)[7] as if they were novels, but they remain little more than collections of short stories which have been loosely linked together by a central device or situation. Matheson, on the other hand, wrote two classic SF/horror novels, *I Am Legend* (1954)[8] and *The Shrinking Man* (1956),[9] but they are both relatively short and highly focused around a central premise. Consequently, they are more like extended short stories than novels.

These writers' preference for the short story is due to the fact that, like the comic, it can operate around a central shock or twist in a way that is difficult to achieve in longer fiction. Indeed, one of the reasons Matheson's two novels read like short stories is that they also work around a central shock or twist at the end. *I Am Legend* even has the punchline so often featured in the comics.

But if these writers were fans of popular culture, they were also critics of mass society. Again and again, their stories attack conformity and conformist perceptions of reality. Indeed while intellectuals often used to beat popular culture with the avant-garde in order to develop their critique of mass society, these writers often beat the middle-class culture of the underinformed with popular culture as an alternative method of attacking mass society. This strategy can be seen in Bradbury's advice to young writers, but can also be seen in their attacks on censorship. Often inspired by the campaigns against the horror comics, these stories suggest that the logical extension of such censorship would also include the censorship of high culture itself. The 'know-nothing' strategy of intellectuals was thereby seen as, at the very least, counter-productive, and possibly even simply another symptom of the conformist tendencies of modern mass society. Like Harold Rosenberg, these critics suggest that the elitist tendencies of mass culture criticism created their own conformity, through its refusal to accept the validity of cultural forms which did not fit their definitions of high culture.[10] In this way, Bradbury and Matheson's fiction not only illustrates that mass culture critics were wrong to assume that mass, commercial or popular culture was necessarily uncritical, but it also actually offers a more sophisticated analysis of mass society and culture, one which presented a critique of mass culture criticism itself.

Of the writers, Bradbury would seem to fit this general category least comfortably. Rather than emphasising his 'trashiness',

Bradbury's writing is most self-consciously 'literary', and for this reason, he 'has become among the most visible science fiction writers'.[11] Nor is his visibility solely within the realm of SF fans. More than any other 1950s SF writer, Bradbury has gained a mainstream literary reputation. If he has not been championed by high theory, his writing is taught widely at the earlier stages of literary education. However, his literary allusions are eclectic, and not restricted to respectable or high cultural texts. They include a wide variety of forms from high and low culture. 'The Exiles' (1950), for example, concerns a conflict between a rocket ship on its way to Mars, and the phantoms of imaginative literature which has been banned on earth. These phantoms are the 'exiles' of the title, and include not only figures from Hawthorne, James and Poe, but also from Stoker, Lewis Carrol, L. Frank Baum, and Lovecraft.[12] Indeed, Bradbury's work also uses this hybridity. It draws together elements from high and low culture and attempts to move beyond the two. Furthermore, as the writer who established this type of writing, Bradbury had to work harder to gain acceptance than Matheson who was able to define himself within a space which Bradbury had opened up for him.

Despite these factors, there are severe problems with Bradbury's work. One of the most central of these that it is contradictory, or simply incoherent. Individual stories can be very effective, but positions are not worked through with any rigour and often conflict with one another in an unproductive way. For example, one of the features which makes *The Martian Chronicles* read like a collection of short stories is that there is no consistency in Bradbury's portrayal of the Martians or their powers. They range from 'sensitive, essentially ordinary families ("Ylla") to shapeless monsters ("The Third Expedition")'.[13] At times they seem a virtually utopian model of culture and tolerance, while in 'The Earth Men' (1948),[14] the crew of spacemen from earth fall victim to rather dubious Martian methods for dealing with the 'mentally disturbed'. It is also rather difficult to see why such an ideal society would produce such 'disturbed personalities' in the first place, or why it would need to incarcerate them in the manner described in the story. As Bradbury would suggest in other contexts, 'insanity is relative. It depends on who has locked the cage.'[15] Such definitions depend on a certain intolerance and a refusal to accept the difference of others.

More significant is Bradbury's confused response to modernity.

As Gary Wolfe claims, many of Bradbury's best stories 'are powerful indictments of unchecked technological progress and question
humanity's ability to deal creatively with the new worlds of which
science and technology hold promise'.[16] Modernisation, technology
and colonisation are frequently related to one another in his fiction
and are presented as alienating and destructive. But Bradbury is also
deeply enamoured with these processes. Thus, while *The Martian
Chronicles* clearly presents the colonisation of Mars as little more
than a process of genocide in which a heroic culture is destroyed
and a beautiful planet is exploited and spoiled, in another story,
'The Strawberry Window' (1959), which seems little more than an
out-take from *The Martian Chronicles*, he suggests that colonisation
is part of a much larger, nobler process of human advancement. As
one character puts it, humanity (or more accurately, men) colonise
Mars not

> to make money, no. Not to see the sights, no. Those are the lies men
> tell, the fancy reasons they give themselves. Get rich, get famous, they
> say. Have fun, jump around, they say. But all the while, inside, some-
> thing else is ticking along the way it ticks in salmon or whales, the way
> it ticks, by God, in the smallest microbe you want to name. And that
> little clock that ticks in everything living, you know what it says? It
> says get away, spread out, move along, keep swimming. Run to so
> many worlds and build so many towns that *nothing* can ever kill man.
> You *see*, Carrie? It's not just us come to Mars, it's the race, the whole
> darn human race, depending on how *we* make out in our lifetime. This
> thing is so big I want to laugh, I'm am so scared stiff of it.[17]

Even at a more basic level, many of Bradbury's stories display a
romanticisation of rockets and gadgets which seems to contradict
the suspicion with which they are treated in other stories.

Nor are these contradictions productive tensions, or even a kind
of internal dialogue between texts. There seems to be little attempt
to explore these contradictions, or their implications. One way in
which Bradbury avoids such an investigation is through a refusal to
make his futures 'realistic' social worlds. For example, they rarely
seem to be developments from the Fordism of the 1950s, but rather
idealised versions of late nineteenth-century middle America with
futuristic trappings such as rockets instead of horses and carts. They
lack most of the social and material features that distinguish 1950s
America. Even in *Fahrenheit 451* (1953),[18] which is both an attack

on mass society and McCarthy era censorship, the social world does not seem to have caught up with the 1950s, never mind the future. For all the references to the fast pace of social life and the decline of community, everyday life seems far more leisurely and social ties far too close for the urban environment in which it is supposed to be set. Who, after all, really thinks of their neighbours as their immediate circles of acquaintances? Furthermore, in stories like 'The Rocket Man' (1951),[19] the rocket ship captain of the title seems like a nineteenth-century sea captain, rather than a 1950s corporation man. In fact, Bradbury's social world is based on such a cosy and romanticised version of 'the every day world of common people' that when he was accused of being 'the Norman Rockwell of science fiction', he took it as a compliment.

Nor are Bradbury's worlds internally coherent. They lack social detail. For example, as Gary K. Wolfe argues of *Fahrenheit 451*:

> The novel is as simple as a parable, and few attempts are made to offer a realistic portrait of an imagined society. The police state, it seems, exists almost solely to burn books, and the society of outcasts that the hero Montag finally escapes to join seems curiously incapable of political action, choosing instead to preserve literary culture by memorizing all the great books.[20]

In fact the terms allegory and parable are often applied to Bradbury's writing, though one might also include the term fable, and it is this approach which accounts for some of the lack of social detail. In his stories, the conflicts and processes which concern him are defined in moral terms, rather than social terms. As Willis McNelly argues, his 'metaphors may well be those of contemporary society, but they are also those of geometrical figures or universal abstractions'.[21] The problem is that there is no clear sense of the relationship between the historical and the transhistorical or universal. The comment above seems to suggest that while Bradbury uses the images of modern society, he is really doing so in order to deal with universal concerns. However, the relationship is actually more problematic. Bradbury seems to be concerned with developments in modern society, but tends to convert them into symptoms of a mythic 'human condition' in a manner that is largely unconvincing. For example, he tends to resolve conflicts into eternal struggles between good and evil, or light and dark. This tendency can be seen most clearly in *Something Wicked This Way Comes* (1962),[22] but it is also a feature of his critique of colonisation. The stories which concern colonisation associate the 'commercial interests', which result in exploitation and destruction, with an eternal dark side of human nature, and this dark side is then opposed to a more positive side associated with humanity's will to achievement. He does highlight the thin and often ambiguous line between these opposed forces, but he still obscures the historical specificity of these 'commercial interests'. This problem is also partly due to a misguided and strained attempt to lend his fiction meaning, significance and even 'literariness'.

None the less, Bradbury is at his best when at his most nightmarish, and his stories often rely on the shock-endings which distinguish the horror comics of which he was so fond. In 'Perchance to Dream' (1959), for example, a marooned astronaut battles to stay awake until a rescue team arrive to save him. He knows that when he sleeps his mind becomes a battlefield for the spirits of the long dead warrior tribes who used to rule the planet on which he is marooned. Unfortunately, when help finally does come, his tiredness and exhaustion render him so wild and emotional that his 'rescuers' forcibly sedate him only to watch him die almost instantly. Not only have his rescuers killed him, but thinking that he has been driven crazy by loneliness and shock, they decide to take advantage of their situation and settle down to spend a night's sleep outside their ship. 'Should be good sleeping tonight,' one says to the other, 'pleasant dreams.'[23]

In another story, 'The Long Years' (1950),[24] one of the tales from *The Martian Chronicles*, a rescue team arrives on Mars to pick up a man who was deserted on the planet twenty years earlier when everyone else returned to earth. The team find him with his 'family', only to discover at the end of the story that his wife and children have long since died, and that the man has actually constructed robot replicas of his loved ones in order to see him through 'the long years'. The shock of the ending is not only that what appear to be humans are actually robots, but also that the leader of the rescue team comes to admire and respect these replicas as entities with their own right to existence or 'life'. In this way, these tales also encourage a sense of unease with regard to appearances. They disturb the reader's perception of reality, and definitions of humanity.

'The Third Expedition' (1950),[25] for example, concerns a colonising force that lands on Mars prepared for alien hostility. Instead they find a welcoming world which is identical to that of their childhoods, a world which appears to be peopled by their loved ones. Lulled into a false sense of security, they accept this world's hospitality only to be murdered in the night by their 'closest relations'. The story does not simply imply that this world is a mere delusion used to fool the invaders; the next morning, after all the crew are dead, the town continues to exist as it was and its people remain the same while funerals are held to bury the dead crew.

'Zero Hour' (1947)[26] also uses a shock-ending which questions appearances. It involves the games of children and their parents' disinterest in what are regarded as infantile fantasies. The parents pay little attention to their children's games or the 'imaginary friends' of whom their children are so fond. They regard these issues as of little importance. In fact, the 'imaginary friends' are aliens and the children are helping them to invade the earth and destroy the adult humans. The children have a far closer relationship with these aliens than with the parents who ignore them.

These techniques challenge the reader's perceptions of normality. Not only does Bradbury often present sanity and insanity as relative terms, he also illustrates that perceptions confine and even construct the world. This issue, for example, becomes the central joke in his humorous SF story, 'Referent' (1959). The story concerns a young boy, Roby Morrison, who lives on Orthopedic Island, an enclosed educational environment through which a highly rationalist society conditions children in isolation from their parents. While alone one day, feeling alienated and confused, Roby encounters an alien which is '*pure* referent'. Initially, Roby perceives the alien as 'the sandman', a fantasy figure which his educators have told him is an unhealthy delusion. His society is hostile to fantasy which is seen as a threat to rationality. As Roby puts it in a moment of rebellion:

> Semantically, our teachers say that ghosts, goblins and fairies, and sandmen are labels, only names for which there aren't any actual referents, no actual objects or things. But to heck with that. We kids know more than teachers about it. You being here proves the teachers are wrong. There are sandmen after all, aren't there?[27]

The problem is that the alien has acquired the form of Roby's perception, though it does protest, crying out: 'Don't *name* me, don't label me.'

As the story proceeds, the alien tries to resist Roby's perceptions but metamorphoses a number of times as Roby perceives him differently. In this story, existence is defined as pure referent and flux which is constructed and defined by thought and perception. As the alien tells Roby, if only Roby could escape his own perceptions and the perceptions of those around him, Roby would become pure referent like the alien:

> The truth, child! Centuries of thought have moulded your atoms to your present form; if you could undermine and destroy that belief, the beliefs of your friends, teachers and parents, you could change form, be pure referent, too! Like Freedom, Liberty, Humanity, or Time, Space and Justice! (p. 71)

In this way, perceptions are seen as ways of dominating and controlling existence, and like many in the 1950s, Bradbury associates freedom with a refusal of conformist thought.

Eventually, Roby grasps Referent's message and steals the alien's spaceship, leaving him stranded on earth where he is found by one of Roby's teachers who sees what he expected to find: Roby alone in the garden. As Referent protests that he is not Roby, but pure referent, the teacher patronises him and calls for the 'psychoward'. Roby and Referent seek to resist the labels of others and establish the right to define themselves and their own perceptions independent of the judgements of others.

In this way, Bradbury's stories are highly sympathetic to those defined as outsiders or aliens. As the captain says of the robot family in 'The Long Years', 'they've as much right to – to life as you or I or any of us'.[28] Indeed Bradbury's story, 'The Fire Balloons' (1952),[29] concerns a missionary who is sent to try and convert aliens to Christianity, but finds that the aliens' difference does not imply their spiritual inferiority. Instead he finds that they are actually spiritually superior to humanity. They have already reached a higher spiritual level.

'The Concrete Mixer', on the other hand, is another humorous story which reverses many of the conventions of the invasion narratives. It concerns an alien invasion of the earth, but is seen from the aliens' perspective. Ettil is branded a coward in his own society for opposing the invasion of earth. He opposes the invasion because he has been reading extensive amounts of SF from earth in which alien threats are 'thwarted by a young man, usually lean, usually

Irish, usually alone, named Mike, or Rick, or Jack, or Bannon'.[30] His opposition fails, however, and the invasion of earth goes ahead only to find that the people of the earth are not hostile to the aliens, but welcome them enthusiastically. Eventually Ettil realises that the aliens have far more to fear from American culture than from American weaponry, and he writes home to his wife:

> Dear Tylla: To think that in my naivete I imagined that the Earthmen would have to counterattack with guns and bombs. No, no. I was sadly wrong. There is no Rick or Mick or Jack or Bannon – those clever fellows who save worlds. No.
>
> There are blond robots with pink rubber bodies, real, but somehow unreal, alive but somehow automatic in all responses, living in caves all their lives. Their derrieres are incredible in girth. Their eyes fixed and motionless from an endless time staring at picture screens. The only muscles they have occur in their jaws from their ceaseless chewing of gum.
>
> And it is not only these, my dear Tylla, but the entire civilization into which we have been dropped like a shovelful of seeds in a large concrete mixer. Nothing of us will survive. We will be killed not by the gun but by the glad-hand. We will be destroyed by the automobile ...[31]

Eventually, Ettil meets an enthusiastic film-maker who wants to make a movie, 'Invasion of Earth by Mars', and to tie the movie into a whole series of merchandising such as the selling of 'a special Martian doll at thirty bucks a throw' (p. 153). It is at this point that Etill has a realisation and asks the producer for his name. On hearing that the producers name is Richard, Ettil starts to laugh. He has realised that he has finally met the Rick of which he had been so frightened. As Ettil puts it: 'So you're Rick. Oh, how different, how funny. No bulging muscles, no lean jaw, no gun. Only a wallet full of money and an emerald ring and a big middle!' (p. 153). In this way, the alien is used by Bradbury not only to parody SF and horror conventions, but to provide a critique of American mass society and culture in the process.

Other stories concern the ways in which humans identify with aliens or outsiders as a way of resisting the destructiveness of 'normality'. In 'And the Moon be Still as Bright' (1948), conflict erupts during a colonising mission to Mars when Spender, one of the team, begins to identify with the aliens whose lives and culture have been destroyed by colonisation. In the process, he comes to oppose the human colonisation of Mars and takes up arms against his fellow humans. Early on he discusses the human mission with his captain, Wilder, a man of similar sympathies to Spender. Again the problem of naming and labelling become central. Spender talks of the signs left by the Martians, and the way in which they had made their planet their own through their material activities, their culture and their language:

> Ask me, then, if I believe in the spirit of the things as they were used, and I'll say yes. They're all here. All the things which had uses. All the mountains which had names. And we'll never be able to use them without feeling uncomfortable. And somehow the mountains will never sound right to us; we'll give them new names, but the old names are there, somewhere in time, and the mountains were shaped and seen under those names. The names we'll give to the canals and mountains and cities will fall like so much water on the back of a mallard. No matter how much we touch Mars, we'll never touch it. And then we'll get mad at it, and you know what we'll do? We'll rip it up, rip the skin off, and change it to fit ourselves.[32]

Wilder refuses to accept Spender's grim prediction of the effect which humans will have on Mars. He argues that the planet is 'too big and too good' to be harmed by humans, and suggests that humans can learn to treat the planet with reverence. But Spender remains unconvinced. Maybe a few will take a moral position, but they cannot hold out 'against all the commercial interests'.[33]

Finally, Spender and Wilder find themselves on opposite sides as Spender deserts and wages war against his old team. Spender even goes so far as to claim that he is 'glad to call [the Martians his] ancestors'[34] so identifying himself with Martian culture, rather than the human culture of Earth. Even Wilder clearly identifies with Spender's position as an outsider in human culture, although he feels obliged to perform his duty and track Spender down. However, when the team have virtually caught Spender, Wilder finds himself pleading for Spender to escape. He even finally comes to believe that 'I'm Spender all over again, but I think before I shoot. I don't shoot at all, I don't kill. I do things with people. And he couldn't kill me because I was himself under a slightly different condition.'[35]

Although Bradbury cannot quite acknowledge it, the problem is that Spender is right. Wilder's moral stand without violent resistance has no effect upon the colonisation of Mars, and he does not appear again in *The Martian Chronicles* until 'The Long Years' in which he is the captain who comes to pick up the survivors. It is here at the end of the novel, that Wilder is finally forced to admit that Spender's predictions were correct. It is also at this moment that he encounters the robot family and learns to value their difference. But Bradbury has no solution. Instead, the reader is encouraged to identify with Wilder's acceptance of the tragic situation, rather than to consider the possibility of any actual solution.

Other stories also concern human identifications with aliens. In 'Dark They Were and Golden Eyed' (1959),[36] humans transform into Martians and lead a much happier life. Indeed, *The Martian Chronicles* finally ends with a family of survivors from the war-torn earth who, having rejected human culture and its destructiveness, travel to Mars. Once on Mars, the father promises his children that they will see some Martians, and he finally fulfils his promise by leading them to one of the planet's canals and showing them their own reflections in the water.

Bradbury was not simply concerned with a defence of other cultures in the abstract. Many of his stories, for example, deal directly with the issue of race. 'Way in the Middle of the Air' (1950) concerns the conflicts and confusions which erupt when the Afro-American population decides to leave the American South and its white population behind for a better life on Mars. Some whites react with confusion, unable to understand why those they regarded as 'like a family member' would reject them, while others react with anger, manipulation and threats of violence in an attempt to make them stay. The central concern of the story is with the ways in which the white characters' sense of identity depends upon the subordination of the Afro-Americans. The white characters are therefore shocked by what they see as a lack of gratitude, and by the ease with which the African-American characters shrug off their servility when presented with an alternative way of life. Bradbury's insights are interesting not only because the book was published in 1950 before developments in the Civil Rights movement galvanised middle-class guilt, but also because he treats black nationalist sentiments as valid. One of the things the whites cannot understand is why the Afro-Americans would want to leave just when whites were beginning to make concessions to them. As one character puts it:

I can't figure why they left *now*. With things lookin' up. I mean, every day they got more rights. What they *want*, anyway? Here's the poll tax gone, and more and more states passin' anti-lynchin' bills, and all kinds of equal rights. What *more* they want? They make almost as good money as a white man, but there they go.[37]

Bradbury makes it clear that even extending Civil Rights will not be enough as long as it is given as a concession by a dominant group handing out favours. Afro-Americans will still exist in a situation of subordination and dependency; they will still desire autonomy, and probably come to believe that the only way out is independence from white society and its history of seeing whiteness as superior. In fact, the story's punchline comes when, having tried to prevent the Afro-Americans from leaving, the main white character says, in a desperate need to assert his superiority, 'Did you notice? Right up to the very last, by God, he said "Mister"!'[38] Bradbury implies that white society is so dependent on its perception of Afro-Americans as inferior that it will resist anything which seeks to challenge that perception.

Similar issues are also dealt with in 'The Big Black and White Game' (1945),[39] but in 'The Other Foot' (1951), the issues are reversed. The story concerns an Afro-American community which is living on Mars and comes into contact with whites for the first time in twenty years. Initially, the story involves the eruption of repressed and long buried hostilities among the Afro-Americans. As one man, Willie, says:

I'm not feeling Christian ... I'm just feeling mean. After all them years of doing what they did to our folks – my mom and dad, and your mom and dad – You remember? You remember how they hung my father on Knockwood Hill and shot my mother? You remember? Or you got a memory that's short like the others?[40]

But the story does not follow this logic through. Instead the anger is dissipated when the community find that the whites have come asking for help. They have destroyed the earth in a nuclear war and need assistance. Most significantly, the tide is turned when the Afro-Americans learn that all the key symbols of the old oppression have been destroyed. For example, the tree on Knockwood Hill where Willie's father was lynched has been burned along with all the other trees on earth. Finally, with all the symbols gone, the Afro-Americans themselves can forgive. They come to see the whites' situation as little different to that under which they themselves had suffered for so many years. In this situation, they recognise that things can begin again afresh. As Willie puts it:

> The Lord's let us come through, a few here and a few there. And what happens next is up to all of us. The time for being fools is over. We got to be something else except fools. I knew that when he talked. I knew then that now the white man's as lonely as we've always been. He's got no home now, just like we didn't have one for so long. Now every-thing's even. We can start all over again, on the same level.[41]

In this way, like other Bradbury stories, 'The Other Foot', is also concerned with perception, and it ends with Willie, as he returns from his encounter with the astronauts, answering those who ask him if he has seen the white man: 'Yes, sir … Seems like for the first time today I really seen the white man – I really seen him clear.'[42]

It is therefore interesting to compare 'Way in the Middle of the Air' with 'The Other Foot' because both stories seem to suggest that the oppressed have far more capacity for altering their perceptions than the oppressors. This is less the case in 'The Rock Cried Out' (1959), which also deals with similar conflicts. However, this story does more to suggest the systems which maintain the presumed superiority of dominant groups, while also showing how deeply ingrained such presumptions are in even those figures who perceive themselves as 'liberal' and 'tolerant'. 'The Rock Cried Out' begins with an American couple who are travelling through South America and are appalled by the smell of the open butchers' shops in the region, even though the male tries to display his understanding and acceptance of alternative cultures. Then, rather conveniently, they hear news that Europe and the United States have been destroyed in a nuclear war. Suddenly, they find themselves on the defensive. As the husband comments:

> We're alone, my God, we're alone. Remember how safe we used to feel? How safe? We registered in all the big towns with the American Consuls. Remember how the joke went? 'Everywhere you go you can hear the rustle of the Eagle's wings!' Or was it the sound of paper money? I forget. Jesus, Jesus, the world got empty awfully quick. Who do I call on now?[43]

Unable to rely on the authority of American political and economic power, they become increasingly vulnerable and paranoid while the people of the region exact revenge on the couple for all that has been suffered at the hands of American power. Finally, the couple find themselves in a hotel where they are offered protection if they will consent to work as menial labourers. They realise, however, that not only do their own feelings of superiority over more overtly exploitative Americans count for very little – they were still part of the system which had exploited other cultures – they also recognise that they are not equipped to deal with a life of menial labour and servile dependence. Finally, knowing that they have nothing to go back to and no way of making a life for themselves in the hotel, they decide to go outside and face the anti-American crowd. And as they do so, they pass an open butcher's shop where the meat 'looked like brutalities and sins, like bad consciences, evil dreams, like gored flags and slaughtered promises'.[44] Faced with both their own guilt and the crowd, they come to their final realisation. As the wife puts it: 'They're all strangers! I don't know any of them. I wish I knew *one* of them. I wish even *one* of them knew me!'[45] It is the Americans' failure to see these people as anything but foreign and different which has led them into this situation. By seeing them as different, these people have remained strangers who do not matter, and now that the situation is reversed, these strangers may not recognise Americans as anything but symbols, representatives of an abusive system of power.

As a result, Bradbury's work presents a critique of white power and privilege, and while his portrayal of other races or ethnic groups may often seem either idealised or patronising, this is not unique to his treatment of these groups, but a more general problem in his writing: for example, it is also a feature of his portrayal of 'positive' white communities. Instead it is around issues of gender that Bradbury has the most problems. His portrayals of women fall into fairly predictable categories such as the understanding, self-sacrificing wife and/or mother and the cold, selfish threat to masculinity. In stories such as 'The Rocket Man',[46] for example, the wife's feelings are merely secondary to the husband's need to travel, and she spends most of her life waiting at home and worrying about his safety. However, this position is never criticised, but instead it is simply presented as the 'tragic lot of women' to maintain the domestic sphere while the husband spends long periods away, advancing civilisation. In fact, Bradbury's concerns are almost entirely and uncritically with his male characters and their preoccupations.

One also finds that the male urge into space is centred around a clear feminisation of other worlds. This feature can be seen most clearly in 'Here There Be Tygres' (1959). The story concerns an expedition to a planet and the discovery that the planet can fulfil every human desire. However, one member of the crew, Chaterton, refuses to trust the apparent benevolence of this new world, and clearly wants to dominate and control it. As he puts it:

> You have to beat a planet at its own game ... Get in, rip it up, poison its animals, dam its rivers, sow its fields, depollinate its air, mine it, nail it down, hack away at it, and get the hell out from under when you have want you want. Otherwise a planet will fix you good.[47]

The metaphor of rape is clearly implied in this passage, but the planet is more clearly associated with femininity by the end of the story.

While Chaterton fears the planet, the rest of the crew all love it and continue to have all their desires fulfilled. Indeed, one character even describes the planet as: 'A versatile world ... A woman who'll do anything to please her guests, as long as we're kind to her. Chaterton wasn't kind.'[48] Eventually, Chaterton is killed by the planet, and the crew decide to leave. However, they do not leave out of fear that they will befall the same fate as their comrade. They know that so long as they continue to treat the planet with love and respect it will continue to grant all their wishes, even women for them to enjoy. Instead they leave because if they stayed they would 'get to liking this world too much'. They have to go or else they would 'never want to leave'.[49] The attractions of the planet and of femininity are ultimately implied to be dangerous. They threaten to divert men from masculine activities such as exploring the universe.

If the appeals of femininity are presented as dangerous in 'Here There Be Tygres', Bradbury's work also presents female dominance as a problem. In *Fahrenheit 451*, Montag's wife is a cold, faithless woman who only values her husband for the possessions and status symbols which his wage can buy her, while 'A Scent of Sarsaparilla' (1959) concerns a man who travels into the past to escape his wife's nagging.[50]

None the less, Bradbury's interest in otherness, aliens and outsiders is part of a more general critique of mass culture. Again and again, his stories concern conformist societies where difference is repressed, and this repression is usually associated with the censorship of imaginative culture. Just as 'The Exiles' concerned phantom characters from imaginative literature who were outcasts from earth, 'The Fox and the Forest' (1950)[51] concerns a man and a women who flee the nuclear weapons and censorship which distinguish their future society for a happier life in 1938, only to be pursued by an enforcer from their own time. It is also worth noting that the enforcer poses as a Hollywood film-maker, and disguises his instrument of control as a film camera. While this does equate the forces of control and censorship with the Hollywood film industry, it should also be noted that Bradbury did not hate films himself, but loved them. In his advice to writers, he told them to 'see every film ever made. Fill up on the medium'.[52] Unlike MacDonald and others who attack the individual products of mass culture as though they were a simple expression of its tendencies, Bradbury can like individual films and even groups of films while still despising the system which produced them. His objection to mass society is that it narrows down the range of materials available, and limits the imagination. It is for this reason that he can be critical of the mass culture theorists who long to see the end of popular forms and who regard the avant-garde as the only forms worth maintaining.

Bradbury's critique of censorship can also be seen in 'Usher II' (1950) which concerns an exile from earth who moves to Mars. Here he builds a monument to the works of imaginative literature (mainly horror) which have been banned on his home planet. This monument is then used to destroy the censors, and to replace them with robot replicas. The man builds a house which recreates many of the death scenes from Poe and other horror writers, and invites guests to come and visit. At first, it appears that the guests watch their own robotic replicas murdered in the various recreations, but it eventually becomes clear that it is the real guests who are being murdered and that it is their robot replicas who are watching. Finally, the house, as in Poe's original story, collapses and the duplicates fly off to take up the positions in society which the dead had occupied. The plan is therefore a revenge against a society of conformity and intolerance which is supposed to have begun in the 1950s and 1960s 'by controlling books of cartoons and then detective books and, of course, films'.[53] This process is also associated with the end of ideology rhetoric of the 1950s to the extent that the term politics 'eventually became a synonym for Communism among the reactionary elements, so I hear, and it was worth your life to use the word!'[54] In such a society, it is suggested, dissent becomes a crime and 'the word "escape" was radical'.[55] Difference was defined as a failure to adjust to reality, and was either prevented or punished.

In Bradbury's work, it is psychology and psychoanalysis which are seen as the main mechanisms for enforcing conformity and an 'adjustment to reality'. In numerous stories, people whose perceptions cannot be tolerated are sent to the 'psychoward' as in 'Referent'. For example, in 'The Exiles', the one earth man who claims to have seen the Emerald City of Oz on Mars is told to 'report for psychoanalysis tomorrow'.[56] Psychology and psychoanalysis, Bradbury suggests, operate by defining difference and different perceptions as matters of individual pathology. The 'norm' is defined as objectively right, and divergence or deviance from it are defined as a problem of individual delusion which must be corrected. In this way, the 'norm' will accept no challenge or even divergence, but must force people to adopt its terms of reference or exclude them.

These issues are also related to anxieties about technology in Bradbury's work. For example, 'The Pedestrian' (1951)[57] concerns a man who is arrested for going out for a walk at night when everyone else in his society is at home watching television. The implications of this story are that in the future community will break down as everyone lives through the 'imagined community' of the mass audience, unconnected to one another except through their common consumption of the same cultural materials. In such a society, it is suggested, a harmless activity such as an evening stroll will be seen as deviant and suspect. It will become something to be corrected either by legal or psychological means. At the end of the story, it is never quite clear if the police are taking the pedestrian to prison or the 'psychoward', but in another story, 'The Murderer' (1953),[58] the arrested deviant is taken to a police cell where a psychiatrist is called in to interview him. The division between psychology and criminology as modes of social control, it is implied, are at best blurred and uncertain. This world is the therapeutic society at its most developed. 'The Murderer' also extends the concerns of 'The Pedestrian' in other ways. In this world, people not only seem to have virtually no interaction with one another, except through machines such as wrist radios, but these machines seem to have the same status as people. The 'murderer' of the story has only killed the machines which dominate his life. In this world, destroying a machine is a crime of murder.

'The Veldt' (1950) takes these concerns with technology still further. It concerns a future world in which machines are able to free humans from mundane manual labour, and 'nurseries' are rooms which can simulate any environment which the child desires. In the story, however, the parents of two children begin to be worried by their children's obsession with the nursery and with one particular environment, an African veldt. Pampered and given everything they desire, the children seem to revert to 'savagery', rather than ascend to a 'higher' level of culture. But the problem is identified with the parents rather than the children. They have overindulged their young children, but only through material gratification. They have allowed the nursery to 'replace' them in their children's affections. The nursery 'is their mother and father, far more important in their lives than their real parents'.[59] As a result, when the parents become concerned by their children's expectations of perpetual and immediate gratification and begin to restrict their children's pleasures, they meet with a horrible fate. They have allowed material and mechanical gratifications to become more important than human interaction in their children's lives, and the children use the machine to kill their parents. In fact, the parents have often wondered what the lions appear to be eating when they enter the nursery's recreation of the veldt. Unfortunately, they only discover at the last moment that it is actually their own bodies. The children have been fantasising about the death of their parents even before the beginning of the story.

However, machines are not irredeemably negative in Bradbury's stories, as is shown by the sympathetic robot family of 'The Long Years'. In fact, in 'Usher II', the robot replacements may even be preferable to their human counterparts. Furthermore, in 'Marionettes Inc.' (1949), a husband, Mr Braling, decides to escape from his marriage for a while and to take the trip to Rio which he had always promised himself. His problem is how to do so without his wife's knowledge. To achieve this end, he uses a robot duplicate who acts as his stand-in while he is away, but on the husband's return, the robot refuses to be put back into its box and locks Braling inside instead. The robot has been used on and off for two years by the husband and has 'grown rather fond' of Braling's wife. Thus while the story does operate in relation to fears of technology out of control, the robot is actually presented as more caring than Braling himself. After Braling has been put in the box, the robot returns to Mrs Braling and gives her the care and attention which Braling has denied her over the years. When Mrs Braling responds by saying 'why – you haven't done that in years', the robot promises to see what he 'can do about that'.[60]

Not only does Bradbury suggest that mass society and its technology are socially and emotionally destructive, his stories are preoccupied with nuclear war and the apocalyptic implications of scientific developments. Ironically, while many humans move to Mars in *The Martian Chronicles* to 'get away from wars and censorship and statism and conscription and government control of this and that',[61] they end up transferring these problems to Mars, at least until war breaks out on earth and most of them return to be annihilated. The problem, it is suggested, is that a mass society not only gives one little to live for, but in the process, devalues human life itself. It is also suggested that the immediate gratifications of mass society encourage people to hide from social responsibilities and political debate. It encourages people to ignore the systems of power on which their luxury and privilege depend. As Montag says in *Fahrenheit 451*:

> Jesus God ... Every hour so many damn things in the sky! How in hell did those bombers get up there every single second of our lives! Why doesn't someone want to talk about it? We've started and won two atomic wars since 1960. Is it because we're having so much fun at home we've forgotten the world? Is it because we're so rich and the rest of the world's so poor and we just don't care if they are? I've heard rumours; the world is starving, but we're well fed. Is it true, the world works hard and we play? Is that why we're hated so much?[62]

For Bradbury, mass conformity and the repression of difference and dissent not only destroy the quality of human life, but also encourage the processes which might lead to the annihilation of human life itself.

Fahrenheit 451

These issues are given their most detailed exploration in Bradbury's novel, *Fahrenheit 451*. Like many of Bradbury's stories the novel plays with perceptions of the world and the difference between appearance and reality, and it does so most clearly through the transformation of the central character, Montag. The narrative concerns a 'fireman', Montag, whose job is not to put out fires, but to burn books, the symbols of all that his society cannot tolerate. During the course of the novel, Montag's perceptions are challenged so that he becomes increasingly dissatisfied with his job, his life and the society in which he lives. In the process, he moves from a position of an insider (who defends his society against the threat posed by literature) to that of an outsider (who is hunted down by all the forces of authority and even the common people). In many ways, this is one of Bradbury's most dark, nightmarish and horrific fantasies, and it seeks to evoke a deep sense of alienation, terror and loneliness that lies buried and disguised behind the apparent pleasures and luxuries of modern life. For example, although Montag's wife seems to live almost entirely for the pleasure given her by her televisual environment, she is driven to attempt suicide on a number of occasions, but is unable to acknowledge these signs of desperation and dissatisfaction to either Montag or herself. Nor is her case presented as an exception. On one occasion, when Montag takes his wife to hospital to have her stomach pumped, he is told by a doctor that they 'get these cases nine or ten a night. Got so many, starting a few years ago, we had the special machines built' (p. 22).

In this way, the normal world is presented as a nightmare while those defined as 'anti-social deviants' are presented as sympathetic and attractive people. For example, Clarisse, the girl who lives next door to Montag and begins his education, is presented as a clear comparison to his wife. Clarisse seems exciting, interesting and happy in her non-conformity. She even challenges the very meaning of the term 'anti-social':

> I'm anti-social, they say. I don't mix. It's so strange. I'm very social indeed. It all depends on what you mean by social, doesn't it? Social to me means talking about things like this … Or about how strange the world is. Being with people is nice. But I don't think its social to get a bunch of people together and then not let them talk, do you? (p. 35)

Not only does Clarisse suggest that the term 'anti-social' is relative rather than absolute, she also criticises the lack of human interaction which distinguishes their social world, a world in which discussion and dialogue are seen as 'deviant' and 'abnormal'.

None the less, Clarisse actually seems a rather bland non-conformist. In many other fictions of the 1950s, she would have seemed the epitome of wholesome young womanhood. She is also opposed to the altogether more monstrous figure of femininity, Montag's wife Mildred. Mildred is presented as selfish and demanding. She is always requiring Montag to conform so that he can continue to satisfy her demands for new consumer goods. For example, while Montag is clearly presented as more than attentive towards her, she is angered by his inability to buy her a fourth TV screen or 'wall' for her 'parlour'. At one point, for example, she says:

> It's only two thousand dollars ... And I should think you'd consider me sometimes. If we had a fourth wall, why it'd be just like this room wasn't ours at all, but all kinds of exotic people's rooms. (p. 27)

Indeed, Bradbury's presentation of Mildred could not be a clearer example of the common association between the conformist consumer of mass culture consumer and the figure of woman.[63]

In fact, as the novel progresses, Mildred increasingly becomes a figure of disgust and horror until Montag has no positive memories of her or his relationship to her, and she is described as a mere object of repulsion:

> Mildred stood over his bed, curiously. He felt her there, he saw her without opening his eyes, her hair burnt by chemicals to a brittle straw, her eyes with a kind of cataract unseen but suspect far behind the pupils, the reddened pouting lips, the body thin as a praying mantis from dieting, and her flesh like white bacon. He could remember her no other way. (p. 52)

It is true that the opening of the book clearly associates the destructive act of book-burning with phallic masculinity, but Bradbury can imagine no positive sexual or emotional relationship between men and women, other than the non-sexual bond between Montag and Clarisse with its associations of childhood innocence. Even then women function positively as nurturers of the male rather than as entities in their own right. In fact, it may not be incidental that Clarisse has learned her non-conformity through her close relationship with a man, her grandfather, and appears to have no significant relationships with other women.

None the less, the major point of distinction between Clarisse and Mildred is the former's love of human interaction as opposed to the latter's obsessive relationship with the televisual images in her 'parlour'. In fact, the lack of any sense of communal interaction is one of the main features associated with mass society within the novel. Clarisse, for example, complains that 'People don't want to talk about anything ... They name a lot of cars or clothes or swimming pools mostly and say how swell! But they all say the same things and nobody says anything different from anyone else' (p. 36). In a conformist world where everyone consumes standardised products, it is suggested, everyone has the same experiences, and hence there is no need for interaction or debate. Everyone thinks and feels the same way, and there is no challenge to their perceptions. In such a world, televisual images replace actual interaction. Not only does Mildred refer to the televisual representations in her parlour as her 'family' but she actually has a far greater allegiance to these images than she has to her husband, Montag. When he asks her to turn the parlour off for him because he is sick, she retorts, 'That's my family!' and only eventually agrees to turn it down. Finally, when Montag is caught hiding books and his home is set ablaze in punishment, Mildred blames Montag for the destruction of her family and rejects him.

Mass culture is also blamed for the loss of community in other ways. In one sequence, Beatty, Montag's fire chief, explains how their society came into being, and he argues that as culture became increasingly homogeneous,

> The mind drinks less and less. Impatience. Highways full of crowds going somewhere, somewhere, somewhere, nowhere. The gasoline refuge. Towns turn into motels, people in nomadic surges from place to place, following the moon tides, living tonight in the room where you slept this noon and I the night before. (p. 61)

Whether television or the structure of the economy is actually responsible for this migration and movement, Beatty is describing the process by which fewer and fewer people continue to live in the place where they were born, and neighbourhoods come to be made up of transitory populations with little shared history or knowledge of one another. This situation is also linked to a critique of the division between work and leisure in modern society, a critique which is common to a whole series of attacks on the modern world including that of Marx.[64] Just as Marx argued that the alienation of labour resulted in leisure being defined as non-activity, so Beatty argues that as work becomes rationalised and routine, life becomes 'immediate, the job counts, pleasure lies all about after work. Why learn anything save pressing buttons, pulling switches, fitting nuts and bolts?' (p. 59). As work becomes devoid of pleasure, leisure becomes the opposite of work, a search for immediate gratification without any expense of effort.

This problem is also related back to the features of mass culture, particularly the dominance of the image. The image, it is argued, offers pleasure without effort. As Faber, the ex-academic in the novel, puts it:

> you can't argue with the four-wall televisor. Why? The televisor is 'real'. It is immediate, it has dimension. It tells you what to think and blasts it in. It *must* be right. It *seems* so right. It rushes you on so quickly to its own conclusions your mind hasn't time to protest, 'What nonsense!' (p. 84)

The apparent realism of the image overdetermines the responses of the viewer, and does not give them enough room to contemplate or consider its implications. This kind of critique is common to mass culture theorists, and it can be found in figures as different as T. W. Adorno and Daniel Boorstin.[65]

For Bradbury, it is this situation which results in the apathy and lack of political debate within mass society. Desiring only immediate gratification, he implies, people lose any sense of responsibility. Indeed, this results in Clarisse extolling the virtues of her childhood in which she 'was spanked when [she] needed it' (p. 36), and so learned to believe in responsibility. Beatty also discusses the ways in which immediate gratification results in callousness:

> For everyone nowadays knows, absolutely is *certain*, that nothing will ever happen to *me*. Others die, I go on. There are no consequences and no responsibilities. Except that there *are*. But let's not talk about them, eh? By the time the consequences catch up with you, its too late, isn't it, Montag? (p. 111)

It is this lack of responsibility which, according to Clarisse, results in the way children callously kill one another or die in car wrecks, and, as Montag complains, the way in which people refuse to discuss the gradual drift towards nuclear war and human annihilation.

In fact it is the fear of human interaction, dialogue and debate which lies behind the banning of books. They are condemned because they are symbolic of these processes. As Beatty observes:

'None of those books agree with each other. You've been locked up here for years with a regular Tower of Babel' (p. 43). The arguments and the differences between books frighten the mass society of Montag's world not only because they require effort in order to think through the opposing positions presented, but also because they challenge people's perceptions and taken for granted beliefs. In this way, Bradbury uses what is often seen as a conservative version of mass culture theory: the critique of mass culture as a tyranny of the masses who stifle complex ideas out of a dread of being inferior. None the less, this does not make his work implicitly conservative. Nor was this appropriation unique to Bradbury. Many mass culture critiques on the left adopted this position whether consciously or not. In fact, it could be argued that it is implicit within all varieties of mass culture theory.

For Bradbury, mass culture 'didn't come from the Government down. There was no dictum, no declaration, no censorship, to start with, no!' (p. 61). Instead, ironically, it was the result of an increasingly various and complex public sphere in which dialogue became a problem exactly because of the variousness of the public. As the markets grew, it is claimed, more 'minorities' (or perhaps more accurately interest groups) were included within it, and there was a danger of causing offence to one section of the market. In this way, Bradbury offers a critique of many liberals who claimed that it was the variousness of social life and the number of vying interest groups which prevented the development of mass society and culture.[66] However, Bradbury is not necessarily arguing against minority movements, but suggests that dialogue between groups is essential. He is arguing for an active public sphere, rather than a defensive preservation of minority identity. As has been argued, others, outsiders and aliens are central to Bradbury's work because they offer a challenge to the norm. The danger, he suggests, is that as minority groups are incorporated into society, they may seek to defend their own identities and perceptions against those of others, rather than challenging others and allowing themselves to be challenged.[67]

None the less, this process is still related back to broader economic and political processes. It is still seen as the product of the industrial revolution with its implications of standardised mass production and standardised mass consumption. It is capital's pursuit of economies of scale in the search for profit, and its use of technology to achieve this end, which is the problem for Bradbury. For this reason, he sees the development of mass society and culture as dating from around the Civil War period, though he also suggests that it was the new technologies of mechanical reproduction such as photography, cinema, radio and television which consolidated this process. The fact that all these cultural forms, except radio, are means of mechanically reproducing images is significant and relates to Bradbury's critique of the image which was discussed earlier. None the less, like many mass culture theorists, he also suggests that these new technologies 'levelled [culture] down' to simplifications. They led to the emergence of 'condensations' and 'digests' which in turn led to a continual decline in the attention span of the audience. It also led to a simplification of narrative patterns in which 'Everything boils down to the gag, the snap ending.'

In fact this is taken so far that at the end of the novel, the authorities, who are televising their hunt for Montag, not only use filmic techniques to dramatise the event, but also fake the ending in order to reach the dramatic resolution before the audience's attention span wanes. As Granger, one of the underground which Montag has joined, observes:

> They're faking it. You threw them off at the river. They can't admit it. They know they can hold their audience only so long. The show's got to have a snap ending, quick! If they started searching the whole damn river it might take all night. So they're sniffing for a scape-goat to end things with a bang. Watch. They'll catch Montag in the next five minutes! ... It'll be you; right up at the end of that street is our victim. See how our camera is coming in? Building the scene. Suspense. Long shot. (p. 142)

In the society of the spectacle, even political events have to be stylised and fictionalised to provide a simple satisfying resolution.

This situation, it is suggested, creates a world of conformity in which people are dominated by technology and controlled by therapeutic technocrats. Clarisse, for example, is forced to see a psychiatrist who 'wants to know what I do with all my time' (p. 29). His job is to 'cure' her of her deviant behaviour and make her adjust to social norms. Montag's society has even 'lowered the Kindergarten age year after year until now [its] almost snatching them from the cradle' (p. 63). It wants to rationalise the socialisation process and avoid the more unpredictable and uncontrollable influence of 'the home environment' (p. 63).

But if psychological control is seen as an insidious form of domi-nation and regulation, technology is seen as a more overt and destructive one. Anxieties about technology are not only displayed through the concern with forms of mechanical reproduction, but also through the figure of the 'mechanical hound' which appears throughout the novel and becomes the major threat to Montag at the end. As the full forces of authority are unleashed in order to track Montag down, it is the mechanical hound which becomes the most tenacious and dangerous figure which pursues him. It has extraordinarily sensitive tracking devices, immense power and a deadly poison which it injects into its victims. As the novel becomes more paranoid and nightmarish, it is this robotic figure which becomes the main force which Montag must escape.

If the mechanical hound threatens Montag, human life itself is also threatened and virtually destroyed by technology in the novel when the move towards war ends in a nuclear apocalypse from which only a few survivors exist with the possibility of starting things over again differently. Unfortunately, while this does illus-trate the destructive tendencies of technology in mass society, it tends to underplay the full horror of such a war and even presents the war as potentially positive: it obliterates a society which is 'shot through' with corruption, and enables the possibility of developing a more humane alternative in its place.

The basis for an alternative is supposedly offered by the under-ground which Montag contacts and joins, a network of individuals who have each memorised the books banned by their society. Books, it is suggested, offer an alternative to mass culture not only because they involve dialogue and debate, but also because they are the products of creative activity. Their production involves the work and struggle of an individual in the production of meaning. For Granger, it is this creative activity that transcends the death of the individual. Through creative activity, the individual makes an impression on other individuals which lives on after the individual's own death. Granger's grandfather, for example, has affected him and passed his thoughts and ideas on to the next generation. This creative act is distinguished by the feature which Faber refers to as 'quality' or 'texture', the telling or fresh detail which makes up the substance of the text. This detail implies concentration and explo-ration, rather than generalisation. As Faber argues:

The good writers touch life often. The mediocre ones run a quick
hand over her. The bad ones rape her and leave her for the flies. (p.
83)

This process of concentration also involves an acknowledgement of
the less beautiful side of life. It does not idealise the world, but presents its imperfections and this feature is explicitly distinguished
from the supposedly idealised images of movie stars: books, it is
claimed, are feared and hated partly because they

> show the pores in the face of life. The comfortable people want only
> wax moon faces, poreless, hairless, expressionless. We are living in a
> time when flowers are trying to live on flowers, instead of growing on
> good rain and black loam. (p. 83)

For Faber, this 'quality' or 'texture' is also related to a second feature of books: leisure.

Here, however, leisure is distinguished from the immediate gratifications associated with mass culture. While mass culture is supposed to overdetermine the audience's responses and deny them
space to think, 'Literature' is supposed to allow them the leisure to
contemplate and consider its features. It allows one the space to
interact with the text and come to one's own conclusions through
the effort of engaging with the text. If quality and leisure are two of
the features which Bradbury sees as missing from mass culture, the
third is 'the right to carry out actions based on what we learn from
the inter-action of the first two' (p. 85). It is here, however, that the
problems of Bradbury's novel become most apparent.

While it is true that Montag's engagement with books does place
him in opposition to society, the novel does not give him any real
basis for action. In fact, the underground are a remarkably passive
organisation who never actually threaten the existing order themselves, but merely preserve the literature of the past in case it might
be needed in some possible future. They do not do anything more
to make that future come about. In fact, Faber himself undermines
his own argument, and that of Bradbury, when he illustrates that
engagement with literature does not necessarily require action, but
may actually have the opposite effect. Faber feels guilty because he
'saw the way things were going, a long time back' but 'said nothing'
(p. 82). He describes himself as

> one of the innocents who could have spoken up and out when no one

would listen to the 'guilty,' but I did not speak and thus became guilty myself. And when finally they set the structure to burn the books, using the firemen, I grunted a few times and subsided, for there were no others grunting and yelling with me, by then. Now, it was too late. (p. 82)

While this is clearly a critique of intellectual quietism over the anti-communist witch-hunts of the 1950s, it does not support the claim that literature requires action. Rather it hints at the political apathy of the literary intelligencia.

Not only has the underground little capacity for political action, it is hardly the preserver of an active living culture. It merely preserves the objects of the past in memory and, even then, these do not exist in relationships of dialogue and debate. They are scattered in 'bits and pieces', individual texts or groups of texts existing only in the memories of individuals who are themselves scattered and dispersed. In this way, the underground hardly offers the image of a culture based on interaction, but only exists as a group of individuals who have fetishised the objects of the past.

It is also rather odd that the terms in which Bradbury attacks mass culture tend to denigrate the very forms which he uses elsewhere to beat mass culture theorists. By directing his critique at the supposed dangers of the 'image culture', he ends up condemning the very forms that he had defended and claimed to love elsewhere, forms such as cinema and comic books. This may also be the reason why this has become one of his most respected novels. In the film version, for example, not only was the prominent French, new wave film maker, François Truffaut, chosen to direct, rather than a mainstream Hollywood director with a feel for SF/horror, but it was the novel's aesthetic pretensions which were emphasised rather than its nightmarish SF/horror elements.

Another problem is that while Bradbury's critique of mass culture does place this phenomenon within social, economic and political contexts, he also shifts in the latter part of the novel towards a more transhistorical analysis of mass culture and society. By the end of the novel, mass culture has simply become one stage in a cyclical historical process rooted in an eternal human condition. It becomes one 'Dark Age' which after a period of renaissance, may be replaced by

another Dark Age, when we might have to do the whole damn thing over again. But that's the wonderful thing about man; he never gets so discouraged or disgusted that he gives up doing it all over again, because he knows very well it is important and *worth* the doing. (p. 147)

Humans may have a tendency towards the darkness of ignorance and apathy, but their aspirations for the light of knowledge and achievement can never be finally repressed.

Something Wicked This Way Comes

Similar problems are also a feature of Bradbury's *Something Wicked This Way Comes* (1962). Often seen as his most overtly horror-based novel, due to its use of Gothic conventions, this novel is neither as nightmarish nor as horrific as other stories such as *Fahrenheit 451*. Its lovely small town setting, its monstrous carnival, and its conflicts are all so allegorical that the story reads more like a parable or fable than a horror story. It lacks the real dramatic tension which makes the last sections of *Fahrenheit 451* so gripping and effective. For all its use of Gothic conventions, the novel has the feel of a morality play in which the issues are just too clear. It also lacks any real narrative, but tends to revolve around a series of situations and images within which discussions of Good and Evil are trotted out in a rather ponderous and pretentious fashion.

In fact, unlike *Fahrenheit 451* the novel does not even try to place its discussion of the 'human condition' within a specific social and historical context. The carnival can be read as an image of modernity in a number of different ways, but the story is removed from any specific historical setting into an unspecified past of childhood which is little more than an idealised fantasy of traditional, small town American life. The concern with modernity and mass culture does remain, but in a form that is so abstract and transhistorical that they are barely recognisable. While *Fahrenheit 451* was a critique of mass culture which ultimately explained its object in terms of a transhistorical 'human condition', *Something Wicked This Way Comes* concentrates on a transhistorical 'human condition' which can be seen to be no more than the problems usually associated with the emergence of mass culture.

The novel concerns a small town which is visited by Coogar and Dark's Pandemonium Shadow Show, a carnival whose name over-explicates its symbolic significance. It soon transpires that the carnival people are figures of Evil who threaten the town, and two boys Jim Nightshade and Will Halloway find themselves in a struggle to save the town and expel the Evil. Like the name of the carnival, the boys' names also over-explicate their significance. Nightshade is the dark side of the two, while Halloway (or Holy way) is the figure of light.

The carnival as an image of modernity is common in American culture, and dates back to the travelling shows with their association of commercial exploitation. Like advertising, they used fantasy, illusion and spectacle to sell people dubious products which they had never previously wanted or thought they needed. This feature is also highlighted in the novel through the emphasis on the carnival's use of technology, especially the carousel, which while invested with supernatural powers is still an image of the seemingly magical powers of technology, particularly for a small town such as Green Town which has hardly been touched by technology or the industrial revolution. Even the various carnival people are associated with technology. Mr Coogar is also Mr Electrico, whose life is sustained through the use of electricity, and even the dwarf's face is described as 'less human, more machine'.[68]

More significantly, the carnival's Evil is that it offers immediate gratification, just as Bradbury had elsewhere implied was the case with mass culture. It awakens fantasies and desires and offers to satisfy them, but in fact the satisfaction of these desires only creates deeper misery, hidden torment and alienation. For example, Miss Foley enters the maze of mirrors and encounters the image of her younger self who taunts her with the line, *'I'm* real. You're not!' (p. 47). This phrase actually describes Miss Foley's own repressed feelings. Saddened by her age, she believes her younger self to be her real self. Having awakened these repressed desires for her younger self, the carnival then offers her the possibility of regaining her youth, but it is a 'gift' that only brings her more misery. As Will's father explains, while it might change her appearance, the transformation cannot make you a child again. Miss Foley becomes cut off from everyone. She is unlike the other children, and has no home to go to. She is even different from her old friends and cannot turn to them for support. She may gain the appearance of youth and happiness, but inside she suffers loneliness, guilt and isolation. Like the people of *Fahrenheit 451*'s mass society, the carnival's victims appear to have their desires satisfied, but this only disguises even deeper suffering.

The association between the carnival and advertising are also obvious. As many critiques of mass culture argued, advertising stimulated dissatisfactions in order to offer one the possibility of satisfaction and self-transformation through the purchase of consumer products. However, as has often been pointed out, not only did this process create and encourage dissatisfaction in order to sell people products for which they usually had not felt a want or a need previously, it also became a self-perpetuating process. The product promises satisfaction, but can never finally fix that satisfaction, while the system has continually to produce new dissatisfactions in order to sell new products. While the 'magic' system of advertising seems to offer a solution to dissatisfaction, it actually needs continually to increase feelings of dissatisfaction. In fact, Miss Foley's encounter in the maze of mirrors seems particularly significant. As Stuart Ewen has pointed out, the mirror is one of the major props of advertising. It is used to encourage people to survey themselves and identify their imperfections, as well as to offer an idealised self which can be obtained through purchasing particular products.[69] It is exactly this kind of encounter which Miss Foley experiences.

But if the carnival is Evil, its association with the immediate gratifications of mass culture, Good is associated with responsibility, the feature Montag identified as missing in his society. In fact, while Evil is associated with pleasure, Good is associated with pain, agony and unhappiness. As Will's father asks him, 'since when did you think being good meant being happy?' (p. 98). Instead of being pleasurable, 'being good' is described as 'a fearful occupation; men strain at it and sometimes break in two' (p. 98). The appearance of happiness is therefore no guarantee of goodness, but quite the reverse; and for this reason, Will's father tells him that there 'are smiles and smiles; learn to tell the dark variety from the light' (p. 98). Hence, while Jim, Will and Mr Halloway do eventually learn to destroy the carnival with smiles and laughter, these are not the smiles and laughter of happiness, not the smiles and laughter encouraged by the fairground amusements. Instead they are signs of acceptance. The carnival feeds on the pain of repressed longings and unfulfilled desires, and the smiles and laughter of the three heroes are an acceptance of life as it is. They are an acceptance of imperfection which no longer desires the pleasures of an unobtainable ideal. In the end, they destroy the carnival with laughter, a laughter which Mr Halloway is finally able to produce through acceptance.

> All because he accepted everything at last, accepted the carnival, the hills beyond, the people in the hills, Jim, Will, and above all himself and all of life, and, accepting, threw back his head for the second time tonight and showed his acceptance with sound. (p. 192)

The problem with this position should be clear. It ends up endorsing the very *status quo* which Bradbury had criticised elsewhere. It endorses the world as it is rather than challenging it and showing that it could be different. The novel does suggest that the dark and the light are inseparable, that we all have a potential for Evil and that it would be easy to 'wind up owner of the carousel, keeper of the freaks … proprietor from some small part of eternity of the travelling dark carnival shows' (p. 214), but here the freaks, the outsiders, the aliens and the purely other are negative. They may be a part of all of us, an eternal element of the 'human condition', but they are things to be resisted, repressed and denied. By *Something Wicked This Way Comes*, Bradbury had subtly changed his position from a critical liberalism to one of acceptance.

Notes

1 Stephen King, *Danse Macabre* (London: Futura, 1982), p. 348.
2 Keith Neilson, 'Richard Matheson', in Everett Franklin Bleiler, ed., *Supernatural Fiction Writers: Fantasy and Horror Vol. II* (New York: Scribner's, 1985), p. 1073.
3 Martin Barker, *A Haunt of Fears: The Strange History of the British Horror Comics Campaign* (London: Pluto, 1984).
4 Richard Matheson, 'Death Ship' (1953), in *Shock!* (London: Corgi, 1962).
5 Ray Bradbury, 'The Concrete Mixer' (1949), in *The Illustrated Man* (London: Corgi, 1955).
6 Richard Matheson, 'The Creeping Terror' (1959), in *Shock!*
7 Bradbury, *The Illustrated Man*; and *The Martian Chronicles* (1950) (also published as *The Silver Locusts*) (London: Corgi, 1956).
8 Richard Matheson, *I Am Legend* (1954) (London: Corgi, 1956).
9 Richard Matheson, *The Shrinking Man* (1956) (London: Sphere, 1988).
10 Harold Rosenberg, 'The Herd of Independent Minds', *Commentary*, VI (September 1948).
11 Gary K. Wolfe, 'Ray Bradbury', in Noelle Watson and Paul E. Schellin-

gen, eds, *Twentieth Century Science-Fiction Writers* (Chicago: St James Press, 1991), p. 71.

12 Ray Bradbury, 'The Exiles' (1950), in *The Illustrated Man*.
13 Wolfe, 'Ray Bradbury', p. 71.
14 Ray Bradbury, 'The Earth Men' (1948), in *The Martian Chronicles*.
15 Ray Bradbury, 'The Meadow' (1947), in *The Golden Apples of the Sun* (London: Corgi, 1956), p. 137.
16 Wolfe, 'Ray Bradbury', p. 72.
17 Ray Bradbury, 'The Strawberry Window' (1959), in *The Day it Rained Forever*, p. 229.
18 Ray Bradbury, *Fahrenheit 451* (1953) (London: Corgi, 1957).
19 Ray Bradbury, 'The Rocket Man' (1951), in *The Illustrated Man*.
20 Wolfe, 'Ray Bradbury', pp. 72–3.
21 Willis E McNelly, 'Ray Bradbury', in Bleiler, *Supernatural Fiction Writers*, p. 920.
22 Ray Bradbury, *Something Wicked This Way Comes* (1962) (London: Corgi, 1965).
23 Ray Bradbury, 'Perchance to Dream' (1959), in *The Day it Rained Forever*, p. 163.
24 Ray Bradbury, 'The Long Years' (1950), in *The Martian Chronicles*.
25 Ray Bradbury, 'The Third Expedition' (1950), in *The Martian Chronicles*
26 Ray Bradbury, 'Zero Hour' (1947), in *The Illustrated Man*.
27 Ray Bradbury, 'Referent' (1959), in *The Day it Rained Forever*, p. 71.
28 Bradbury, 'The Long Years', p. 165.
29 Ray Bradbury, 'The Fire Balloons' (1952), in *The Illustrated Man*.
30 Bradbury, 'The Concrete Mixer', in *The Illustrated Man*, p. 141.
31 *Ibid.*, p. 150.
32 Ray Bradbury, 'And The Moon Be Still As Bright' (1948), in The Martian Chronicles, p. 54.
33 *Ibid.*, p. 54.
34 *Ibid.*, p. 64.
35 *Ibid.*, p. 71.
36 Ray Bradbury, 'Dark They Were and Golden Eyed' (1959), in *The Day it Rained Forever*.
37 Ray Bradbury, 'Way in the Middle of the Air' (1950), in *The Martian Chronicles*, p. 96.
38 *Ibid.*, p. 102.
39 Ray Bradbury, 'The Big Black and White Game' (1945), in *The Golden Apples of the Sun*.
40 Ray Bradbury, 'The Other Foot' (1951), in *The Illustrated Man*, p. 29.
41 Bradbury, 'The Other Foot', p. 38.
42 *Ibid.*

43 Ray Bradbury, 'The Rock Cried Out' (1959), in *The Day It Rained Forever*, p. 205.
44 *Ibid.*, p. 222.
45 *Ibid.*, p. 222–3.
46 Bradbury, 'The Rocket Man'.
47 Ray Bradbury, 'Here There Be Tygres' (1959), in *The Day It Rained Forever*, p. 128.
48 *Ibid.*, p. 137.
49 *Ibid.*, p. 138.
50 Ray Bradbury, 'A Scent of Sarsaparilla' (1959), in *The Day It Rained Forever*.
51 Ray Bradbury, 'The Fox and the Forest' (1950), in *The Illustrated Man*.
52 Wolfe, 'Ray Bradbury', p. 71.
53 Ray Bradbury, 'Usher II' (1950), in *The Martian Chronicles*, p. 105.
54 *Ibid.*
55 *Ibid.*
56 Bradbury, 'The Exiles', p. 105.
57 Ray Bradbury, 'The Pedestrian' (1951), in *The Golden Apples of the Sun*.
58 Ray Bradbury, 'The Murderer' (1953), in *The Golden Apples of the Sun*.
59 Ray Bradbury, 'The Veldt' (1950), in *The Illustrated Man*, p. 16.
60 Ray Bradbury, 'Marionettes, Inc.' (1949), in *The Illustrated Man*, p. 162.
61 Ray Bradbury, 'The Taxpayer' (1950), in *The Martian Chronicles*, p. 31.
62 Bradbury, *Fahrenheit 451*, p. 74.
63 See, for example, Andreas Huyssen, 'Mass Culture as Woman: Modernism's Other', in Tania Modleski, ed., *Studies in Entertainment: Critical Approaches to Mass Culture* (Bloomington: Indiana University Press, 1986).
64 Karl Marx, 'Economic and Philosophical Manuscripts (1844)' in *Early Writings* (Harmondsworth: Penguin, 1975).
65 See, *The Dialectic of Enlightenment* and *The Image*. However, it is worth noting that these claims are also common within much of the work on postmodernism. See, for example, Mark Poster, ed., *Jean Baudrillard: Selected Writings* (Cambridge: Polity, 1988).
66 See, for example, Daniel Bell, 'America as a Mass Society: A Critique' in Bell, *The End of Ideology: On the Exhaustion of Political Ideas in the Fifties* (Cambridge, Mass: Harvard University Press, revised edition, 1988).
67 Indeed, Bradbury's would seem to be criticising the liberal positions which Homi Bhabha has referred to as diversity and to be promoting a position which is similar to Bhabha's conception of difference. See, Homi Bhabha, 'The Third Space: Interview with Homi Bhabha', in

Jonathan Rutherford, ed., *Identity: Community, Culture, Difference* (London: Lawrence and Wishart, 1990).

68 Bradbury, *Something Wicked This Way Comes*, p. 124.

69 Stuart Ewen, *Captains of Consciousness: Advertising and the Roots of the Consumer Culture* (New York: McGraw-Hill, 1976).

The familiar becomes strange for Scott Carey in *The Incredible Shrinking Man* (1957), Jack Arnold's film version of Richard Matheson's novel *The Shrinking Man* (1956).

Chapter 4

The dilemmas of masculinity:
the fiction of Richard Matheson

If Bradbury defined and legitimated this type of horror fiction, it was Richard Matheson who realised its potential. As King and others have argued, it was Matheson who brought together the elements which would distinguish modern horror literature and differentiate it from the horror writing of earlier periods. If he is less famous than Bradbury outside horror and SF audiences, this is partly because he did not feel the pressure to legitimate his work according to the terms of more 'literary' varieties of fiction. Bradbury had established the area and Matheson was content to explore its possibilities on its terms.

The differences between Bradbury and Matheson are also related to another distinguishing feature of Matheson's work. He has a far less romanticised and idealised approach to 'the everyday world of common people' and his work is far more clearly placed within specific social contexts. There is a clear focus on the modernity of 1950s America in his fiction, and this is particularly evident in his characters' social and economic situation. For example, while Bradbury's characters seem to be the products of turn-of-the-century, rural, middle-American small towns, Matheson's characters are usually defined in relation to suburban domesticity and corporate employment.

In fact, Matheson's fiction seems to be preoccupied with the male anxieties of the 1950s, although he does not necessarily endorse these anxieties. More commonly, he explores and criticises the conceptions of normality upon which these anxieties are often founded. Normality is always relative within his fiction and, usually, it is monstrous. For these reasons, his fiction displays a general concern with paranoia, loss of control and estrangement.

As Keith Neilson puts it, 'the common situation in Matheson's fiction' is that of 'the man in the trap'.[1] However, while Neilson also argues that these stories are almost always told from the male point of view, this point of view is usually used to explore male anxieties, particularly sexual anxieties. Matheson's stories usually place their male figures in a position in which their perceptions of the world are challenged. The world becomes strange and unfamiliar to them, and their ways of relating to the world become redundant. Whether it is they who change or the world around them, the certainties on which they had previously depended disappear, and they are thrown into confusion. For this reason, Matheson's fiction usually concentrates heavily on the mental processes of his male characters and their intellectual and emotional responses. Matheson's concerns with social and mental breakdown, or 'madness' are frequently related to another feature: these stories were often 'unusual for their time in their open discussions of sexual longings' (p. 534), discussions which are used to explore his characters' sexual anxieties and the way in which they are related to definitions of masculinity.

Despite such concerns, Matheson's work does not have the strained seriousness of Bradbury's fiction. He is quite at home within the genre, while able to maintain a self-consciousness about the workings of genre and popular culture in general. In fact, several of his stories are overtly parodic in form. In 'Mantage' (1959), for example, a writer comments on a movie he has just seen and complains that film makers 'gloss over everything'.[2] The complaint is not simply directed at the content of the individual movie, but at the styles and structures of movies in general, particularly the use of montage, hence the title of the story. The writer's complaint is that montage allows the film so to condense an activity that it loses any sense of the 'experience' of that activity. As he complains,

> This writer the picture was about ... He was a lot like I am; talented with plenty of drive. But it took him almost ten years to get things going. *Ten years*. So what does the stupid picture do? Glosses over them in a few minutes. A couple of scenes of him sitting at his desk, looking broody, a couple of clock shots, a few trays of mashed-out butts, some empty coffee cups, a pile of manuscripts. Some bald-headed publishers with cigars shaking their heads no at him, some feet walking of the sidewalk; and that's it. Ten years of hard labor. It drives me mad. (p. 51)

However, Matheson's story goes on to pursue these issues in more depth. The writer ends up wishing 'that life could be as simple as a movie. All the drudgery set aside in a few flashes of weary looks, disappointments, coffee cups, and midnight oil, trays of butts, no's and walking feet' (p. 51). And his wish seems to come true. The story then becomes a series of scenes and images which tell the story of the writer's later life. However, as the story unfolds, the writer begins to feel that 'time has quickly passed'. Eventually, he begins to find the passage of time increasingly disorienting, and cannot remember the intervening periods between the key moments of his life. His life is experienced as though it were a movie: scenes even

fade just before he has sex. In the process, the story not only foregrounds the conventions of narrative itself, but also comments back
on the writer's own critique of the movies. Life can travel by so fast
that one doesn't know where it has gone, and one feels as though
one has bounced from one significant moment to another. In fact,
the story maintains a sense of uncertainty as to whether the writer's
life is being constructed like a film or whether this is merely his
'experience' of life. In this way, it not only parodies the forms of
popular narrative, but also comments upon the experience of life in
the modern world.

'The Creeping Terror' is perhaps more overtly parodic and takes
as its object of parody the forms of SF/horror itself. In this story, it
is discovered that California is actually a disease which is rapidly
spreading and taking over the whole of America. In this way, it not
only parodies the genre itself, but also offers a social satire of Cali-
fornian culture and its impact upon American culture in general. In
'Advance Notice' (1959), on the other hand, a writer of SF/horror
finds that his invented situations are repeated in reality. The shock
of this realisation not only makes him a hot property in publishing,
but also ends his publishing career. As he writes to his editor:

> you better get another boy. Why? Goddam it, man now that my files
> are all factual, *what in hell am I going to write about? You know I can't
> write nonfiction!*[3]

The story even includes a moment when an editor, who is so excited
by the opportunities offered by the situation, tells the writer, 'We'll
kill a Matheson story and stick in your piece instead' (p. 98).

'Advance Notice', like many other Matheson stories, also works
around a shock-ending or punchline which challenges the reader's
perceptions. In Matheson's fiction, these shock-endings can be relatively simple, as in the case of 'No Such Thing as a Vampire'
(1959). In this story, a man initiates a hunt to track down a vampire,
but at the end it is revealed that he has actually used the whole hunt
in order to revenge himself on a man who has slept with his wife.[4]

'Legion of Plotters' (1953), on the other hand, concerns a man
who feels victimised and harassed by those around him. He believes
that he is the victim of a conspiracy which is designed to drive him
mad, and even works out a system which, he believes, is being used
to drive him insane. Eventually, he is so paranoid that he believes
that everyone is out to get him, and attacks six people in self-

defence before he himself is killed. In this way, the story draws one
into the paranoid perceptions of a person who may or may not be
mad, but it does so in such a way that one identifies with him and is
never finally sure whether he is mad or not. The story places the
reader in an uncertain relationship to the man's perceptions.[5]

Other stories such as 'Third From the Sun' (1950) also use similar techniques. In this story, the crew of a space ship travel through
space in search of a habitable world. Eventually they find one in an
alien solar system, a planet with one moon that lies third from the
sun. In this way, it reveals that the travellers are not 'humans' but
are aliens who are travelling to 'our' world. None the less, the story
carefully establishes the aliens as points of sympathy and identification and so questions what it means to be 'human'.[6]

In this way, these stories also seek to challenge our perceptions of
'reality' and 'normality'. In 'Shipshape Home' (1953), for example,
a couple begin to suspect that their apartment is not what it appears
to be, and they eventually realise that the whole building is actually
an alien spaceship.[7] 'F——' (1951), on the other hand, involves a
more detailed examination of social codes of normality. It concerns
a scientist who travels to the future in a time machine. Once there
he is arrested for a heinous crime – the possession of food. In the
future, food is banned and eating is seen as an obscene activity.
Instead of eating, the people of the future inject themselves with the
nutrients necessary for survival. As a result, pictures of food have
come to occupy the status which pornography occupied within
Matheson's own period, and the desire to eat is a guilty secret
indulged, when possible, in private.[8]

The challenge to perceptions of 'normality' is also tackled by
Matheson through his interest in outsiders, aliens and others. His
first published story, 'Born of Man and Women' (1950), for example, is told from the point of view of a monstrous child who lives in
a cellar where it has been chained up by its parents. It is also told in
the first person, through the child's strange, almost alien, version of
English. But if the child appears hideous and monstrous to its parents, the story presents him as a sensitive victim of abuse, while the
normal world of the parents is presented as a monstrous culture of
complacency, cruelty and intolerance. The child is ignored, chained,
and viciously beaten by those people to whom it looks up, but at
last, it decides that if 'they try to beat me again Ill hurt them. I will'
(p. 4).[9] In the context of the story, and from the position of the

child, this response is not only presented as an understandable and even justifiable response, but also as a heroic rejection of the values of the supposedly 'normal' world.

'Blood Son' (1951) also concerns a youthful outsider, Jules, who we are told, 'wanted to be a vampire'.[10] Most of his life he had disgusted people, and from an early age his sexual curiosity had been punished. However, at the age of twelve, his life is changed forever when he goes to see *Dracula*. The film gives him an image of otherness with which to identify, and so define his difference from the 'normal' society which has oppressed him. After stealing a copy of Stoker's novel, and reading it again and again, he feels strong enough to respond when his teacher asks him to read out a composition in which he has outlined his ambitions. His composition states:

> When I grow up I want to be a vampire ... I want to live forever and get even with everybody and make all the girls vampires. I want to smell death ... I want to have a foul breath that stinks of dead earth and crypts and sweet coffins ... I want to sink my terrible white teeth in my victims' necks. I want them to ... I want them to slide like razors into the flesh and into the veins ... Then I want to draw my teeth out and let the blood flow easy in my mouth and run in my throat and ... And drip off my tongue and run out of my lips and down my victims' throats! ... I want to drink girls' blood. That is my ambition! That is my ambition! *That is my ambition!* (p. 84)

If this event makes him even more of an outsider to 'normal' society, it does give him a positive image of himself. His only problem is that he does not know how to become a vampire. At least, he doesn't know until he is finally attacked by a vampire one night, a vampire who, after the attack, gently lifts him up and calls him 'my son' (p. 89). In this story, Jules is certainly seen as perverse, but his perversity is given meaning and significance. It is presented as an understandable response to a sterile and hostile 'normality'.

In 'Mute' (1961), on the other hand, the 'normal' characters are not presented negatively, but they are still ill-equipped to deal with otherness. Though they mean well, their effects are potentially damaging and destructive. The story concerns a young boy whose parents die in a fire. He is then taken in by a young couple who try to give him love and understanding. Unfortunately, the boy's parents were part of a group who were experimenting with telepathy, a talent which they believe is suppressed by society and language, but which can liberate consciousness. As a result, the parents had taken part in an experiment in child development. They had cut themselves off from society and had raised their son so as to develop his telepathic abilities. The boy's problem, once his parents die, is that to develop his telepathic powers his parents have raised him in isolation from language, and as a result, the forms of 'normal' human interaction are merely painful experiences to him. Any attempts to teach him to speak are a form of violence which threaten to send him mad. He is eventually 'saved' from this predicament by one of his parents' associates who comes to take him to a place where he will be safe and secure with other children raised in the same way. Even when society means well, its practices and standards may be cruel to those who are different.[11]

In other stories, such as 'Miss Stardust' (1955) and 'SLR AD' (1952), conflicts between 'normality' and otherness are dealt with humorously. In 'Miss Stardust', a beauty competition is forced to accept entrants from the whole universe, a situation which raises severe problems for the standards of beauty on which the competition is based.[12] In 'SLR AD', on the other hand, a man answers a personal ad from a Venusian girl. However, he starts to worry when she promises to come and visit. He has fears about what she will look like, and is worried by the demands she might make on him. But by the end of the story the situation is reversed. She rejects him as too 'fragile and pale', and she comments that she considers it 'doubtful that the whole race can last'.[13] Meanwhile, he becomes hopelessly infatuated with her, and writes letters which beg her to come back to him. He apologises for his initial reaction to her, which had seemed like disgust or fear, but claims that he just 'didn't know you were so big and beautiful' (p. 48).

Even in stories such as 'Being' (1954) in which a huge, bubble-shaped monster feeds on humans, there is an interesting reversal. The story plays with the conventions of the 1950s invasion narratives, but it is revealed at the end that the monster is actually man-made, the product of a scientific experiment which has gone wrong. In fact, the being was a creation of 'tumorous hydroponics', and was designed as a food for humans.[14]

These concerns with otherness, outsiders and aliens are not only associated with issues of race, but also with issues of gender and sexuality. Stories such as 'From Shadowed Places' (1960) do concern the failure of modern white America to accept or understand the beliefs of other races and cultures, but even in this story, these issues are related to issues of gender. It concerns a man who has been hexed or cursed by a witch-doctor for an offence committed on a trip to Africa. The hex has powers that the victim's white friends refuse to accept, and they have to call in a black, female anthropologist to help save his life. But the anthropologist does not use Western rationality to deal with the problem. She has not only come to believe in juju, the form of African magic involved, but has also been initiated into its secrets. She insists that juju has real power, and that most witch-doctors are women. She challenges the whites' assumption that scientific explanations offer truth and uses her knowledge of juju to cure the victim. This story concerns powers which modern American culture cannot accept or understand, powers which are claimed to be at least as valid as those of scientific rationality.[15]

There are a number of stories which present women's power over men negatively, but many stories also present men's power over women at least as negatively. In fact, many stories present men as lacking in empathy or understanding with regard to women. Even many of the stories which concern women's power over men actually challenge assumptions about women. In 'The Likeness of Julie' (1962), for example, a young male notices a girl in his English class and becomes excited. Initially, he sees her as a 'child afraid to show her ripening body'.[16] He sees her as an innocent and this is part of his objectification of her. He sees her as an object to be used, abused and 'degraded' by him, but does not assume that she might have desires of her own. As a result, he plans to 'invite her to a drive-in movie, drug her Coke there, take her to the *Hiway Motel*' (p. 57). Also to protect himself against any repercussions, he decides to 'take photographs of her and threaten to send them to her parents if she said anything' (p. 57). At the end of the story, however, it is revealed that the girl is a telepath who has been controlling him for her own ends and desires. She may seem the height of innocence and passivity, but is actually the subject of her own desires, not the object of his.

'Lover When You're Near Me' (1952) also concerns a telepathic female but this story is somewhat different. It involves David Lindell who is stationed on an alien world with an alien culture for six months. All the men who had been stationed on the planet before him had gone mad, but Lindell thinks that he will be different. His job is to oversee the Gnees, the alien work-force, who 'don't have much family life'.[17] He is told that the males of this race are few and 'all pretty dumb', but he is not prepared for the fact that the females have a telepathic power which he cannot resist. They can enter his mind at any time, and he has no privacy from them. This situation is made worse when one of the Gnee women becomes infatuated with him. In this way, the story raises fears about female dominance, particularly when Lindell

> thought of what Martin had said about the women outnumbering the men. And a phrase entered his mind – *matriarchy by mind*. The phrase offended him but he was suddenly afraid it might be true. It would explain why the other men had cracked. For, if the women were in control, it might well be that, their inherent lust for dominance, they made no distinction between their own men and the men from Earth. A man is a man is a man. (p. 27)

None the less, the story makes it quite clear that Lindell's sense of masculinity is also based on an assumption of his own superiority.

He is horrified by 'the idea of being considered on a level with the dolts [the male Gnee] who lived in the village' (p. 27). In fact, not only is he initially pleased by the alien woman's attentions – she waits on him hand and foot – but it is his patronising humour and easy superiority which cause the problem in the first place. Used to casually treating women as objects, he calls her 'lover' and so gives her the impression that he is interested in her. It is also significant that the final straw is not so much her behaviour – she never does anything but dote on him – but his own realisation that he has fallen for her. It is his own thoughts of love which are the 'new shock that would topple his already shaking edifice' (p. 33). It is this realisation which is the final terror which he is never able to forget, even after he leaves the station forever.

Matheson's analysis of assumptions of male privilege are also found in other stories which do not concern female power, but male control. This is sometimes humorously handled as in 'A Flourish of Strumpets' (1956) where a couple find that prostitutes have started to ply their trade door to door. Initially the husband pretends to be shocked in order to humour his wife, while secretly indulging his fantasies. But as his fantasies become more powerful, he eventually finds he cannot resist them. In order to compensate for his feeling of guilt he then begins to do 'a little dusting and vacuuming',[18] and starts to bring his wife flowers, actions which his wife sees as unusual behaviour. But his final shock comes when a handsome, young, male prostitute turns up at his house and asks for his wife. In this way, the story not only deals with male sexual hypocracy, but also with the double standard. It is acceptable for him to see prostitutes in secret, but he is horrified by the prospect of his wife having the same choice.

If 'A Flourish of Strumpets' is humorous, 'Girl of My Dreams' (1963) is a much darker picture of the exploitation of women by men. It concerns a young man who is living with a woman whose dreams predict real-life disasters. He stays with her not out of love – he is actually disgusted and repulsed by her – but so that he can exploit her gift to blackmail others. He will only give them the information which they need to protect themselves, if they will pay him the money which he demands. When his partner questions his actions, and tries to resist him, he violently attacks her, releasing all his repressed feelings of repulsion. This attack causes her death, and as she dies, she has a vision of his death, a vision which she is unable to finish describing before she dies. He is finally left with only a partial knowledge of his own end, and lacks the information which he needs in order to save himself. In the process, the story clearly places the reader's sympathy with the ugly, 'freakish' female, rather than with the handsome, 'normal' male. It is the man's assumption of superiority in relation to the woman which is not only seen as exploitative and responsible for his feelings of repulsion, but also as the cause of his own downfall.[19]

Male lack of sympathy and empathy is also an issue in 'Trespass' (1953), although it is not as darkly portrayed as in 'Girl of My Dreams'. In this story, a man returns home after six months away to find that his wife is pregnant, despite the fact that he could not possibly be the father. Initially, he suspects her of having an affair, until the symptoms of the pregnancy become too unusual. The entire story is told from his point of view, but it is handled in such a way as continually to undermine his interpretations and perceptions. Again and again, it is clear that he perceives the events purely in terms of himself, unlike his wife who is constantly concerned about how the situation affects their relationship to one another.[20]

If these stories are suggestive about issues of masculinity, the most common preoccupation within Matheson's fiction is around male feelings of powerlessness, alienation and estrangement. It is this preoccupation which concerns both his major novels of the 1950s, *I Am Legend*[21] and *The Shrinking Man*,[22] but it can also be identified in a number of short stories. This concern is also directly related to concerns about the 1950s corporation man, the major image of conformity in the period. 'Clothes Make the Man' (1951), for example, is about an advertising executive called Charlie. The figure of the ad executive is significant. For many in the 1950s, it was this figure which not only epitomised the corporation man, but also the 'other directed' man who managed people rather than things, and was bound up with the society of the image, rather than the world of reality and substance. He dealt with the manipulation of appearances and style. It is therefore pertinent that the story concerns the executive's relationship to his clothes. Charlie is always well dressed and his identity is so much a product of the clothes he wears that he cannot do without them. When on a trip to the country, his friends go swimming, but he won't join them because it would mean undressing. His wife even complains that she doesn't 'know whether [she is] married to a man or a wardrobe'.[23] By the end of the story, he can't function without his clothes. He can't walk without his shoes and is literally powerless without his suit. His wife even begins an affair with the suit and tells 'all her friends the damn thing has more sex appeal than Charlie ever had' (p. 81). The story implies that, in the modern world, image is everything and people's identities are produced by the commodities which they consume, commodities which seem to have more life than the humans who possess them.

Other stories also deal with a male's gradual loss of identity. 'Disappearing Act' (1953), for example, is supposedly taken from a notebook found in a candy store and it involves an unsuccessful writer who also makes money through a part-time typing job. After a row with his wife over money, he goes out with a friend and becomes involved in an extra-marital relationship. For the 1950s males whom Barbara Ehrenreich discusses, this might have been an act of self-assertion against the demands of women,[24] but for the character in Matheson's story, it is a confusing, if pleasurable, experience which only reminds him of his love for his wife. His problem is that he feels inadequate because he is unable to perform the role of breadwinner which he expects of himself as a man. Unable to perform this function, he tries to hold on to a sense of his own masculinity, but finds it gradually slipping away. First, the woman with whom he has had the affair seems to vanish; then, bit by bit, other parts of his life disappear; until mid-way through a sentence in the notebook, which he is using to record these events, he disappears entirely. In this way, the story plays with the anxieties associated with certain definitions of masculinity and upon one man's alienation and estrangement as he finds himself unable to live up to those definitions.[25]

This concern can also be found in 'The Curious Child' (1954), though it does offer an SF interpretation of the process. Again the main character, Robert Graham, is a corporation man who works in an office. Slowly he starts to lose his memory. He can't remember what his wife asked him to bring home; where he left his car; or even what kind of car he drives. He even loses his wallet in which were cards that at least established some record of his identity. As a result, his feelings of panic and disorientation increase until he is finally confronted by a man who explains that as a child of two, Robert had wandered into a time machine and travelled back to 1919 where he had become lost. Since then he has been living in the 'past'. His loss of memory and identity had been caused by the fact that as the people of his own time tracked him down and got closer and closer to him, his 'past and present was jumbled up' in his mind until he finally 'lost hold of everything'.[26]

'The Edge' (1958) is a similar story but, unlike 'The Curious Child', it lacks a scientific explanation. It starts with a man greeting a friend, Don Marshall, only to have Marshall deny that he knows him. Initially, the man thinks that he has mistaken someone else for Marshall, but finds that while he really is talking to Marshall, Marshall has no recollection of him. Eventually, the man leaves and Marshall, perplexed, goes home where he is greeted by his wife. All seems to go well until she answers the phone and he hears her say almost automatically, 'Yes, darling ... You – won't be home until late?' She then turns to Marshall and asks, 'Who are you?'[27]

As in the other stories, Marshall is a corporation man – he works for 'American Pacific Steamship Lines'. However, although the story does raise the possibility of a scientific explanation – the possibility of an alternative universe – this is neither confirmed nor explored. The impact of the story is related to the ways in which it deals with male anxieties in the 1950s, particularly fears about the loss of identity due to the demands of the corporate workplace and the suburban home. The corporate workplace threatens to absorb the male into a characterless mass, while the male finds it harder and harder to meet the expectations of himself and others within the suburban home.

In Matheson's fiction, this preoccupation with paranoia, alienation and estrangement is also related to a concern with madness. In 'Nightmare at 20,000 feet' (1961), for example, a plane passenger thinks he sees a man on the wing of the plane, but cannot get anyone to believe him. Eventually, realising that it is probably a gremlin, an impish demon which wrecks planes, he finds himself even more isolated, and tries to kill it himself, only to be dismissed as a suicidal lunatic. The story has become a classic of the era after it was used as the basis for a *Twilight Zone* episode and was later remade by George Miller in the homage to the series, *Twilight Zone: The Movie* (1983). Its main strength is the purity of its mounting sense of paranoia and isolation in which it is never clear whether Wilson is actually mad or the only person who actually knows what is going on. In this way, it is both troubling and exhilarating. It places the reader in a position of intense, but uncertain identification with a character whose perceptions are fundamentally untrustworthy, but who none the less has the courage to stand by his own perceptions against the common perceptions of 'normality'.[28]

This preoccupation with insanity is also present in 'Therese' (1969) which again challenges the reader's perceptions. It is presented as the diary of Millicent, a malcontent, who plots the murder of her sister Therese. By the end of the story, however, it is revealed that the author is in fact a multiple personality, Millicent Therese Marlow, and that in plotting to kill her alter-ego, she has also killed herself. One of the interesting features of the story is that it relates this murderous insanity back to the family. Therese is Millicent's sexual self, a figure which Millicent must define as corrupt and depraved, probably as a way of dealing with an experience of child abuse. Millicent hates her father whom she describes as a 'vile man'. But while she claims that her father was 'brutish, carnal and disgusting',[29] she also admits that her sister loved him, and even suggests that they may have slept together. The implication is that the multiple personality is a way of dealing with and disavowing the fact that her father had sexually abused her by associating this abuse with her fictitious 'sister'.

Insanity and monstrous families are also related to one another in 'Graveyard Shift' (1960),[30] a story which came out the same year as

Hitchcock's *Psycho* (1960), but also bares a strong resemblance to 'Miss Gentilbelle' which was written by Matheson's close friend, Charles Beaumont, and was published in 1955, five years earlier.[31] The story is told through a series of letters which discuss the fate of a young boy, Jim. At the start of the story, Jim is found by some neighbours. He seems quite mad, but it has also been discovered that his mother is dead, her throat having been cut with a razor. Initially people assume that she had been murdered, and when a whole series of devices are found which she had used to frighten and disturb her son, people begin to suspect Jim. It is presumed that he may have killed his mother out of revenge for these abuses.

Finally, however, it is suggested that these abuses were part of a particular plan on the part of his mother. She had been overly dependent on her husband and had never loved the boy, particularly when she became jealous of her husband's feelings towards his son. But when her husband died in order to save the child from drowning, her feelings turned to hatred and she devised 'a whole, monstrous world of horror' for the boy so that he would have 'trust and need for only one person – her' (p. 53). She placed the child into the same position of dependence as that which she had occupied in relation to her husband; and then, having made herself the child's 'only shield against these horrors', she took her own life. In this way, she deprived him of the one person on whom he had come to depend, just as she felt that he had deprived her of his father. She had planned it so that 'when she died, Jim would go completely mad because there wouldn't be anyone in the world he could turn to for comfort' (p. 53).

However, these stories are not necessarily an example of the anti-maternal strand of 1950s thought with its attack on 'Momism'. In 'Therese', the abusing parent is male. It is not so much the gender of the parent which matters in these texts but rather the growing awareness that human consciousness and identity were being produced and managed by social forces coupled with an increasing sense that they were inherently unstable and uncertain.

In fact, this concern with the production and management of identity and consciousness is found in a number of stories. 'When the Waker Sleeps' (1950), for example, appears to be the story of a heroic struggle between two mighty powers, one good and one evil. But it is eventually revealed to be an induced fantasy which the workers of this world are fed while they perform the boring, mundane task of fighting the rust which threatens their machines. Not only does this story involve an image of humans dominated by technology in which individuals have become drones which merely exist to serve and care for machines, but it also evokes a society in which consciousness is managed and controlled for efficiency. The story even includes an implicit critique of 1950s anti-communism in which the heroic struggle against the evil other is simply a delusion used to ensure conformity and obedience.[32]

A similar concern is also to be found in 'Full Circle' (1953) in which a journalist is sent by his editor to do a story on a show, 'Larg and Fellow Martians in *Rip Van Winkle*' which is presented by 'Terwilliger's Living Marionettes'. Initially the journalist is reluctant, but when he meets Larg, one of the Martian performers, his views change. He learns that the performers are exiles from Mars who are forced to present themselves as humorous spectacles for the amusement of human audiences. Larg tells the journalist of the exploitation and virtual genocide which had accompanied the colonisation of Mars by Earth, a colonisation which has turned Mars into an underdeveloped region dependent upon Earth. Larg talks of his wife whom he has not seen for fifteen years. He doesn't even know if she is alive or dead. This interview makes the journalist 'ashamed – terribly ashamed. For myself and my people'.[33] He no longer sees Larg as a 'funny little guy from Mars' (p. 185), and the encounter creates a friendship between the two men.

But when the journalist writes about the show, his editor tells him: 'cut out all that stuff about the murder of a race. Larg and his noble character. Handle it straight. The show, the kids' reactions. That's all we want' (p. 186). The journalist complains, and states that he 'thought this was a newspaper. Not somebody's propaganda sheet – not some rich man's solace' (p. 186). But the editor is less than impressed by this response. He insists that it is not he who makes policy, and claims that most journalists learn the job and get this sort of thing 'out of [their] system after college. They don't let it linger inside them until they're married and have a kid like you' (p. 187). The criteria of the newspaper is not 'truth', and as the editor points out, it probably never was. Both editor and journalist are caught 'in a trap' and 'can't afford to tear ourselves loose' (p. 187). As the journalist comes to realise, things have come 'full circle':

> Larg couldn't do anything about it. *He* couldn't do anything about it.
> Both of them, knowing the situation for what it was, were powerless
> to change it. They were hemmed in. Bound within an enchanted circle
> of economics, of policy. (p. 188)

The system has becomes self-regulating and the newspaper doesn't
exist to inform. Rather it exists to manage the consciousness of the
population; to amuse and entertain; to give the appearance of social
responsibility; but not to criticise and challenge people's perceptions of their world.

Even in 'The Conqueror' (1954), a western short story, one finds
these concerns. It involves a young man from the East who arrives
in the Wild West and challenges a gunfighter to a showdown. The
town is worried and confused. They can't fathom the young man's
motives, and fear that he will be killed. In the event, he is actually
successful, but is later killed by his victim's friends, a response that
he had clearly failed to predict. After his death, the narrator goes
through the young man's bags in search of an explanation for the
incident. What he finds are newspaper-clippings and a diary. They
make it clear that the young man had become obsessed with the stories of gunfighters which he had read in the papers, 'holding up as
idols those men whose only talent was to kill',[34] and in an attempt
to emulate them, he had 'brought himself pistols and practised
drawing them from their holsters until he was incredibly quick'
(p. 62). Finally, it also becomes clear that inspired by these stories,
the young man had developed 'a projected odyssey in which a city
boy would make himself the most famous pistol fighter in the
Southwest. It listed the towns this young man had meant to conquer' (p. 62–3). Unfortunately, the town he had died in was only the
first on the list. The young man's sense of identity was learned and
produced from the journalistic accounts of the early mass media,
but relying on these accounts as a guide to reality, he had not been
able to predict the actions of others. He only thought about the dramatic event of the gunfight on which the press had concentrated,
not on the context of relationships and responses which might sur-
round this event.

'The Holiday Man' (1957) also concerns consciousness, but
instead of focusing on how it is produced or constructed, it concentrates on how it can be threatened and destabilised. It begins
with a man leaving for work and taking a commuter train. He seems

the epitome of the corporation man, an advertising executive, but something is troubling him. He is frightened of driving and cannot bear to go up to his office. But while he 'always tried to break away from' his job, he finally 'never could'.[35] Once in his office, he becomes overpowered with anguish: 'It trickled on his brain like melting ice' (p. 85). Eventually, it is revealed that his job is bound up with the prediction of deaths. His job is to watch every incident, however ugly or tragic, so that the unpredicted can be calculated, controlled and accounted for. It is this routine handling of the horrific which is wearing at him, alienating him from his labour and threatening his sanity so that all he can do is look forward to his holidays.

Indeed, the critique of rationalisation is found again and again in Matheson's fiction. 'The Test' (1954), for example, concerns a society in which elderly people are tested to see if they can still function as productive members of society, and are sentenced to death if they fail. This situation results in the elderly having to cram for tests like youngsters who struggle to pass academic exams.[36] 'Shock Wave' (1963) also concerns a man who unconsciously turns an old church organ into an instrument of destruction out of his 'fear of being also scrapped, replaced; his dread of being shut out from the things he loved and needed; his hatred of a world that had no use for aged things'.[37] These stories are a critique of a modern world which tends to sweep away and destroy everything that is not new and efficient, which feels no debt to, or respect for, that which is old.

'The Thing' (1951), on the other hand, concerns a group of non-conformists who oppose the tyranny of scientific rationality. They eat food when science has insisted that people live on a diet of 'pills, venous banquets and gourmets' nightmares of concentrated vitaminic juices'.[38] As one man puts it, it is 'a brutal comment on the times that the simplest and most ordinary of pleasures can assume such vast, incredible proportions' (p. 37). The rationalisation of social and cultural life has become a nightmare, but as another man argues 'its our own fault. We've outdone our selves. Built ourselves such a rock-ribbed and Simon-pure system that its become a cage' (p. 37). While this process is associated with women who are described as the ideal scientists, Matheson undermines his male characters. Their non-conformity seems self-satisfied and even smug, and it does not involve any actual resistance. Instead they merely affirm their opposition to authority through the act of taking their children to see 'the thing', a machine which seems to be in a state of perpetual motion and so seems to flout the official scientific 'truth' as defined by the 'Policy Boards'.

Not only is this non-conformity basically the passive act of watching a spectacle, it is also undercut in other ways. First, the 'proof' which contradicts the 'Policy Boards' is itself a machine. If scientific rationality is the problem, the non-conformists are still obsessed with technology. They even seem to deify the thing, and confer almost religious significance upon it. Second, this pseudo-religious awe also raises another problem – it is unclear whether or not the group, unable to accept a challenge to their beliefs, are actually faking their own evidence. As one father says when his sons ask if the thing will ever stop, 'No Billy ... We'll never *let* it stop' (p. 44). It is unclear if this is a heroic assertion of their non-conformity or a hint that this secret organisation may be interfering with the machine so that it will not challenge or contradict their faith.

If Matheson criticised the conformist and rationalist tendencies of modern society, he did not indulge in the kinds of aesthetic outrage practised by others. In 'To Fit the Crime' (1952), for example, a man complains about mass culture's degradation of the English language so often that he alienates almost everyone who knows him. Finally, when he dies, he is consigned to hell where he is endlessly tortured with clichés and bad English.[39]

Indeed when he does attack mass culture, Matheson usually concentrates on the effects of technology, not the lack of aesthetic standards. In several stories, this preoccupation with technology is dealt with through the figure of the robot. In 'Brother to the Machine' (1952), a figure wanders the city, alienated from everyone else. He can see no distinction between the humans and the robots which inhabit his world. The 'common classes did the same work as the robots. Together they walked or drove through the streets carrying and delivering.'[40] The city becomes a nightmare of domination in which being human is not 'a blessing, a pride, a gift' (p. 8). Instead, humans are merely a 'brother to the machine, used and broken by invisible men who kept their eyes on poles and their fists bunched in ships that hung over all their heads, waiting to strike at opposition' (p. 8). Finally, his desperation is such that he commits suicide in a lake. It is only at this point that it is revealed that this character is a robot who thought he was a man. In this way, the figure of the robot is used to question our perception of what it means to be human. If a robot can't tell the difference and if it is able to have greater revulsion to the dehumanising conformity and domination which distinguishes its society than most humans, the distinction between human and machine becomes uncertain and unclear.

'Deus ex Machina' (1963) also deals with this dilemma. It concerns a man who cuts himself shaving one morning, and finds that underneath his skin, he is only steel and wire – he is a robot who thinks he is a man. Shocked and confused by this discovery, he goes on with his daily routine only to find that the whole world has been replaced by robots who believe themselves to be human. Slowly he begins to realise that nothing is as it appears to be. His chewing gum is actually a lump of grease. His food and drink at the diner merely 'plates of grease' and 'cups of oil'. Even the rain is now oil. Finally, he recalls a passage from the Bible: *'And God said let us make man in our image'*.[41] The implication is that the God of science and technology has replaced humans, starting with those in authority, and as a corporation man, an accountant who is 'a part of the basic commerce system' (p. 31), he would have been one of the first to be replaced.

If this story deals with these issues on a global scale, 'Lazarus II' (1953) places them within a much more personal context. It concerns a young man who wakes to find himself alive after an attempted suicide. The demands of his parents have not only driven him to suicide, but prevented him from dying. They have saved his mind and built him a robotic body. Worse still, he is unable to kill himself now. It is true that the boy's father blames the mother for forcing him to save her son in this way, but even the son does not accept this excuse: 'You did this for yourself – for the pleasure of experimenting.'[42] If the mother overinvests in her children and in the domestic sphere, the father overinvests in the public sphere of science and is quite willing to use his child in the pursuit of its activities. But eventually the boy comes to realise that 'I am now as I have always been … A well-controlled machine' (p. 77). The dominance of science and technology only confirm the relationships in which the child is dominated and controlled by its parents' desires, ambitions, and expectations.

These issues are further developed in 'The Doll that Does Everything' (1954) in which two parents decide to keep their child quiet by giving it an expensive robotic doll. They have chosen to have a child but are both too self-absorbed to see it as anything but a nuisance, a distraction. It is a figure of disruption and disorganisation which they try to control unsuccessfully. Eventually they decide to buy 'the doll which does everything' as a way of pacifying the child. It is a doll which acts like a real child in every way, and they believe that the influence of the plaything will calm their child down. The plan seems to work for a while, but the child begins to act up again and this time the doll imitates him. At this point the parents realise that while the robot doll can do everything a child can do, it has one difference: it can be controlled. Finally, they decide to secretly replace the child with the doll, a plot which is only uncovered 'twenty years later, when a college-going Gardener Benson met a wriggly sophomore and blew thirteen gaskets and his generator [and] the ugly truth came out'.[43]

Indeed Matheson's concentration on the intimate effects of modernity means that he is less preoccupied with its apocalyptic consequences than Ray Bradbury. Stories such as 'Descent' (1954)[44] and 'The Last Day' (1953)[45] do involve apocalyptic destruction, but Matheson is more interested in the effects of modernity on particular individuals, and seems to imply that its implications are quite bad enough without 'the end of civilization as we know it'. In fact, Matheson even parodies the despairing 'end of the worlders' in 'When the Day is Dun' (1954). The story involves a lone survivor of an apocalypse who sits writing rather awful poems which bemoan the end of the world. However, when another survivor appears and calls him friend, 'something suddenly snapped within the poet's brain'.[46] He shoots the stranger 'neatly between the eyes', settles down to write another poem, and thinks to himself: 'for this moment, to have this glorious, shining doom alone – it was worth it' (p. 127). The literary and intellectual condemnation of the apocalyptic tendencies of modern society, the story implies, may have their share of romantics, and these romantics may secretly welcome the destruction of a corrupt society and aggressively defend their sense of uniqueness and difference from others. There is a danger in the 'outsider' defending his own uniqueness. The role of the outsider may be adopted as a way of defending one's own privilege from others.

I Am Legend

This concern with the privileged trying to maintain their privilege is one aspect of Matheson's novel, *I Am Legend*. This novel has acquired the status of one of two or three classics of 1950s horror novels and it concerns a man, Richard Neville, who is the last human alive after the world has been taken over by a plague of vampires. Despite the presence of the vampire, the novel breaks with the traditional gothic trappings of vampire fiction and it is clearly located within modern suburban America. Neville attempts to survive in the new world by turning his house into a fortress against the mighty onslaughts of the vampires, and this situation is used to examine and challenge notions of normality.

The novel achieves this aim by placing its readers in an uneasy relationship to Neville in which they are not only deeply involved in his thought processes and responses, but are also able to identify their limitations and omissions. It is also stressed that Neville is a deeply conformist figure who seeks to maintain his concepts of normality, routine, and order – even in a world which has been overrun by vampires. As a result, while some commentators have been critical of the novel's lengthy descriptions which detail Neville's everyday routines, these details are central to the novel. Neville is a man of preconditioned habit who unquestioningly accepts received, commonsense notions of normality, and cannot accept or even imagine alternatives. He is a man who is threatened by anything which challenges his assumptions, and regulates his life according to futile and obsessive routines.

These habits are often humorously detailed as in the case of his preparation for bed where he continues to wear pyjama bottoms despite the fact that he 'never wore pajama tops; it was just a habit he'd acquired in Panama during the war'.[47] He even continues to drive a station wagon, *the* family car of the 1950s, and refuses to use any other vehicle, despite the fact that he has to travel long distances to find replacements when his old models are inoperative. Even his task of making stakes to kill vampires is reminiscent of the workshop carpentry which became a popular pastime for 1950s middle-class males who were concerned to prove the masculine skills absent from their office jobs.

Nor does Neville take advantage of 'the end of civilization as we know it' in the ways one might expect. He stays in his suburban home and decides against the idea of 'moving to some lavish hotel suite'. His excuse is 'all the work he'd have to do to make it habitable' (p. 39), but this evades the issue. He has to do a whole number of jobs in order to secure his house, including destroying the houses next door, boarding the windows, sound proofing, etc. His real reason for not moving is a reluctance to give up what he knows in favour of that which is unfamiliar. So routinised is his life that his shopping list includes a category simply referred to as 'Usual'. He even continues to rely on the sun as a means of judging nightfall, a dangerously inaccurate practice given that after nightfall the vampires wake and take over the streets.

In fact, Neville is portrayed as an average lower middle-class WASP who has no real distinguishing features except for his 'long, determined mouth and the bright blue of his eyes' (p. 8). His need to hold on to that which he knows and the contradictions into which this leads him can also be seen in his relation to authority. When the vampire plague is under way and his wife suggests that they protect their daughter by keeping her home from school, he rejects the idea and tells her, 'Unless the health authorities say schools have to shut down, I don't see why we should keep her home' (p. 45). But when his wife dies, he cannot throw her body into the flames as ordered by the health authorities. Instead he insists on burying her body despite the fact that people are being shot for this crime. He is only prepared to do as the authorities tell him if it conforms to his sense of the normal way of doing things. Even his insistence on burying his wife is not motivated by any religious conviction, but merely by a sense that this is the way things are done.

This refusal to accept change and the conformist forms of thought on which it is based, are shown to be dangerous. Not only does it prevent him from recognising the significance of the differences between the living and the dead vampires, but it also leads to his eventual destruction. He has identified the difference between the living and the dead vampires, but he does not consider it of much importance: they are all simply vampires to him. As a result, he is unprepared for the emergence of the new social order built by the living vampires. More significantly, even when Ruth, one of the living vampires, has warned him about the new society and advised him to escape from the city and into the country, he refuses to go and is eventually captured and sentenced to death. Nor has he much reason for this decision, other than his tentative and uncertain explanation to Ruth:

> I ... couldn't ... I almost went several times. Once I even packed and ... started out. But I couldn't, I couldn't ... go. I was too used to the ... the house. It was a habit, just ... just like the habit of living. I got ... used to it. (p. 137)

Instead he remains to carry on a task which he recognises is futile. He spends his days hunting down individual vampires and killing them.

Even this task is a routine. He knows that he will never be able to kill all the vampires, and while he tells himself that he does it to defend himself, the novel itself suggests quite different motivations. In fact the novel is divided into four stages of Neville's life: January 1976; March 1978; June 1978; and January 1979. In the first of these stages, Neville is trying to find a way to deal with his situation. He creates routines for himself, but he is also angry and frustrated. His attacks on the vampires are attempts to both satisfy his need for vengeance, and to give himself a regular routine to replace work and family life. In the second stage, it is the routine which becomes most important. He no longer feels the bitterness and confusion of the previous period. Instead he begins to treat the problem of the vampires rationally and 'scientifically'. This involves a repression of emotion and it is the reawakening of his feelings which is the focus of the third section.

His meeting with Ruth, whom he initially believes to be human, forces him to question his way of living. She enables him to see that he has lost contact with his own 'humanity'. When he first meets her his voice 'is devoid of warmth'; it has become 'the harsh, sterile voice of a man who had lost all touch with humanity' (p. 102). When he finally gets her back to his house, he is not particularly excited by the prospect of ending his loneliness. In fact, he finds it very hard to feel any positive feelings towards Ruth:

> Robert Neville sat there wondering why he didn't feel more compassion for her. Emotion was a difficult thing to summon from the dead, though. He had spent it all and felt hollow now, without feeling. (p. 107)

He has become so cold and rational that he no longer knows how to interact with other people. Indeed, the only thing he really feels is fear. He is worried that Ruth's presence will disrupt his well-ordered routines. His old fantasies of finding another person with whom to share his life is replaced by a desire for things to continue as they are without posing any threat to his 'schedule or standards' (p. 114). He even dreams of killing Ruth, though he knows that these 'thoughts were a hideous testimony to the world he had accepted; a world in which murder was easier than hope' (p. 115).

Ironically, he argues himself out of such action by telling himself that he is 'a man, not a destroyer' (p. 115). But while he says this to assert his humanity, one of the central points of the novel is that 'a destroyer' is exactly what he has become. He has become the mirror image of the vampire. To the vampires, he is the dark spectre who stalks and kills defenceless sleepers. Again and again, the novel emphasises the similarity between his actions and those of the traditional vampire. Not only does he kill his victims while they sleep, his activities are also regulated by the sun. His house is described as a 'sepulchre', and he doesn't just kill for survival, but also for pleasure. Even his early addiction to alcohol is paralleled with the vampire's need for blood.

In the process, the novel illustrates that definitions of the monstrous are always relative and social; a monster is a definition given by a particular society to that which it finds threatening. If the vampires appear monstrous to Neville because they threaten his world, he appears monstrous to them because he threatens their's. Even Neville eventually comes to this realisation in the final stage of the novel when he is captured by the society of living vampires. Earlier he had jokingly argued a defence of the vampire as a minority group who were victims of prejudice, but he comes to acknowledge that this is exactly what they had been. Suddenly he realises that 'I'm the abnormal one now. Normalcy was a majority concept, the standard of the many and not the standard of just one man' (p. 140). It is at this point that he realises that, as an object of fear and disgust, he occupies the same position in their society as the vampire had occupied in his own. It is here that the meaning of the title becomes clear. When he realises this fact, he decides to commit suicide rather than be executed, and as he does so, he converts himself into myth. 'Full circle', he says to himself as he dies,

> A new terror born in death, a new superstition entering the unassailable fortress of forever.
> I am legend. (p. 141)

While this relativisation of 'normality' does not simply imply that the human and the vampire can overcome prejudice and learn to live with one another in harmony, it does illustrate that definitions of right and wrong, normal and abnormal, are not absolute.

As a result, the novel undermines many of Neville's responses. For example, he is horrified by the 'brutality' with which the living vampires kill the dead vampires in order to establish their new society. He questions their actions and finds that he

> didn't like the looks of them, he didn't like the methodical butchery. They were more like gangsters than men forced into a situation. There were looks of vicious triumph on their faces, white and stark in the spotlights. Their faces were cruel and emotionless. (p. 131)

But as Ruth points out, Neville had been little different. He had killed many times, and she says to him, 'Did you see *your* face when you killed? I saw it – remember? It was frightening. You weren't even killing then, you were just chasing me' (p. 138).

She even justifies their actions and explains their motives, and while she does acknowledge that they may have gained pleasure from the act, she sees this as both unsurprising and as little different from Neville's own behaviour:

> Maybe you did see joy on their faces ... It's not surprising. They're young. And they *are* killers – assigned killers, legal killers. They're respected for their killing, admired for it. What can you expect from them? They are only fallible men. And men can learn to enjoy killing. That's an old story, Neville. You know that. (p. 138)

Neville's response to the violence is based on an assumption of superiority and difference in which he defines his own responses as being normal and legitimate and the reactions of those whom he defines as different from him as being abnormal and illegitimate.

In this way the novel explores the oppositions on which Neville's sense of identity is based, and this is most clearly seen in his distinctions between rationality and irrationality as exemplified by his attitudes towards scientific thought and sexuality. Though Neville defines himself in opposition to science at the opening of the novel, he does not associate himself with the irrational, but with practical common sense. He 'had loathed his father and fought the acquisition of his father's logic and mechanical facility every inch of the way' (p. 19). At this stage, he objects to science as a 'mindless' and 'mechanical' process, but he is not as different from his father as he believes. By the point at which he meets Ruth, he is forced to admit that 'I don't believe anything unless I see it in a microscope. Heredity triumphs again. I'm my father's son, damn his moldering bones' (p. 111). His practical common sense has gradually developed into a cold, scientific rationality. His obsession with science is both a ritual which gives his life order and routine, and a search for a means of control, a way of ordering the world according to his interests and desires. Scientific discovery gives him a 'quiet, well modulated satisfaction' which comes to replace his need for inter-action with others. With the acquisition of knowledge, his 'life was becoming almost bearable' (p. 96).

This concern with science is also related to his sense of identity in other ways. It is related to his definition of himself as human, and more significantly a man. For Neville, both humanity and masculin-ity are associated with the capacity for rational thought, and this association allows him to distinguish himself from the vampires. He even dismisses the living vampires as mindless and irrational, though this mistake will later prove his downfall:

> He was certain that all the living who came to his house at night were insane, thinking themselves true vampires although actually they were only demented sufferers. And that would explain the fact that they'd never taken the obvious step of burning his house. They simply couldn't think logically. (p. 95–6)

In this way, Neville's situation also implies a critique of many vari-eties of mass culture criticism.

Like Neville, many mass culture theorists felt themselves to be besieged by a mindless mass culture which threatened their world and its values, and was incapable of providing the basis for a new culture. For example, many believed that the working class were no longer the agents of historical change who would form the basis for an alternative society, but were merely a mindless, undifferentiated mass who were now fully integrated into the debased culture of contemporary society.[48] But Neville is wrong in his assessment of the vampires. He fails to acknowledge the living vampires' capacity for thought and is unable to predict that they will produce a new soci-ety in which he is both redundant and even monstrous.

He holds on to rational thought because it gives him a sense of an identity which is superior to that of the vampires, but also because he is unable to acknowledge states of being that exist outside his terms of reference. He refuses to accept difference as valid in any way. Throughout the novel, he has to provide a scientific explanation for the vampire plague. He cannot accept a mythological explanation which would force him to admit the existence of anything that might exist outside his experience, comprehension or control. However, just as when he succeeds in providing a scientific explanation, he himself is converted into myth and legend.

If science and rational thought are associated with masculinity for Neville, sexuality is associated with femininity and otherness. He identifies sexual desire and physical sensation as a threat to be repressed and controlled. He most especially fears the female vampires and the desires which they excite within him, desires which he regards as an alien invasion against which he must defend himself. Not only does he find that it is 'the women who make it so difficult' for him to feel secure from the vampires outside, but he also opposes sexual desire to rational thought. Distracted by the vampires outside, he finds himself unable to read, and finds that

> All the knowledge in those books couldn't put out the fires in him; all the words of centuries couldn't end the wordless, mindless craving of his flesh. (p. 12)

Sexual desire is opposed to language and rationality, and he claims that desire is 'an insult to a man' (p. 12). It may be defined as natural, but for Neville, the rational mind exists to order and control the natural world. 'You have a mind, don't you' he tells himself. 'Well *use* it!'

Indeed, throughout the book, Neville experiences physical sensations as destructive forces which threaten to disrupt his rational thoughts: pain 'flares' or 'explodes', and his screams come 'ripping back his bloodless lips' (p. 36).

Neville's need to define himself as superior to women can also be seen in his need to define women as victims. He takes it as significant that in the mornings, the vampires who have been left for dead after the previous night 'were almost always women' (p. 16). He even chooses women as the objects of his experiments almost without fail. The reason for this is made clear in one particular passage:

> He took the woman from her bed, pretending not to notice the question posed in his mind: Why do you always experiment on women? He didn't care to admit that the inference had any validity. She just happened to be the first one he'd come across, that was all. What about the man in the living room, though? For God's sake! he flared back. I'm not going to rape her.

Crossing your fingers, Neville? Knocking on wood?
He ignored that, beginning to suspect that his mind was harboring an
alien. (p. 48)

Neville's choice of women as the subjects of his experiments is
sexual. The act of staking is an act of phallic penetration which reaf-
firms his position of dominance over them. Even when he is not
using the stake, his experiments on them are used to confirm his difference from them. He makes them victims and so asserts his power
and lack of vulnerability.

He is disturbed, however, when he realises that all these victims
remind him of his daughter, Kathy, and this emphasises another feature of his relationship to women. Neville remembers his wife and
child as almost idealised figures whom he contrasts with the vampire females outside his house. They never challenged his authority
and remained passive figures who lacked any distinguishing personal features. At least, that is, until his wife dies and returns as a
vampire in a particularly telling example of the 'return of the
repressed'.[49] Indeed, these features are foregrounded by her name,
Virginia. His wife even insists on making him breakfast when she is
sick with the early stages of the plague. But, for Neville, these forms
of passivity are positive qualities. They are seen as the appropriate
forms of female behaviour. For this reason, the perceived similarity
between the sleeping female vampires whom he tortures and his
own daughter is a significant detail. It not only hints at his incestu-
ous desires for his daughter, but also at the fact that his need to
assert his power and authority over women has made his wife and
child into little more than victims.

Neville's relationship to the male vampires is also significant.
Unlike the female vampires who are seen as an undifferentiated
mass and as objects of fear, disgust and loathing, Neville's relationship to the male vampire, Ben Cortman, is based on a sense of
respect and even affection. Nor is this fact simply due to his friendship to Ben before the plague transformed him into a vampire.
Neville not only shows his affection for the vampiric, Ben, by com-
paring him with the comedian, Oliver Hardy, but he consciously differentiates him from the other vampires. Ben, he believes, has more
of a 'zest for life', despite the fact that the phrase is 'such an obvious anachronism' (p. 97). For Neville, Ben operates as a male antag-
onist against whom he can test and prove his own masculinity.

Neville even knows that killing Ben would actually be difficult for him because he enjoys, and even needs, the competition. Without the struggle with Ben, his life and his identity would lack definition.

The entrance of Ruth disturbs Neville's preconceptions and the distinctions on which they are based. If Cortman acted as a challenge to Neville which affirmed his sense of himself as a man, Ruth acts as a challenge which disturbs it. His interaction with her not only shows him how cold and brutal he has become, but she also illustrates again and again that his actions are not so very different from those of the vampires. She offers the other's perception of himself, a perception which contradicts his own self-image. As they talk, he begins to feel guilty for the first time. As the novel puts it:

> In the years that had passed he had never once considered the possibility that he was wrong. It took her presence to bring about such thoughts. And they were strange, alien thoughts. (p. 121)

Not only does she challenge his self-image, she also challenges his perceptions of the vampires. It is through her that he learns of the living vampires' plans to build a new society and this knowledge contradicts his view of them as mindless beings. He is forced to accept that the living vampires may be different but that they are not necessarily inferior to him either.

The same is true of his views of women. The new vampire society is not hierarchically organised along gender lines, and Ruth is 'a ranking officer in the new society' (p. 139). She has power, authority and capabilities which Neville had not associated with women or even believed to be either appropriate or possible. But while she is confident and able in this new role, she also possesses the qualities of empathy which Neville lacks.

Despite her difference from Neville, and even despite the fact that he had killed her husband, she is able to sympathise with his plight and recognise that 'you were just as much forced into your situation as we were forced into ours' (p. 127). She is able to care for him and even love him without seeing his difference as either a sign of inferiority or a cause for loathing and disgust. She encourages him to escape from the city and save himself, and even when he is captured and condemned to death, she offers him a way of avoiding the humiliation of a public execution. She gives him poisoned pills to swallow, and comforts him. While Neville might display a fear of female sexuality, the novel does not endorse his fears.

Instead it offers a critique of the definitions of masculinity upon which these fears are based, and presents powerful women such as Ruth as potentially positive figures with a capacity for the empathy which is lacking in contemporary constructions of masculinity.

The Shrinking Man

If Neville is estranged by changes in the outside world, Scott Carey in *The Shrinking Man* is estranged by changes within his own body. A freak combination of factors causes him to grow smaller as he loses one seventh of an inch per day. But along with this physical reduction in size, a whole series of changes occur in his social relationships. Most particularly, he loses confidence in his masculinity and becomes intimidated by his wife. The position of authority and control which he had assumed to be his right as a man gradually seems to slip away as his height decreases and until he finally falls into the basement and is totally displaced from his position within the home. He now perceives the once familiar cellar as a strange and alien world, and apparently normal objects become terrifying: the floor of the basement becomes a huge desert; the boiler becomes a giant, thundering tower; the walls become vast cliffs; and he becomes the prey of a normal house spider which now acquires the appearance of a gigantic monster.

Barbara Creed has related Carey's fear of the spider to a fear of women.[50] In the film version, she claims, the spider is frequently associated with Carey's wife. But the book makes it quite clear that neither the spider nor the wife are inherently monstrous or threatening. On the contrary, Carey is frightened by them because of his own anxieties, anxieties which he overcomes at the end of the novel. His fears are presented as the result of his failure to recognise and dispense with his concepts of 'normality', particularly those concepts of normality which are associated with the role of 'normal' middle-class masculinity in the 1950s.

Carey's loss of height is related to concerns about the 1950s in a number of ways. Not only is it supposed to be the result of environmental pollution – he is subjected to a freak combination of radiation and insecticide – but it is also associated with his fears of failure. He believes that as a man he must provide for his family and supply them with all that was expected of the prosperous middle classes of the 1950s. To achieve this end, he has devised a plan:

First working for his brother, then applying for a GI loan with the idea
of becoming a partner in Marty's business. Acquiring life and medical
insurance, a bank account, a decent car, clothes, eventually a house.
Building a structure of security around himself and his family.[51]

But rather than providing security, this plan puts more and more
pressure on him.

For example, this plan is so dependent upon receiving a GI loan
that he becomes ever more anxious about whether his application
will be accepted. Commitment to this plan also places him in greater
and greater debt until he feels that every 'bill was a chain that
weighed him down. He could almost feel the heavy links forged
around his limbs' (p. 11). His need to prove himself as a man also
requires him to refuse to let his wife get a job. He believes that he
must be able to provide for his family without his wife having to
work. But these anxieties are products of his own need to live up to
a particular definition of masculinity. It is a pressure he puts upon
himself. The novel resists the common claim within the 1950s that
it was women's demands for security and material comfort that was
responsible for the emasculation of men.[52] Indeed, as Carey
becomes more and more anxious and as the pressure of the medical
bills associated with his loss of height make the situation still worse,
he is clearly shown to transfer his blame on to his wife as a way of
escaping responsibility. It is not a pressure placed on him by women
which the novel presents as the problem, but the pressure that men
place upon themselves. It is his fear of failing to live up to an internalised definition of masculine success.

His loss of height only increases his anxieties about his masculinity. As his wife becomes more and more upset at his refusal to seek
medical help, he wants to comfort her but is 'able only to look up
at her face and struggle futilely against the depleted feeling he had
at being so much shorter than she' (p. 27). As he shrinks, he starts
to feel more and more inadequate beside her, particularly in their
sexual life. Everything she says and does, he begins to interpret as
though she were patronising him or treating him as a child, and this
only confirms his feelings of sexual inadequacy:

Imagination it might be, but that didn't prevent him from feeling like
a boy – indecisive, withdrawn, much as though he'd conceived the
ridiculous notion that he could somehow arouse the physical desire of
a full-grown woman. (p. 37)

Indeed, Carey is presented as being incredibly self-centred. He perceives everything in terms of himself.

Even his desires to provide for his family are less the product of
a desire to see them happy, than a desire to prove his own powers
as a man. As he makes plans for them in the event of his death, he
angers his wife who notices that he is treating them like objects or
'bric-a-brac to be disposed of' (p. 41). He also expects his wife to
be able not simply to respond to his own needs and desires, but to
be able immediately to know what they might be from one minute
to the next. For example, due to his feelings of sexual inadequacy,
he breaks off sexual relations between himself and his wife, and
refuses her even 'a kiss or an embrace', but when he eventually
needs comfort and sexual contact, he is infuriated when she does
not immediately know what he desires and respond accordingly.
Even when she does understand his desires and responds, he does
not concern himself with her anxieties and fears:

> When, too soon, it ended and the night had fallen black and heavy on
> his mind, he slept, content, in the warm encirclement of her arms. And
> for the measure of the night there was peace, there was forgetfulness.
> For him. (p. 43)

He expects his wife to comfort his anxieties, but does not even reg-
ister the fears which she is harbouring.

Carey's notion of masculinity is therefore based on a sense of his
superiority and significance as a man, and it is these privileges which
he fears losing along with his height. If he is not a success and loses
his size, he fears that he is becoming something other, something
non-masculine; something which he sees as childlike or feminine.
Initially he begins to feel like a boy, but gradually he also becomes
concerned that he is becoming the object of others' desires, rather
than the subject of his own. As Barbara Ehrenreich has argued, one
of the ways in which male roles were defined in the 1950s was
through an implicit distinction. If one was not successful in one's
work and was therefore unable to provide for one's family, it was
suggested that one was less than a man, a position which was associated with homosexuality through the following logic: 'I am a failure = I am castrated = I am not a man = I am a woman = I am a
homosexual.'[53] Hence Carey's panic over the homosexual advances
of a man from whom he accepts a lift, and his fear of becoming a
media spectacle. Carey is terrified of becoming an object of others.

He fears losing his feeling of superiority and significance as a man, and becoming subordinate to others' power and authority.

This does lead him to recognise, briefly, that while 'poets and philosophers could talk all they wanted about a man's being more than fleshy form, about his essential worth, about the immeasurable stature of his soul', it 'was rubbish' (p. 42). He recognises that human beings' identities are not simply fixed and inherent, but are defined by social relations with others, social relations which are based on subjective perceptions and more objective forms of economic power. But as his size decreases, he finds that both other people's perception of him changes and his economic power disappears. He can no longer do his job, and he is forced to rely on his wife's income.

As a result, he tries to compensate for his feelings of powerlessness and inadequacy through his objectification of his daughter's babysitter. He spies on her and maintains some sense of power by seeing her as a sexual object. However, this solution is hardly rewarding and it eventually backfires when the girl finds out about his behaviour, a situation which only adds feelings of embarrassment and shame to his already depleted ego. As a result, he becomes ever more childish. Feeling that he is unable to assert power and authority over his wife, he flies into tantrums and whines in his various attempts to manipulate those to whom he feels that he must now defer.

On one occasion, he insists on being taken along to a carnival when Lou, his wife, takes their daughter, Beth, despite the fact that he can't enter the carnival with them. But this journey has positive results for him. He finds himself at a freak show and meets 'Mrs Tom Thumb' or Clarice, a midget who is part of the carnival troop. Not only does he find that her size means that he can relate to her without feeling abnormal or strange, but she also helps him to take control of his life again. For Scott, there was 'nothing lower for a man than to become an object of pity ... When a man became pitiable, he was lost. Pity was for helpless things' (p. 93). But Clarice does not consider herself an object of pity, despite her size. She has a sense of confidence in herself and she gives Scott the confidence to refuse the role of object. Instead of existing as an object of the mass media, he begins to write his own story. He becomes the subject of his own life once more, and is able to make enough money from the book finally to provide for Lou and Beth.

However, this change does not prevent him from shrinking, and he eventually becomes so small that his wife has to buy a doll's house for him to live in. Finally, he is chased by the family cat and ends up trapped in the cellar while his wife and child presume him to be dead. It is the time which he spends in the cellar which frames the majority of the narrative, most of the earlier periods of his life being presented in flashbacks; and in this alien world, he faces the final challenge to his notions of masculine supremacy in his conflict with the spider. If the spider is clearly presented as female, the novel also makes it quite clear that it is not inherently monstrous. Not only does it only acquire a monstrous status when Carey has become small enough to perceive it as such, but it also becomes a displacement of, and a focus for, all of Carey's anxieties. Carey needs to prove himself against it to give himself some sense of superiority and importance. It is merely something which Carey needs to conquer in order to hang on to some sense of masculinity.

Indeed the situation is also charged with significance. Not only were cellars often converted into workshops by men in the 1950s, so that they would have a male refuge where they could prove their traditional masculine skills to themselves, but the cellar had also been a refuge for Carey in the earlier stages of his shrinking. It was 'the last refuge to which he always fled in those days' (p. 112). Deprived of every other sphere, he becomes trapped in the cellar, and believes that he must master this environment through rational thought, just as Robert Neville had tried to master his world:

> All right. He had a brain. He'd use it. After all, wasn't this his universe? Couldn't he determine its values and its meanings? Didn't the logic of a cellar life belong to him, who lived alone in that cellar? (p. 142)

But Carey is not alone. The spider also occupies the cellar and it is a threat not only to his life, but perhaps more importantly, to his sense of male dominance. The spider is 'every anxiety, insecurity and fear in his life given a hideous night black form' (p. 170). It is an object on to which he has displaced all his fears about the threats to his masculinity, and which he must destroy to affirm his sense of himself as a man.

Unfortunately for Carey, not only does killing the spider have no impact on his decreasing size, but almost as soon as he has killed the creature, he comes to recognise the irrelevance of his previous fears.

After his encounter with Clarice, Carey has realised that a 'man's self-estimation was, in the end, a matter of relativity', but he still believed in hierarchies of value; to be smaller than others was to be less than others. He had also assumed that 'zero inches means nothing' (p. 216), that when a certain day came he would shrink into non-existence. But after killing the spider, he finally loses his last seventh of an inch and finds that he still exists. His perception of size was based on everyday calculations of measurement. The concept of 'microscopic and submicroscopic worlds' had never occurred to him. Only once he has killed the spider does he realise that

> Existence went on in endless cycles. It seemed so simple to him now. He would never disappear, because there was no point of non-existence in the universe. (p. 216)

Initially, he is frightened by the endless and perpetual change that this existence would mean, but then it occurs to him that if 'nature existed on endless levels, so also might intelligence' (p. 216). Instead of trying to desperately hold on to the values and standards of his old life, he is finally liberated from them and runs towards 'the new world' which is described as a 'wonderland', a place of new and exciting sensations:

> There was much to be done and more to be thought about. His brain was teeming with questions and ideas and – yes – hope again. There was food to be found, water, clothing and shelter. And, most important, life. Who knew? It might be, it just might be there.
> Scott Carey ran into his new world, searching. (p. 217)

At the end, Carey has finally abandoned his old desire to assert masculine dominance and rationality upon the world. He comes to recognise the value of alien worlds and forms of existence, and revels in the new sensations and experiences which they offer.

Notes

1 Keith Neilson, 'Richard Matheson', in Everett Franklin Bleiler, ed., *Supernatural Fiction Writers: Fantasy and Horror Vol. II* (New York: Scribner's, 1985), p. 1074.

2 Richard Matheson, 'Mantage' (1959), in *Shock!* (London: Corgi, 1961), p. 51.

3 Richard Matheson, 'Advance Notice' (1959), in *Shock 4,* (London:

Corgi, 1970), pp. 99–100.

4 Richard Matheson, 'No Such Thing as a Vampire' (1959), in *Shock 2* (London: Corgi, 1965), pp. 13–22.

5 Richard Matheson, 'Legion of Plotters' (1953), in *Shock!*, pp. 101–9.

6 Richard Matheson, 'Third From the Sun' (1950), in *Third From the Sun* (New York: Bantam, 1955), pp. 1–4.

7 Richard Matheson, 'Shipshape Home' (1953), in *Third From the Sun*, pp. 146–166.

8 Richard Matheson, 'F——' (1951), in *Third From the Sun*, pp. 84–102.

9 Richard Matheson, 'Born of Man and Woman' (1950), in *Third From the Sun*, p. 4.

10 Richard Matheson, 'Blood Son' (1951), in *The Shores of Space* (London: Corgi, 1958), p. 82.

11 Richard Matheson, 'Mute' (1961), in *Shock 2*, pp. 91–123.

12 Richard Matheson, 'Miss Stardust' (1955), in *Shock 3*, pp. 153–72.

13 Richard Matheson, 'SLR AD' (1952), in *Third From the Sun*, pp. 47–8.

14 Richard Matheson, 'Being' (1954), in *The Shores of Space*, pp. 7–35.

15 Richard Matheson, 'From Shadowed Places' (1960), in *Shock 2*, pp. 123–47.

16 Richard Matheson, 'The Likeness of Julie' (1962), in *Shock 2*, p. 55.

17 Richard Matheson, 'Lover When You're Near Me' (1952), in *Third From the Sun*, p. 15.

18 Richard Matheson, 'A Flourish of Strumpets' (1956), in *Shock 2*, p. 156.

19 Richard Matheson, 'Girl of My Dreams' (1963), in *Shock 3*, pp. 7–21.

20 Richard Matheson, 'Trespass' (1953), in *The Shores of Space*, pp. 90–123.

21 Richard Matheson, *I Am Legend* (1954) (London: Corgi, 1956).

22 Richard Matheson, *The Shrinking Man* (1956) (London: Sphere, 1988).

23 Richard Matheson, 'Clothes Make the Man' (1953), in *The Shores of Space*, p. 79.

24 Barbara Ehrenreich, *The Hearts of Men: American Dreams and the Flight from Commitment* (London: Plugo, 1983).

25 Richard Matheson, 'Disappearing Act' (1953), in *Third From the Sun*, pp. 120–36.

26 Richard Matheson, 'The Curious Child' (1954), in *The Shores of Space*, p. 136.

27 Richard Matheson, 'The Edge' (1958), in *Shock!*, p. 116.

28 Richard Matheson, 'Nightmare at 20,000 Feet' (1961), in *Shock 3*, pp. 189–208.

29 Richard Matheson, 'Therese' (1969), in *Shock 4*, p. 109.

30 Richard Matheson, 'Graveyard Shift' (1960), in *Shock 2*, pp. 48–54.

31 Charles Beaumont, 'Miss Gentilbelle' (1955), in Roger Anker, ed., *The*

Howling Man (New York: Tor, 1992), pp. 1–24.

32 Richard Matheson, 'When the Waker Sleeps' (1950), in *Shock 3*, pp. 122–37.

33 Richard Matheson, 'Full Circle' (1953), in *Shock 3*, p. 185.

34 Richard Matheson, 'The Conqueror' (1954), in *Shock 4*, p. 62.

35 Richard Matheson, 'The Holiday Man' (1957), in *Shock!*, p. 85.

36 Richard Matheson, 'The Test' (1954), in *The Shores of Space*, pp. 61–77.

37 Richard Matheson, 'Shock Wave' (1963), in *Shock 3*, p. 121.

38 Richard Matheson, 'The Thing' (1951), in *Shock 4*, p. 33.

39 Richard Matheson, 'To Fit the Crime' (1952), in *Third From the Sun*, pp. 107–14.

40 Richard Matheson, 'Brother to the Machine' (1952), in *Shock 2*, p. 8.

41 Richard Matheson, 'Deus Ex Machina' (1963), in *Shock 4*, p. 31.

42 Richard Matheson, 'Lazarus II' (1953), in *Shock 2*, p. 69.

43 Richard Matheson, 'The Doll that Does Everything' (1954), in *The Shores of Space*, p. 176.

44 Richard Matheson, 'Descent' (1954), in *Shock 2*, pp. 23–38.

45 Richard Matheson, 'The Last Day' (1953), in *The Shores of Space*, pp. 144–58.

46 Richard Matheson, 'The Day is Dun' (1954), in *The Shores of Space*, p. 127.

47 Matheson, *I Am Legend*, p. 14.

48 See, for example, Adorno and Horkheimer, *The Dialectic of Enlightenment* (London: Verso, 1979).

49 This term is drawn from Freud but has been used by Robin Wood in his work on the horror genre. See, Robin Wood, *Hollywood from Vietnam to Reagan* (New York: Columbia University Press, 1986).

50 Barbara Creed, *The Monstrous-Feminine: Film, Feminism, Psychoanalysis* (London: Routledge, 1993).

51 Matheson, *The Shrinking Man*, p. 12.

52 See Ehrenreich, *The Hearts of Men*.

53 *Ibid.*, p. 25.

Kay and the creature in a publicity shot for *Creature from the Black Lagoon* (1954).

Chapter 5

The critique of maturity:
the films of Jack Arnold

In the realm of film, during the mid-1950s, the sympathetic handling of aliens, outsiders and others is most directly associated with the films directed by Jack Arnold and produced by William Alland at Universal Pictures, and they owe a clear debt to the writers previously discussed. Not only was Arnold's first major film in the genre, *It Came from Outer Space*, based on a story by Ray Bradbury, but Arnold's last major film, *The Incredible Shrinking Man*, was based on Matheson's novel and scripted by Matheson himself. These two films are generally recognised as two of Arnold's best, but he was not completely dependent on the talents of these writers. The film that has become his most enduring classic, *Creature from the Black Lagoon*, had no creative involvement from these writers. In fact, it was the remarkable success of this film which prompted Universal to invest heavily in the production of SF/horror films after 1954, many of which were to be directed by Arnold.

However, the importance of these films was not limited to their immediate commercial success. For many horror fans, Arnold's films have become some of the most fondly remembered horror films of the period. *Creature from the Black Lagoon*, for example, has been referred to in Leonard Wolf's Horror as 'a darling of horror film aficionados. And for good reason'.[1] David J. Skal goes somewhat further to include *Creature from the Black Lagoon* alongside EC Comics, *The Twilight Zone* and *Shock Theatre* as the 'most vivid formative memories' of 'a large segment of the [American] population'. Indeed, he implies that for many people these texts became the basis for 'mass media rituals'.[2] Many contemporary figures such as Stephen King, John Carpenter, and Stephen Speilberg often refer to particular Arnold films as formative moments not only in their experience of horror (and often film), but of childhood itself. For both King and Carpenter, individual Arnold films provided them with the first cinematic experiences, experiences which, they believe, changed their lives forever. For King, it was The *Creature from the Black Lagoon* which had the most profound effect; for Carpenter, it was *It Came from Outer Space*. Both may only have remembered a particular sequence or emotional response after their first viewing, but they emphasise that these responses and scenes remain the epitome of everything to which they aspire as writers and directors.

Nor was their experience unique. As Thomas Docherty has

pointed out, birth rates in America during the war years showed a marked increase, and this produced a generation which was to constitute a small baby boom just prior to 'the great baby boom of 1946–57'. It was the children of this wartime baby boom, he argues, which reached 'adolescence in the latter half of the next decade' – the latter half of the 1950s – and would 'become the original teenagers'.[3] For many of these 'original teenagers', the films of Jack Arnold were amongst their first cinematic experiences, and occupied a privileged place in their terms of cultural reference. The cultural tastes and activities of this generation of 'original teenagers' also became the tastes and activities with which the children of the great baby boom would grow up, and to which they would aspire. In this way, these films have acquired a central place in the cultural memory of a whole generation, and have thereby influenced film and culture since the 1950s. Not only are films such as Stephen Speilberg's major hit of the 1970s, *Jaws* (1975), clearly and self-consciously marked by stylistic debts to *Creature from the Black Lagoon*, these films are endlessly recycled at cinema clubs and every ten to fifteen years there seems to be a revival of interest in their original 3D versions.

Their use of 3D seems to be of particular importance, maybe because it emphasises the ritual aspect of the cinema experience. Audiences become more self-conscious about themselves both as a group and as individuals within a group. The glasses look and feel awkward and silly, and many people know the photographs of 1950s audiences wearing their glasses at 3D movies and find these pictures amusing. For this reason, these films become even more of a collective event and experience than the more usual forms of film exhibition, and the activity of seeing one's first 3D movie has become, for many, an event in itself, a virtual rite of passage.

These films also become actively bound up with youth cultures through their preoccupation with alienated outsiders. Their isolated figures who were abused by the guardians of normality, for no other reason than their freakish difference, was a point of identification for a generation of youth who were trying to articulate their dissatisfactions with the values of middle-class America. Indeed, these films covertly discussed these issues of difference in terms of developmental metaphors which explored the standards of 'maturity' which regulated the social codes of 1950s behaviour.

As Barbara Ehrenreich has argued: 'It is difficult, in the wake of the sixties' youth rebellion, to appreciate the weight and authority that once attached to the word "maturity.'"[4] If maturity meant acceptance of established social codes, any deviance from these codes was defined as invalid, a failure to develop, immaturity. Yet in Arnold's films, the adult world of the developed and the mature has little appeal, while the worlds of the underdeveloped and immature 'deviants' are treated with sympathy, dignity and even romance. Again and again, his films display a fascination with, and respect for, the integrity of alternative worlds most particularly in his use of atmospheric and 'alien' locations, such as the desert or the upper Amazon. Audiences are encouraged to identify with alternative life-forms and lifestyles in a number of ways. They are encouraged to perceive events, at least in part, from the perspective of the alien-ated and abused outsider.

The particular appeal of the 'creature' movies is also the way in which these concerns are related to issues of gender, sexuality and sexual difference. In these films, the outsider is not only abused for its difference, but often denied emotional and sexual companion-ship as well. This did not simply provide a point of identification for the adolescent male because the creature's difference from adult males is also associated with females' difference from these males. In these films, both the creature and the female characters recognise a point of identification through their sense of difference and sub-ordination to the authority of the male values of 'maturity'.

Thus, while James B. Twitchell might refer to these films as 'silly',[5] a better term might be 'childish' or 'adolescent', but not in the pejorative sense. These films not only present a critique of the values of maturity, but overtly flout the 'sensible' and the 'realistic' in favour of a world of childlike imagination and awe.

Not only have these films acquired a cult status among youth cul-tures, they have also been surprisingly well received by critics. Geoff Andrews, for example, refers to Arnold as 'one of the best Sci Fi directors of the 1950s',[6] while Tony Rayns discerns 'sparks of authentic pulp poetry throughout' *It Came from Outer Space*.[7] *The Encyclopedia of Science Fiction Movies*, on the other hand, describes Arnold as 'a striking, often brilliant, fantasy director'.[8] Critics not only claim that his use of 3D creates 'compositions in depth [that] are constantly interesting',[9] but also praise his use of locations. Describing *The Incredible Shrinking Man*, for example, Kim Newman argues that Arnold 'persists in his discovery of the beauty and weirdness of familiar locations',[10] while *The Encyclopedia of Science Fiction Movies* describes *Tarantula* as 'a compelling film, less for the subject matter – a giant tarantula on the rampage – than for director Jack Arnold's eerie use of the desert landscapes, a feature of his best work'.[11] It is possible that the positive response to Arnold's work is due to the central position which these films had for this generation of film critics. However, it is ultimately their sympathetic focus on alienated and estranged outsiders which these critics all mention and praise, although, unfortunately, this is often used as a way of privileging them over other forms of 1950s horror.

It Came from Outer Space

Such cultural distinctions between Arnold's movies and other 1950s horror films can be seen in Biskind's account of *It Came from Outer Space*. The film concerns an amateur astronomer and writer on space, John, who lives on the outskirts of a small town in the desert. One night, he sees something crash in the desert and goes to investigate. Deep within a crater, he sees an alien ship just before a rockfall covers the craft in rubble. He tries to tell the local townspeople, but no one will believe him because they perceive him as 'odd' and therefore refuse to trust him. Even the scientists don't think they can rely on him: they need facts and see John as just too imaginative to be trustworthy. His attempts to rouse the town fail, but he continues to investigate until the aliens contact him and explain that they are peaceful and need time to repair their ship so that they can leave earth. They fear humans who, they believe, are not ready to accept their difference. Even John is shocked when he finally gets to see them as they really are. Soon John finds himself trying to pacify the town, rather than rouse it. Too many people have noticed that odd things are happening, and John has to try to defend the aliens and prevent a clash between the aliens and the humans which might destroy them both. Finally, he succeeds in giving the visitors from outer space enough time to get away, but afterwards, he speaks with excitement and anticipation of the day when humans and aliens will be able to meet in harmony, good will and understanding.

Biskind presents this film, along with *The Day the Earth Stood Still*, as the critical and left-wing examples of 1950s SF films by playing them off against what he terms 'right-wing' and 'centrist' films, films which, he implies, constitute the majority of the genre's output in the period. For example, he compares *It Came from Outer Space* with *Invasion of the Body Snatchers*, a film which he regards as a relatively positive example of the 'radical right-wing' science fiction film:

> At the beginning of *Invasion of the Body Snatchers*, Miles Bennell wasn't different. He didn't think unconventional thoughts, wasn't equated with aliens, and while the film attacks conformity, it doesn't defend non-conformity, the right to be alien. On the contrary, it uses the concept of 'alien' to derogate those it dislikes. In *It Came from Outer Space*, on the other hand, John Putnam was estranged in the first place, long before the lost-in-spacelings made their way to Earth. He is an Einstein, and Oppenheimer. Neither an expert nor a professional, he is an amateur, the genius that centrist films distrusted.[12]

Just as Biskind's comparison between *The Thing from Another World* and *The Day the Earth Stood Still* unsuccessfully tried to privilege the latter over the former, so does his attempt to distinguish *It Came from Outer Space* from *Invasion of the Body Snatchers*.

As has already been argued, the alien in *Invasion of the Body Snatchers* is associated with developments within American society, particularly the tendency towards conformity. By opposing the alien, Miles *is* defending the right to be different, his non-conformity. John, on the other hand, is not just acting to protect the aliens, but also the townspeople. He even turns on the aliens on certain occasions and actually kills one in order to defend the community. At this moment, he is partly concerned with the safety of his girlfriend, but he is also concerned that the hostility of the humans might lead the aliens to destroy them.

Even more unsuccessful is Biskind's attempt to link *It Came from Outer Space* with *The Day the Earth Stood Still*. They may both defend the alien against human hostility, and even present the human world as barbaric and dystopian, but their politics are actually very different. The aliens in *It Came from Outer Space* just want to be left alone to follow their own course, while the aliens of *The Day the Earth Stood Still* demand that the humans accept the 'rational' way of doing things or perish. These films may both share a rather naive faith in the benevolence of science, but this faith is ultimately very different in the two films. In *The Day the Earth Stood Still*, science is rational. It is above individual or special interests, and is therefore justified in imposing its order upon humanity. But in *It Came from Outer Space*, John's science is carefully distinguished from the science of experts like Dr Snell who works at a nearby observatory. Snell wants facts, while John talks of 'imagination, the willingness to believe that there are lots of things that we don't know anything about'. Biskind does discuss this exchange, but he does not appreciate how differently it presents John's interest in science from that of Klattu in *The Day the Earth Stood Still*. For John, science is a quest for alternative perceptions and new ways of seeing the world, while the science of Snell and Klattu is a rigid, objective structure which invalidates alternatives.

In fact, while the film does present the earth as essentially 'primitive' in its failure to accept otherness, John is anything but the serious, grim patriarch represented by Klattu. He is not only a deviant, but by the standards of the 1950s, he is 'immature'. The surest sign of this 'immaturity' is in the film's emphasis on his status as an unmarried man. If marriage was a sign of maturity, single men like John were suspect, even if they did have girlfriends. Not only has John avoided the responsibility of family life and the role of breadwinner, he has not shrugged off infantile 'romanticism' in favour of a 'realistic conception of marriage'.[13] He and Ellen, his girlfriend, may have a 'working partnership', but this relationship is the outcome of a romantic love for one another, rather than the more practical relationship between men and women described by the defenders of 'maturity'.

The conflict between John's immaturity and concepts of maturity is also highlighted through his conflict with Matt, the town's sheriff. Matt had previously worked under Ellen's father, and replaced him when he died not only as sheriff but also as Ellen's unofficial guardian. Taking responsibility for Ellen, Matt repeatedly assumes the role of patriarch, and tries to prevent John from leading Ellen astray. For example, a conflict arises when Ellen, a teacher, 'skips' school to help John pursue his interest in the crater. Certainly, John is not directly responsible for her action, but Matt holds John responsible for Ellen's behaviour and argues that Ellen has 'adult responsibilities' and that the town will turn against her if she does not live up to them. Significantly, it was the acknowledgement of responsibility which was the surest sign of maturity in 1950s America.

However, Matt is not simply worried about Ellen taking time off school, but he is more generally worried about her relationship with

John. John is 'different' from the townsfolk. They don't understand him, and what they don't understand makes them frightened. This situation not only directly associates John with the aliens, but also identifies him as a 'deviant'. People think he is 'crazy'. For example, he is ridiculed by the papers who report his story about the aliens with the headline, 'Stargazer sees Martians'. But if the townsfolk are frightened by what they don't understand, there is also the threat that they may not only ridicule and ignore him, but actually try to destroy him just as they attempt to destroy the Martians.

John is disappointed by this situation. He has left the city to escape this kind of prejudice, his action implying a rejection of the modern American world, particularly the conformity of the corporation and the suburbs. In selecting a small isolated community in the desert, he hopes that he will be allowed to think for himself. As a result, John rejects the maturity of the conformist corporation man for the immaturity of the inner-directed thinker, and if the film had not made this clear enough, the comments of Snell make it explicit: 'He's more than odd. He's individual and lonely – a man who thinks for himself.'

The town, on the other hand, represents conformity and intolerance. They are afraid of things that are different. It is suggested that they have already seen John as a threat, and have talked about him behind his back long before the crash of the space ship, but when he insists on telling them 'the truth' as he sees it, they ridicule him. The press publishes their sensational headline and a helicopter pilot tells John, 'you've been up in the stars too long'. In fact such is their intolerance of difference that when John asks the helicopter pilot what he would do if there really were alien visitors from space, the man replies that he would 'hold them for a circus'. He would confine them and turn them into spectacles for amusement and exploitation. John, of course, suggests that it would be better to 'find out what they're doing here first'. To him, the aliens are not just freaks, but may have valid goals from which humans can learn.

For John, the problem with the town is summed up in his opening remarks. The town may 'know its past', but unfortunately, it is also 'certain about its future'. As a result, when the aliens begin to 'replace' the townspeople with replicas so that they can move around freely and repair their spaceship, John positively relishes the confusion, chaos and uncertainty that this situation causes. For example, when Matt starts to realise the implications of John's claims, he comments that if John is right, there is no way that Matt himself could even be sure that John was actually John and not some alien in disguise. At this moment, John takes advantage of the situation to confuse Matt still further. Yes, he says, Matt couldn't be sure that he actually was John and not an alien sent to give Matt a series of false leads.

For John, the town's certainty about the future is a problem. It is confident that its values and perceptions are incontrovertible, and is therefore intolerant. Not only does this result in a lack of enthusiasm, energy and imagination, but also in a hostility to that which is different and a fear of having its values and perceptions challenged. In fact, not only does the film identify John with the aliens, presenting them both as outsiders that the townspeople don't understand, but John and the aliens identify with one another. When the aliens explain their purpose on earth to John, they claim that they don't want to hurt anyone, but least of all him. They recognise him as a kindred soul and trust him with their secret knowledge. Finally, when John does confront the aliens, their leader has even assumed John's own image, and the conversation between them is presented as an exchange between like-minded beings. Like John, they are reaching for the stars in a search for new experiences and perceptions, and even when John is forced to kill one of them, its death is sympathetically handled.

If the film resembles the depersonalisation narratives in which the townspeople are replaced by apparently cold, robotic aliens, this situation is not used to suggest the 'rational conformity' of the aliens, but rather it is used to play with the audience's perceptions and expectations. Despite appearances, it is revealed, the aliens are dreamers like John who feel like little more than frightened children on earth. Unfortunately, this is perhaps the least effective aspect of the film due to the rapid transition from the presentation of the aliens as cold and robotic replicas to the proud and expressive replica of John at the end of the film.

None the less, the film does emphasise that the alien is uncertain and unpredictable. It can appear to be one thing and then suddenly change into something else, and this feature is most clearly dealt with through the handling of the desert locations. Not only is the desert associated with the aliens in a number of ways throughout the film, it is also used to illustrate the insignificance of the town and its experiences in comparison with the vastness of nature. Visually the town is presented as merely a small outpost in a gigantic alien world which cannot be fully known or predicted. As John puts it, the desert may look dead but it is alive. It is 'waiting for you', and will kill you if you go too far. He also stresses that it has any number of ways in which it can kill you.

The alien desert is dangerous, unpredictable and various, but these are not necessarily negative features. They offer the challenges, uncertainty and heterogeneity that John misses in the culture of the town. In fact, both John and the film present the desert as a place of beauty and mystery, but not a beauty which is safe and conventional. Rather the desert's beauty is one which has the associations of terror and limitlessness which define the sublime. These qualities are best evoked by a sympathetic telephone repairman when he describes the desert to John: 'You see lakes and rivers that aren't really there, and sometimes you think the wind gets into the [telephone] wires and sings to itself.' It is therefore no surprise that the aliens use the desert to hide from humans, and that John himself lives outside the town on its fringes.

Creature from the Black Lagoon

While *It Came from Outer Space* has acquired the status of a cult classic within the genre, it is *Creature from the Black Lagoon* which became a major hit, and along with *The Incredible Shrinking Man* has been the most highly praised by critics. Its popularity and power are largely related to its concerns with sexuality and gender. In *It Came from Outer Space*, Ellen was somewhat independent, but mainly through her association with John. It is his interests which she pursues, rather than her own. Furthermore, while there is an element of threat towards her when she is captured by the aliens, this threat is not primarily sexual. Even John and Ellen's relationship lacks a sexual charge: he seems more interested in staring at the stars and interacting with aliens than spending time with Ellen. In this way, John's immaturity is more prepubescent than adolescent. In contrast, the immaturity of the creature from the Black Lagoon is adolescent. If the world of *It Came from Outer Space* is largely sexless, the world of *Creature from the Black Lagoon* is unremittingly sexual.

The film concerns a group of mostly male scientists who travel deep into the upper Amazon in a search for evidence of animal life's earliest attempts to make the transition from the water to the land. They are hoping to find fossils, but they actually encounter a living example, the gill-man. The creature reacts violently to their invasion of his world and a conflict develops between the male scientists and the creature. This conflict becomes particularly intense when the creature becomes attracted to the only female on the expedition, Kay. Most critics read this attraction as simply a male desire to possess the female body with an implied threat of rape. In this way, the conflict within the film is interpreted as one between human and non-human males for the possession of the woman's body as object. For example, Biskind claims that the creature is 'driven into a frenzy by the proximity of Julia Adams in a one piece bathing suit'.[14] The final destruction of the creature and the establishment of the heterosexual couple of David and Kay is therefore read as a confirmation of the patriarchal nuclear family.

However, there are problems with this kind of interpretation. First, it does not explain why the creature is presented with such sympathy and dignity. Most critics acknowledge this aspect of the film's presentation of the creature, but if the creature simply represents the threat of sexual violence which female sexual independence must evoke and males must learn to repress, there is no reason to present the creature as positive in any way. In fact, if the film simply works to claim that male and female sexuality need to be contained in the mature relationship of the patriarchal nuclear family, the sympathetic portrayal of the creature only seems to get in the way, and it would have been so much easier for the film to have simply presented it as an unqualified monstrous threat.

Second, the creature is clearly distinguished from Mark, another scientist on the expedition. While Kay's boyfriend David is the nominal hero, Mark is the leader of the expedition and clearly interested in Kay himself even before there is any encounter with the creature. However, his aggressive attempts to compete with David for Kay's affections are presented as negative, and clearly distinguished from the behaviour of the creature. In fact while Mark is in competition with David for Kay, he also competes with David over the best way of dealing with the creature.

Mark is presented as an acquisitive, goal-oriented male scientist. He is more concerned with the dollars which publicity will attract than with research itself, and he values the money because it will enhance his power and prestige. In fact, David claims that Mark has even taken credit for specific findings in order to promote himself and extend his reputation. There is also the implication that it is Kay's findings for which Mark has taken the credit. Not only are these features related to a contempt for everything that is different – he despises both the *Rita*, the boat on which they travel down the Amazon, and its owner, Louis – it is also related to a form of science which is only concerned with dominance and control.

Rather than study the creature in its natural habitat as David suggests, Mark wants to capture it as proof of his discovery. He is less concerned with learning from the creature's difference than with converting it into an object with which to enhance and display his own power. As David complains, Mark sounds 'like a big game hunter' out for 'trophies'.

In fact, Mark clearly fetishises his harpoon gun as a display of phallic dominance and aggression. He praises its efficiency and refers to it as 'a positive weapon' while he both displays its power and boasts that it makes no difference what he shoots at. This latter phrase not only emphasises his indiscriminate use of violence in order to prove his masculinity and power, but is also directed at David who has just been sharing an intimate moment with Kay. The remark is a thinly veiled threat. However, Mark's aggressive use of the spear-gun against the creature also identifies David with the creature: at one point, when David criticises Mark for firing at the creature, Mark responds by saying, 'you sound as though I put the harpoon through you'. But the most developed associations are between the creature and Kay. Mark wants to convert both into objects or trophies through which to display his power and prestige.

As a result, the ways in which Mark is distinguished from the creature further undermine claims which suggest that the creature is simply motivated by a male desire to dominate or possess the female body. If Mark is clearly associated with an aggressive assertion of dominance and control, the creature is only hostile to those humans who have invaded his world. He is trying to defend his space rather than extend his power and control. He also directs no violence towards Kay. In fact, the relationship between the creature and Kay is dealt with not as an attempted rape, but as a tragic romance. Unlike male figures such as Mark, the creature displays a fascination and affection in relation to Kay, and she also shares a bond with the creature. She may tend to scream a lot when the creature goes after her, but she constantly tries to defend the creature from the other humans. She tells the men that if they would only leave it alone, the creature would not bother them, and when the men defend an attack on the creature by claiming that it could have harmed her, she simply responds, 'But it didn't!' It may have killed one of the men in the struggle, but it did not intend violence towards Kay.

In fact, there are numerous occasions when Kay and the creature are shown staring at one another as if they both recognise something of themselves in the other through their difference from the men around them. Indeed, the creature is first drawn to Kay when she is swimming on the surface of the lagoon, on the boundary between his world and that of the human males. She is swimming alone, and gaining pleasure from both herself and the water. In doing so, she displays a different relationship to the water from that of the men. The males literarily penetrate the water, while carrying spear-guns and cameras in a manner that is clearly associated with masculine aggression, control and objectification.

During this sequence between Kay and the creature, the creature does not directly threaten Kay, but cautiously reaches out to touch her leg. It appears almost nervously shy and even flees once it has touched her. Its hesitation and uncertainty are not due to any fear of physical aggression from Kay, though. It shows little fear of fighting with the human males, even when they are heavily armed. Instead it is a 'childlike' uncertainty about itself in relation to others, particularly a sexual uncertainty.

Still wary of contact with Kay, the creature then begins to swim along below her and mirrors her movements in a manner that implies an identification with her, rather than a desire to dominate her. This identification is hardly surprising. Like Kay, the creature is distinguished from 'mature' masculinity. His 'childlike' immaturity is associated with pre-phallic or pre-genital sexuality, and this association can be related to the heroine's movements in the water, movements through which she experiences pleasure without recourse to males, a pleasure which is not genitally centred.

Debates about sexuality frequently assume a fundamental difference between male and female sexuality in which male sexuality is aggressive, goal-oriented and genitally centred, while female sexuality is none of these but altogether more diffuse and *fluid*. However essentialist these arguments may be, they are fundamental to a whole series of debates about masculinity and femininity, even many

supposedly critical varieties such as post-structuralist psychoanalysis.[15] As a result, this distinction suggests the main point of identification between Kay and the creature. Kay's relationship to the
water is closer to that of the creature than the human males. He
lives in harmony with the water, despite the fact that water is clearly
associated with the feminine. At the opening of the film, the audience is told that it was within the 'warm depths' of the water that
life was born, and the lagoon itself is shaped like a large womb with
a narrow neck at one end. Even the photography distinguishes
between the world above the surface of the water and the world
below it. While the former is 'shot in flat matter-of-fact black and
white' like many other 1950s SF movies, the underwater sequences
were strikingly photographed by William E. Snyder. This photography is frequently praised by critics, and it presents this world as a
fabulously romantic space through its use of shimmering light and
flowing movements, an atmosphere which is more than comple-
mented by the film's music.

The creature's 'deviance' from the norms of masculinity is also
defined in terms of 'immaturity' in other ways. At the opening, an
omniscient narrator describes the process of evolution, and the start
of this process is visually represented by what appears to be the Big
Bang. As the narrator announces in order to explain this image, 'In
the Beginning, God created the heaven and the earth'. This moment
is then followed by the claim that initially 'the earth was without
form and void' before the narrative moves on to describe how the
'seas rose, found boundaries and were contained'. The story so far
is one of creation and definition as the world takes shape, but this
process is followed by the 'miracle of life' which, it is claimed, was
born within the 'warm depths' of the seas and developed in 'infinite
variety'. If the process of creation was initially associated with definition and containment, the creation of life is distinguished by heterogeneity and the crossing of boundaries.

The narrator describes how life moved on to the land and
declares that it is here that different life forms left 'a record of their
coming, their struggle to survive and their eventual end. The record
of life is written on the land, where 150 million years later, in the
upper reaches of the Amazon, man is still trying to read it.' At this
point, the film cuts to an aerial shot of the Amazon which eventually closes in to reveal a human expedition which has not been visible previously and which still remains dwarfed by the vastness of

the natural scenery. In this way, both visually and verbally, the film emphasises the insignificance of human existence against the variety and magnitude of nature.

Not only does this passage describe humanity's development, it also contextualises the creature's place in the process of evolution. It is one of nature's first attempts to make the transition from the water to the land, from the feminine origin of life to the masculine attempt to rationalise and control existence. It is a hangover from an early point of evolutionary history, and it lives in a part of the world which is described later as being 'exactly as it was 150 million years ago'. This place is, as David says, inspired by the world below the surface of the lagoon, 'like another world' or at least another time. If this world is deadly and all the things in it are described as 'killers', it is also associated with a lost stage of innocence and perfection. It is described as a 'paradise', an Eden before the fall during which humans acquired knowledge. In this way, the film does not present immaturity as a negative condition, but as potentially positive. It is associated with the origin of life as well as the threat of death, but even the threat of death need not be seen negatively. Like the desert in *It Came from Outer Space*, the Amazon jungle is dangerous, unpredictable and various; and as such, it offers challenges, uncertainty and heterogeneity. It is a sublime place of terror and limitless beauty.

If immaturity has positive connotations, the mature world of modernity and science are more negatively presented, particularly through their association with Mark. It is associated with dominance, control and the destructive invasion of alternative worlds. The scientists not only destructively invade the creature's world for their own ends, but are often shown as callous and dismissive of other cultures. Not only does Mark hate the *Rita* and its captain, Louis, but the other scientists refuse to heed his warnings and dismiss them as mere superstition. Unfortunately, Louis's myths and legends prove a lot more appropriate than their science. Therefore, while the film tries to preserve a sense of the positive potential of science by highlighting the difference between Mark and David, this is only partly successful and is only achieved by emphasising David's own immaturity and his identification with the creature.

When David is first introduced in the film, he is immediately identified as immature through his avoidance of marriage. As Ehrenreich argues, 'the average age of marriage for men in the late fifties was twenty-three, and according to popular wisdom, if a man held out much longer, say even to twenty-seven, "you had to wonder"'.[16] But David is clearly holding out. Maia and Kay tease him about his avoidance of marriage, and Kay reports that his only real defence is that they are 'together all the time anyway'. But David's immaturity is not presented negatively. Even if Mark is not married, he is the main figure of mature masculinity, a figure whose maturity is both proved and denigrated through his conformity to the systems of authority and power associated with capitalist enterprise and professional hierarchy. David, on the other hand, is a free thinker like John in *It Came from Outer Space*, and as such, he becomes a virtual rebel. Unfortunately, according to many 1950s psychologists, 'the rebellious person [was] also an immature person'.[17]

Like *It Came from Outer Space*, the opposition between David and Mark is also an opposition between two different views of science. Like Snell, Mark wants the facts and proof which will gain him respect from the scientific and economic communities, and it is for this reason that he wants to objectify the creature by capturing or killing it. David, on the other hand, is like John to the extent that he is little concerned with the ridicule of others, and sees such ridicule as the result of a lack of imagination. While Mark feels the need to capture the creature to make people believe him, David asks: 'Why won't they believe you?' After all, David argues, science should acknowledge and recognise the possibility of things which might exist outside its knowledge. As with John in *It Came from Outer Space*, David regards science as a quest for new perceptions and experiences, rather than a sterile accumulation of facts and findings. For this reason, Mark and David clash over the appropriate response to the creature. While Mark wants to objectify it and literally turn it into a dead fact, David wants to learn from it. He values its otherness and difference, and wants to protect its distinctive existence.

In fact, David is not only identified with the creature through his immaturity and through the way in which Mark displaces his aggression towards David on to the creature, but it is also David who finally stops the other humans from firing at the creature at the end of the film. He lets it return to the lake and relinquishes the scientific demands that he and Mark had made upon the creature. The creature is allowed to return to its own world, and despite the fact that it appears to be dying, David does not try to appropriate its body either as scientific proof of its existence, or for further study and examination.

However, David is less a point of identification within the film than an attempt to resolve the conflict between Mark and the creature, the conflict between the rational and the irrational, or maturity and immaturity. Unfortunately, this resolution does not quite work. The creature remains the main point of identification and sympathy, while David remains rather dull, boring and one-dimensional. The film also doesn't finally succeed in disassociating David from the negative connotations of dominance, control and exploitation associated with Mark. If David argues that humans have much to learn from the difference of less developed species, it is only so that humanity itself can develop. By learning how nature managed to adapt to life on the land, he suggests, humanity may learn how to adapt to life on other planets. Not only does this argument still associate David with the goals of development and progress rather than 'immaturity', it also associates him with the very exploitative and colonialist ambitions which the film attacks elsewhere. The scientists' journey into the Amazon is an invasion which is presented as both exploitative and destructive.

To some extent, the film does suggest that David may have renounced these ambitions by the end of the narrative, but it is unclear. As a result, the establishment of the heterosexual couple at the end of the film is hardly convincing. It is never quite clear what Kay actually sees in David, but it is not really intended to present the triumph of the patriarchal nuclear family anyhow. There is no indication that David has learned the error of his bachelor ways and will now do the 'mature' thing by marrying Kay. Instead, the end of the film is more concerned with the tragic destruction of a pre-phallic sexuality. It is the image of the creature slowly sinking down through the water which closes the film, not the image of David and Kay united. In fact, the creature's death is presented, partly through Kay's sorrow, as the destruction of alternative or even oppositional possibilities, not merely the loss of an earlier stage of development from which one must inevitably grow away.

As a result, the fact that the film proved so successful with teenage audiences, and that this group particularly identified with the creature's victimisation by the adult males, should hardly be a surprise. But it is also worth noting that the film associated its concerns with 'immaturity' with the two other major issues of political and cultural opposition which were to emerge through the course of the 1950s: race and sexuality/gender. The creature is not only associated with the oppression of women, but also the tyranny of WASP culture over other ethnic and racial groups, particularly through the film's concern with colonisation.

Revenge of the Creature

The sequel to *Creature from the Black Lagoon*, *Revenge of the Creature* (1955), was released the following year and was also directed by Arnold. Though much less evocative, it did develop the first film's concern with gender, again using an identification between the creature and a female character to achieve this end. The film opens with another trip up the Amazon in which a big game hunter and a scientist go in search of the creature. However, on this occasion, they have been sent by an American marine institute with the explicit task of capturing the creature and bringing it back to America. There is no struggle between the scientist and the hunter on this journey, and the tension between science and commercial exploitation seems to have completely passed. Science is now fully integrated with the commercial exploitation of the creature and vice versa. Despite warnings from Louis, the *Rita*'s captain, who tells them the story of the previous film, the expedition eventually captures the creature and transports it back to the marine centre where it is put on display for the public and experimented on by scientists.

As in the previous film, the creature becomes the victim of abuse by humans who try to condition it, through the use of a large phallic bullprod, in an attempt to calculate its intelligence. The creature also becomes fascinated with a female scientist, Helen Dobson, who is working for her Masters degree in Ichthyology. Helen also seems to become fascinated with the creature, and frequently spends her time watching it through the windows of its tank.

Helen is confused about her direction in life. She wonders how she got started as a scientist and where it will lead her. All the other women whom she knows have already got married and had babies, and she senses that she is reaching a crisis point, uncertain whether she wants to be a scientist or a wife and mother. It is made quite clear, however, that this is only a dilemma which women face. As the male scientist, Clete, acknowledges, 'Its tough on you girls. I'm not saying it should be. Just that it is.' Helen's problem is that the role of wife and mother, on the one hand, and that of scientist, on the other, are incompatible within her society and she feels trapped in a double bind: damned if she does and damned if she doesn't. She can't decide what she really wants because her desires are socially incompatible. Like Kay, she identifies with the creature because both share the same sense of being different from those around them. In fact, not only is the creature trapped like Helen in so far as it is chained to the base of its tank, but as Helen claims, 'I pity him. He's so alone. He is the only one of his kind in the world.' Like the creature, Helen is also unique. She has no female friends who share her experiences of uncertainty and indecision, nor any role models to whom she can aspire. The scientific norm is completely male, and she too feels herself to be alone and the only one of her kind.

But Helen is not entirely a victim in this world. She is successful and respected as a scientist, and is able to hold her own with the men. At one point, she explains to one of the officials at the centre that they are drugging the creature so that they can analyse its brain-waves, but points out that they would get better results if they could only test the creature while it was conscious. The official, who has been patronising her, comments that everyone knows that the brain shuts down when one is asleep. Helen begs to differ, and explains that the brain-waves simply become erratic when one is asleep, like the brain-waves of those who are insane. The official reacts with horror, and asks if that means that he is insane while he is asleep. Helen responds by politely reassuring him that, in his case, there would be little difference between his sleeping and his waking states. She then returns to her work before he has time to realise that she has got the better of him.

None the less, her proficiency in the male world does not completely compensate for the deprivation in other areas of her life. Finding that, unlike the men, she has a conflict between her public and private life, she refers to a dog as 'my one true love and favourite boyfriend', at least until she develops a relationship with the male hero, Clete. She also differs from her male colleagues because she is uncomfortable with the unfeeling, callous and even cruel experiments which are performed on the creature, experiments which the men excuse through concepts of scientific objectivity. Clete may claim that he 'sure hate[s] to use' the bullprod on the creature, but accepts it as an inevitability. Helen, on the other hand, is referred to sarcastically as a 'fine scientist' for being 'squea-mish about doping a fish' with which to drug the creature. As Clete observes, for a scientist, she is very 'sentimental'.

But Helen's emotional qualities are not presented negatively in the film. Rather it is their absence in the males which is presented as a problem. As Helen points out, science has its own inadequacies. It is only concerned with the empirical or factual, and it ignores sub-jective experiences. It is concerned with rational control, rather than emotional interaction. As she observes when she and Clete become romantically involved: 'Scientists are funny. They are as stupid as cavemen when it comes to important things. They can't explain love.' Not only does this highlight the limits of scientific rationality, but it also compares it with the 'ignorance' of the unde-veloped. The primitive, undeveloped and immature may not have the knowledge offered by science, but science has its own deficien-cies. In fact, the deficiencies of science are its very detachment from the spheres of emotional and sexual interaction with which both Helen and the creature are associated. In fact Helen refers to the definition of love which she has found in Webster's dictionary where it is defined as 'an attraction based on sympathetic under-standing', the very relationship which the film establishes between Helen and the creature.

One of the problems with the film, or at least one of the features which makes it less effective than *Creature from the Black Lagoon*, is that the bond of sympathetic understanding between Helen and the creature is simply a matter of their shared feelings of being iso-lated and trapped by the demands of a male world. Unlike *Creature from the Black Lagoon*, it does not raise the more positive and utopian image of the pleasures which are shared both by Kay and the creature in the waters of the lagoon. The identification is simply established through dissatisfaction, not through the image of any alternative mode of existence. As a result, the relationship also loses its emotional charge, and in comparison with Kay, Helen seems a very conventional, vulnerable heroine with little sense of her own sexuality. She may be aware of the male's desires for, and designs upon, her, but she seems far more passive in relation to them than was the case with Kay.

Another problem is that there is no image of 'mature' masculin-ity against which the hero, Clete, is defined. There is a brief rivalry over Helen between Clete and the hunter, Joe Hays. But Joe is quickly killed off, and offers no real threat to Clete. He does not have the authority which Clete enjoys, and their rivalry is friendly, rather than overtly hostile. Hays never even seems really to resent Helen's growing affection for Clete.

Nor is Clete's mode of science defined in relation to a more authoritative version of science. He is not really distinguished from the exploitative aspects of science, and it is Clete himself who uses the bullprod in his experiments. In fact, Clete's science is not the search for new perceptions and experiences, but rather the attempt to consolidate and justify the sense of human superiority over other species. His job is to establish the distinction between humans and animals. This attempt is thwarted in his encounter with the creature as he finds that 'every test, every reaction, just misses being human'. Unfortunately, this challenge to his assumptions does not require him to accept and value the creature's difference, but rather to recognise its similarity. This similarity may challenge his assumptions of human superiority, but it only blurs the line between man and nature. It does not require Clete to recognise difference as a valid condition from which humans can learn.

This presentation of the creature also contradicts Louis's warnings at the start of the film where he claims that the creature 'doesn't belong in our world'. He is not only warning the hunters against the creature's power, but also against violating the difference and integrity of its world. But if Clete discovers that the creature is similar to humans, the sense that the humans are violating its difference is undermined and even lost. None the less, Louis does make other claims which suggest how the creature is meant to be read. He argues that the creature is stronger than the force of evolution, that it is something that the process of development is unable finally to eradicate. It is these forces which rationality may attempt to repress or contain, but cannot finally erase.

Not only is the creature associated with the emotional and sexual spheres from which science remains detached, but much of its antagonism is directed against the symbols of modernity. Not only does it vent its rage on the modernist cage of the marine tank in which it is imprisoned, but its actions immediately after it escapes are significant. As it is walking towards the sea, and the visitors to the park are running with fear, a small child falls in front of it and blocks its path. The creature does nothing to harm the child but simply waits until its mother has got her out of the way. But on reaching the beach it finds that its way is blocked by parked cars and it proceeds to overturn one of the vehicles which is standing in its way. The refusal to harm the child is therefore contrasted with the aggression directed against the car, one of the central symbols of modernity in the 1950s.

The creature's 'immaturity' is therefore associated more directly with resistance to the rationalisation of modern America than with the issues of masculinity which distinguished the original film. As a result, its association with teenage anxieties about sexual and gender roles is less clear, though it is hinted at in one scene. After the creature has escaped, it makes its way to the hotel where Helen is staying. As it emerges from the water, the scene shifts to a teenage couple who are necking in the boy's car. Instead of being attacked by the creature, they are interrupted by a policeman who orders them to stop what they are doing and go home. Both are clearly disappointed. The girl complains that they weren't doing anything wrong, but after further orders from the policeman, the boy grudgingly says, 'anything you say officer'. The scene seems to have little function in the drama of the overall sequence, but it does mirror the creature's disappointment when its desires for Helen are frustrated by the intervention of both Helen's dog and Clete. Later in the film, the creature is also interrupted by two teenage boys both of whom it kills, but while they are in no way used to mirror the creature's plight and become its victims instead, they are given much more characterisation than is necessary. The film dwells on their conversation as they debate whether or not to follow their fathers' advice and attend college. In fact, at this particular moment, their sense of indecision about what it is that they want out of life is actually quite close to that of Helen, though the gender differences are still significant.

Tarantula

If *Revenge of the Creature* is not as evocative as *Creature from the Black Lagoon*, *Tarantula* (1955) is probably the least interesting of all Arnold's 1950s SF/horror movies. It concerns a scientific attempt to develop an artificial form of nutrient which goes horribly wrong. The nutrient, which has a radioactive base, causes animals to grow to fantastic proportions, but when two of the scientists experiment on themselves, it causes them to develop monstrous deformities and drives them mad. One scientist dies, but the other attacks a third scientist, injects him with the nutrient and starts a fire before he too finally dies. The surviving scientist, Deemer, realises that he is doomed to the same fate as his colleagues and tries to develop an antidote. Unfortunately, he is unaware that a tarantula on which they had been experimenting with the nutrient had escaped from the laboratory during the fire, and that it is growing to a fantastic size. A young doctor who is investigating the strange deformities of the first victim soon becomes aware that strange things are happening in the countryside, and eventually pieces the story together in time to call in the air force who kill the giant tarantula before it can destroy the small desert town where he lives.

The majority of the film is a quite standard version of the kind of invasion narrative exemplified by *Them!*, but it also includes an interesting, though undeveloped, metamorphosis narrative in which the surviving scientist gradually transforms from a mild mannered, if somewhat arrogant, figure into a deformed autocrat. This particular narrative strand does create some sense of sympathy with the alien or outsider in a way that the narrative of the spider's destruction does not.

Deemer is actually presented as different right from the start of the film, but not in a sympathetic way. He is mild and relaxed, but only because he is safe in his assumption of authority and superiority over others. This assumption also makes him arrogant, detached and somewhat disdainful. As the sheriff puts it at one point early in the narrative, 'some of these big brains never learn manners'. He even lives out of town like John in *It Came from Outer Space*. But unlike John, Deemer is not an imaginative outsider who wants to learn from the differences of others and who is perceived by the town as a threat. Instead, he is a man who is searching for ways to control and dominate the world; who cannot imagine the dangerous implications of his work; and who is too preoccupied with the importance of his own work to consider others as important.

At one point, after the fire in the laboratory, he goes outside to bury his colleague in the desert. He does not want an investigation into the death to threaten or even interrupt his research. After he has finished coldly disposing of the body, he turns his attention to one of the laboratory monkeys and lavishes it with the affection which is absent in his relationships with other humans. As one of his experiments, the monkey has more significance for him than any of

the humans with whom he is obliged to interact. Despite these feelings, the townspeople do not perceive him as a threat, but rather
accept and even maintain his authority over them. As the sheriff says
when the hero, a local doctor called Matt, is troubled by Deemer's
explanation of his colleague's death, a 'young fellow like you can't
stack up what he knows against the professor'.

Indeed the film sets up a conflict between the local GP, with his
practical medical knowledge and his close personal interactions
with others, against the international expert with his specialised
knowledge and his sense of detachment from, and authority over,
others. Deemer's transformation is therefore presented as both an
intensification of his alienation from others and a result of his own
hubris. Horrified by the transformation of his features, he becomes
both increasingly authoritarian in his relationships with others and
pathetically frightened by their reaction to his appearance. At one
moment, he is hiding himself away so that Matt will not see his
deformity, and the next, he is accusing his new female assistant,
Stephanie, of betraying his confidence.

However, this preoccupation with the psychological effects of
physical transformation are never a feature of the giant spider's
transformation. It is not a sympathetic creature like the aliens from
It Came from Outer Space or the creature from the Black Lagoon,
but neither is it portrayed as simply negative. As is stressed by a scientist whom Matt visits, tarantulas are neither good nor evil, but
'just part of the world around us'. Each living thing, he claims, 'has
a function in its own world'. Difference is not the problem, but valid
and necessary. Instead, the problem is that like the creature from the
Black Lagoon, the tarantula 'doesn't belong in our world' and has
been displaced from its natural environment and relationships to
nature through its increase in size.

In this way, the threat posed by the spider is similar to that posed
by Deemer himself. While Deemer's sense of superiority over others
detaches him from relationships with them, his experiments on the
spider have detached it from its relationships with nature and placed
it in a position of dominance over humans. It uses them for food and
can dismiss their presence with one swat of its giant legs. In this way,
the spider's actions become a commentary upon Deemer's relationship to others. Indeed not only does Deemer have to confront his
own developing monstrosity, but he is eventually killed by his own
creation which returns to his house and crushes him.

The spider is also associated with the desert, and as with much of Arnold's work, the use of this landscape is significant. As with other films, *Tarantula* presents the human world as one that is dwarfed by the natural world which surrounds it, a world which is terrifyingly unpredictable and virtually limitless. If Matt does describe it as 'evil', this term is not weighted with purely negative connotations. Matt uses it when trying to describe the sense of awe and beauty which it evokes. It is alien and unknown, but by implication, it is also fascinating and attractive for that very reason. As he puts it, the desert is 'like something from another life. Serene and quiet, yet strangely evil – as if it were hiding its secrets from man'. Of course, what Matt doesn't know at this point is that the desert is actually hiding the tarantula, but without the element of danger and potential terror, it would not be sublime.

The desert is also associated with an early stage of development. As is pointed out, it was once an ocean, and the place where life began. The spider is of that desert, and Deemer's crime is partly to accelerate its development. The rational, adult world is thereby contrasted with the irrational, underdeveloped worlds which are still connected to the origins of life. Unfortunately, while Matt's status as a young, small town doctor opposed to the older, austere father figure, Deemer, connects him with the world of the immature, the film does not develop this much further, and he remains a rather bland and one-dimensional figure as does Stephanie, despite her position as a female scientist.

The Incredible Shrinking Man

For many critics, Arnold's next film, *The Incredible Shrinking Man*, was one of his best. If he had begun his work in SF/horror films with a film version of a short story by Ray Bradbury, his return to form drew upon a novel by Richard Matheson. But while the film was written by Matheson, it changed the emphasis and concerns of the original novel in significant ways. Most obviously, the process of transformation prior to Carey's descent into the world of the basement is of much less importance than his struggles once he find himself in the cellar. The film is also far less concerned with a critique of Carey's need to hold on to specific notions of masculinity. Instead it presents the story as a regression from civilisation to primitivism, and ends up with a clearly religious return to the blissful union of man with the cosmos prior to the 'fall'. In a sense, Carey's fall into the basement is a reversal of humanity's fall from grace. Indeed, Carey's shrinking is not associated with the pressures which he experiences in trying to live up to certain definitions of masculinity. Instead Carey is presented as a well-to-do advertising executive: a grey flannel man who exists in a state of complacency until he begins to shrink, a process which causes him to feel increasingly isolated and estranged from the normal world.

However, this does not mean that issues of gender are unimportant in the film. The opening of the novel is changed so that Carey is actually on board the boat with his wife when the radioactive cloud appears and engulfs him. Just prior to its appearance, he has been persuading his wife, Louise, that it is her duty to bring him a beer, despite the fact that the seriousness of his expectations are disguised with humour. Even when she objects, he claims that he is on holiday and she has to remind him that she is supposed to be on holiday too. Eventually, he makes a deal with her: if she will get him a beer, he will make dinner for them in return. As she goes to get the beer, he then begins jokingly to assume the role of a feudal master. He refers to her as his 'wench' and orders her to fetch him a 'flagon'. The scene is used to illustrate his complacency about his own position as a man, but as he begins to shrink, this complacency is replaced by panic. He becomes more 'tyrannical, more monstrous in [his] treatment of Louise'.

This concern with gender roles is also highlighted in his relationship with Clarice, the midget. Probably due to the film censorship of the period, this relationship is made straightforwardly platonic. None the less, Clarice teaches him that difference from others need not be seen as inferiority. He even comes to feel that 'everyone else is out of step except' the two of them, but when he realises that his continual shrinking has now made Clarice taller than he is, he runs from her. He is both horrified by his lack of control over the shrinking process, and by the thought that this change in size will make her dominant over him.

The film is also more overtly critical of the media than the book. While Clarice tries to teach Carey to recognise his worth, the media turns him into a 'freak' whose story can be exploited for entertainment and commercial gain. They make him a figure of fun which is used to affirm people's sense of their own normality, at least until he is presumed dead at which point they change their approach. Suddenly, Carey's story is an example of human courage and dignity. It is presented as a tragic but heroic tale of the 'human spirit' struggling against adversity.

However, the film develops its main focus once Carey has fallen into the cellar. Jack Arnold not only 'forces us to see life from the perspective of the ever-diminishing central character',[28] but he also manages to transform the familiar setting of the basement into a landscape almost as sublimely alien as the upper Amazon or the desert. Both effects are achieved by filming the sequences almost entirely according to Carey's sense of scale. The boiler towers above; the floor stretches out into the distance; and the spider with which Carey fights looms over the camera as he does battle. By adopting Carey's sense of scale, the film also succeeds in creating the very sense that 'everything else is out of step' which Carey has referred to earlier. The section set within the cellar environment also acquires a more focused narrative. While earlier parts of the film are broken up into short moments from different stages of Carey's decline, the sequences in the cellar are able to track the gradual process of decline in a far less disjointed fashion. The novel had avoided the problem of presenting these earlier stages in a disjointed fashion by using the cellar narrative as a framing device for a series of flashbacks, but without this type of organisation, the film seems much more assured when it concentrates on Carey's struggle to survive in the cellar.

In fact, this struggle is far more positively portrayed in the film than it is in the novel. The novel presents Carey's need to dominate and control his environment as a hangover from his previous existence. It is presented as a need to assert his authority and superiority over the world of 'nature' in order to affirm a sense of his own masculinity. In the film, the emphasis seems somewhat different. Carey's struggle to survive is presented as a return to a more primeval or primitive existence in which his civilised identity has been stripped away. In fact, one of the first things Carey has to do on reaching the cellar is to recognise that his civilised clothes are inappropriate, and to dispense with them in favour of a piece of cloth which pointedly resembles a caveman's bearskin. This reinterpretation changes the implications of many of Carey's comments. For example, when he declares that 'as man had dominated the world of the sun so I will dominate my world', the implication is less that he needs to prove his masculinity, and more one of forging an existence in a primitive and hostile landscape. In fact, again and again, the film emphasises the almost instinctive and primordial nature of his motivations, particularly with regards to the spider. He experiences 'some new source of power urging him to the death struggle' as he goes after the spider, and he even likens himself to the spider by claiming that he is less driven by decisions than by reflex.

This might seem to suggest that the basement becomes a 'new frontier' in which he is able to act out a heroic civilising process associated with masculinity, but it is actually a movement away from the process of civilising and modernising the world. It is a return to a moment which is 'purer' because of its primitiveness, not a prelude to further civilising or dominating nature. Indeed, once Carey has actually killed the spider to obtain food, the food itself becomes meaningless and unimportant to him. As Carey puts it, 'even as I touched the food, I no longer felt hunger or fear of shrinking'. Instead he turns, leaves the food behind him and goes to watch the stars. What had seemed instinctual behaviour is now referred to as some 'great directing force' which is soon identified as God. Just as eating the apple of Eden had caused the fall, Carey's failure to eat the food is related to a reversal of the fall. If eating the apple had given humanity the knowledge that separated it from nature, then by dropping the food, Carey is able to become one with existence.

Rather than maintaining his hierarchical view of existence and desiring domination over those defined as inferior to him, Carey comes to accept a universe without hierarchies in which he does not need to assert his dominance and independence. He comes to see existence as a 'gigantic circle' in which 'the infinite and the infinitesimal' meet. Instead of the novel's endless layers of existence each with its own value, the film suggests that the cosmic and the microscopic meet. As Carey disappears into nothingness, he attains cosmic stature and is finally at one with existence. If God is invoked at this moment, He is not a patriarch who exists independently from creation, but is the cosmic universe itself. In this way, the film values innocence over knowledge, the undeveloped over the developed, and immaturity over maturity. While Carey is not a child at the end, he rejects the values of adult masculinity and maturity in favour of a blissful union with creation.

Notes

1 Leonard Wolf, *Horror: A Connoisseur's Guide to Literature and Film* (New York: Facts on File, 1989), p. 49.

2 David J. Skal, *The Monster Show: A Cultural History of Horror* (New York: Norton, 1993), p. 364.

3 Thomas Docherty, *Teenagers and Teenpics: The Juvenilization of American Movies in the 1950s* (Boston: Unwin Hyman, 1988), p. 45.

4 Barbara Ehrenreich, *The Hearts of Men: American Dreams and the Flight from Commitment* (London: Pluto, 1983), p. 17.

5 James B. Twitchell, *Dreadful Pleasures: An Anatomy of Modern Horror* (New York: Oxford University Press, 1985), p. 60.

6 Geoff Andrews in Tom Milne, ed., *The Time Out Film Guide* (London: Penguin, 1989), p. 586.

7 Tony Rayns in Milne, *The Time Out Film Guide*, p. 293.

8 Phil Hardy, *The Encyclopedia of Science Fiction Movies* (London: Octopus, 1986), p. 139.

9 Tony Rayns in Milne, *The Time Out Film Guide*, p. 293.

10 Kim Newman, 'The Incredible Shrinking Man' in Jack Sullivan, ed., *The Penguin Encyclopedia of Horror and the Supernatural* (New York: Viking, 1986), p. 219.

11 Hardy, *Encyclopedia of Science Fiction Movies*, p. 154.

12 Peter Biskind, *Seeing is Believing: How Hollywood Taught Us to Stop Worrying and Love the Fifties* (London: Pluto, 1983), p. 150.

13 Ehrenreich, *The Hearts of Men*.

14 Biskind, *Seeing is Believing*, p. 121.

15 The problem with such claims is that it is usually unclear whether these supposed differences between male and female sexuality are 'natural' or 'cultural'. Indeed, not only is there a tendency to privilege a 'real' and 'natural' female sexuality which exists outside 'patriarchal' domination as superior to male sexuality, but also a tendency to dismiss women whose sexuality does not conform to this model. Furthermore, it has also been pointed out on a number of occasions that such claims, despite their supposedly radical and critical politics, are little more than a reproduction of traditional, conservative claims about sexual difference. None the less, the claims continually reappear with feminist debates. See, for example, Ellen Willis, 'Sexual Politics' in Ian Angus and Sut Jhally, eds, *Cultural Politics in Contemporary America* (London: Routledge, 1989); and Carol S. Vance, ed., *Pleasure and Danger: Exploring Female Sexuality* (Boston: Routledge, 1984).

16 Ehrenreich, *The Hearts of Men*, pp. 14–15.

17 Ehrenreich, *The Hearts of Men*, p. 22.

18 Hardy, *Encyclopedia of Science Fiction*, p. 169.

Drive-in horror: a publicity still for AIP's classic, *I Was a Teenage Werewolf* (1957).

Chapter 6

Teenagers and the independents:
AIP and its rivals

W hile Arnold was making his films on low budgets at Universal, independents like AIP (American International Pictures) began attracting audiences with even cheaper productions. However, despite their low budgets, these films were not necessarily of poor quality; indeed, in different ways, many were formally innovative. It was simply that AIP developed and spearheaded the move towards 'high concept' films: films that sold themselves on clearly defined sensational premises. The company often designed the advertising campaigns first, tested the campaigns, and then, if these campaigns were successful, hired someone to make the film. It was led by Samuel Z. Arkoff, a former studio lawyer, and James H. Nicholson, a film marketing and sales executive, and its success was based on low budget productions which were clearly directed, through the use of 'state of the art' marketing campaigns, at the teenage audience. In fact, Arkoff and Nicholson's AIP has often been credited both with developing the forms and strategies which would save the industry as a whole (as the mass audience was gradually replaced by a predominantly teenage clientele), and with laying the foundations for the 'New' Hollywood of the post-1960s. As Thomas Docherty has argued:

> Nicholson and Arkoff decided early on that teenagers made up the only market that could sustain the motion picture business. In the 1950s, AIP perfected the exploitation strategies that throughout the next decade it would ride to ever-increasing fortune and legitimacy.[1]

In fact AIP was to become one of the most important stables for the development of young talent in the 1950s and 1960s, and it gave figures such as Roger Corman, Jack Nicholson, Francis Ford Coppola, Martin Scorsese and John Milius some of their first work in the industry.

Initially set up as a distribution company, AIP began in 1954 as the American Releasing Corporation, and its first releases were three productions by Roger Corman: the drag racing feature, *The Fast and the Furious* (1954) and two westerns, *Five Guns West* (1955) and *Apache Woman* (1955). By 1956, however, they had 'moved away from producing antiquated "formula" pictures with narrative roots in the old studio system's B picture in favour of the new gimmick or exploitation pictures aimed at teenagers'.[2] For example, Corman began to produce a series of alien invasion narratives such as *The Day the World Ended* (1956) and *It Conquered*

the World (1956) along with other teen-oriented films, and he has
been credited as the figure who 'set in granite the teenage exploitation style'.[3] However, Corman was not the only film-maker associated with AIP; for example, in 1957, Bert I. Gordon directed *The
Amazing Colossal Man* and followed it up in 1958 with a sequel,
The War of the Colossal Beast. These two films clearly drew on
Arnold's *The Incredible Shrinking Man*, but reversed the basic
premise. A similar tactic was also used by AIP's chief competition,
Allied Artists, which released *Attack of the 50 Foot Woman* in 1958.

 1957 also saw one of AIP's greatest successes, *I was a Teenage
Werewolf* which was released in June, just one month before the
equally phenomenal success in the US of Hammer's *The Curse of
Frankenstein*. *I was a Teenage Werewolf* also predated the phenomenal success of the first television showings of Universal's classic
gothic horror films of the 1930s which were broadcast in October
of the same year. Indeed the television broadcasts of Universal's
gothic horror films were to become 'the seasons biggest sensation'
according to the *TV Guide*.[4] But if the aliens, outsiders and others in
1950s horror had often been a point of identification for teenagers,
the success of the AIP films was often due to their willingness to
tackle this association directly. They often presented a direct identification between the teenager and the monstrous outsider. As
Thomas Docherty has observed:

> Having better reason than most to feel a kinship with malformed and
> hyperthyroidic humans, teenagers were faithful followers of and sym-
> pathetic onlookers to the plight of the hormonally disadvantaged;
> their own biological state must have seemed equivalently capricious
> and uncontrollable. The sudden swellings and shrinkings of adoles-
> cence, the inhabitation of a body with a mind of its own, beset all sorts
> of screen creatures, but the unadorned human frame grew and waned
> with a distinctly genital sense of proportion. The remarkable devel-
> opment of *Cyclops* (1957), *The Amazing Colossal Man* (1957), and
> *Attack of the 50 Foot Woman* (1958), and the disheartening diminu-
> tion of *The Incredible Shrinking Man* (1955), *Attack of the Puppet
> People* (1958), and even *Tom Thumb* (1958) are elastic expressions of
> the ebb and flow of pubescent development.[5]

But these films were not just concerned with teenage anxieties about
their bodies, but more particularly with teenagers' relationships to
both adults and their peers. These films directly focused on the feeling of being alien, on the problems of 'fitting in' or 'adjusting' to the

demands of the social world; and they often gave a far more agonised, pessimistic and critical portrayal of these problems than the
more respectable productions of the bigger studios.

Unlike many of the productions by the major studios, *I was a
Teenage Werewolf* is not seen from the position of an investigating
adult, but from the perspective of the teenage protagonist, Tony. In
fact the film is not concerned to 'interpret' teenage lifestyles and
tastes for an adult audience, but 'takes teenage subculture on its
own terms'.[6] Even in a classic such as *Rebel Without a Cause* (1955),
James Dean's character, Jim Stark, is not so much at odds with the
adult world as he is denied his 'proper' entry into this world by the
absence of a positive male role model. In fact, Jim desperately wants
a 'normal' family with a strong father and a supportive mother, and
actually creates a surrogate family for himself through his relationship with the loving Judy and the childlike Plato. In *I was a Teenage
Werewolf*, on the other hand, Tony has no significant problems with
his home life. His mother may be dead, but he does not want a
replacement. He even has a very affectionate and caring relationship with his father. Tony's problem is that he doesn't want to conform or adjust to either the world of his peers or that of adults. He
is a genuine outsider who only wants people to recognise and
respect his difference, a desire which is ultimately frustrated and
denied him.

In fact, the very 'trashiness' of these films allowed them more
space to be critical and subversive than many more mainstream
films, as well as the opportunity to be more timely and topical. The
films were not only promoted with often outrageous advertising
campaigns, but were themselves usually quite clearly humorous and
tongue-in-cheek. As a result, the producers could ward off criticism
from the Hollywood censors and other guardians of morality. It
would have been difficult for these groups to have taken these films
too seriously, and even if they had, it would have been difficult to
persuade others to take them seriously. In fact, Arkoff and Nicholson maintained a good relationship with the Production Code
Administration. In any event, AIP would not have been very worried by some criticism. It would not have come from their target
audience, and would probably have only increased the films'
teenage appeal.

The humorous, tongue-in-cheek quality of these films also had
other implications. For example, the films were often clearly self-

parodic, and self-reflexive: they repeatedly reflect upon their status as cinema with their monsters striking at victims in dark theatres or drive-ins. Even in cases when the narrative did not draw attention to the cinematic experience, they compensated for their low budgets and bad special effects by using these features to create humour. These films often relished their own ludicrousness and artificiality even while dealing with strongly contentious or emotive issues, and often without detriment to these issues. Certainly there are some extraordinarily 'bad' films, but these cannot be discussed in isolation from the series of films as a whole. While critics usually praise Roger Corman's films because they are so clearly self-conscious and self-parodic, the majority of these films are far more difficult to classify. It is often difficult to tell a movie which is simply humorously inept from one that is self-consciously parodic. However, audiences which were used to the parodic films could usually still read inept examples for the sheer humour of their ineptness. In short, the intention of the film-maker was often irrelevant.

In fact, the ludicrousness and artificial aspects of these films often evokes the same kind of affection as their pathetic and monstrous outsiders, and in this sense, the form and context were often directly linked. As a result, it is interesting that when the big studios tried to get back in on the act – for example, 20th Century Fox's *The Fly* (1958) – it was the most ludicrous aspects of these films which were both the most effective and the most affectionately remembered.

Colossal Men and 50 Foot Women

The Amazing Colossal Man was the first of the cheapies to draw upon Arnold's *The Incredible Shrinking Man*, and it concerns Colonel Glen Manning who is exposed to a new type of radiation when he tries to save a crashed pilot from a plane just before a plutonium bomb test. The radiation causes rapid growth and he is secretly relocated to a government research centre where scientists try to identify the source of this problem. As he feels increasingly hopeless and isolated, Manning starts to go 'mad', and when he eventually escapes from the centre, he is hunted across the country until he reaches Las Vegas. A series of rather appalling special effects then catalogue the destruction and havoc which he causes in the city. Finally, however, the action moves to the Hoover Dam, where he is shot by the army and falls to his death.

Though generally inept, the film does try to evoke some sympathy for Manning's plight. From the start, Manning is presented as a loner. His fiancée points out that he has no family, and that he is 'alone except for me'. In fact, he seems to have lost almost every human contact which he has ever made. While still in a coma after the explosion, he dreams of Korea where, amidst the destruction, he shares a bond of friendship with a fellow soldier who is then killed before his eyes. The scene has no real function except to detail this loss, and it is presented as a particularly traumatic moment in Manning's past. Even Manning's attempt to save the pilot from the bomb fails, and initially, he seems more horrified by his failure to save the unknown pilot than by his own fate. Manning's isolation is not simply externally imposed though. He deliberately disobeys orders in order to try to save the pilot, and he separates himself from his fiancée by signing up to fight in Korea. She wants him to stay at home with her, but he insists on going. He is therefore an individualistic loner who refuses to accept discipline from above, and rejects the comforts of the domestic sphere for the more masculine activities of war.

The process of enlargement only exaggerates this sense of isolation. Manning finds the world around him strange and alien, and he begins to realise that he has lost any possibility of domestic happiness. He asks his fiancée if there is any life which they could possibly share together, and he finds that seeing her is so painful that he tries to drive her away from him. He even feels isolated from his previous self, and says that everything which came before he started to grow now seems like 'another life'.

In the process, the film does take some suggestive positions with regard to concepts of 'normality'. Manning begins to recognise that he is seen as a 'freak', and in an argument with one of the soldiers assigned to keep watch on him, he says that the tent in which he is kept makes him feel like a 'circus freak' or a 'clown'. This feeling is partly a display of his developing 'insanity', but this 'insanity' is the result of his growing recognition that he has become an object of fascination and curiosity for other humans. As a result, he taunts the soldier by asking him: 'Why don't you ask me what it feels like to be a freak?' Finally, he changes his approach, and informs the soldier: "I think you're the freak ... I'm not growing; you're shrinking!" The film's handling of these issues is not particularly original and it draws most of its ideas from Arnold's *The Incredible Shrinking Man*, but it does have one interesting moment of its own. When he describes himself as feeling like a 'circus freak', he suggests that his freakishness could be exploited as a spectacle for paying customers. At this point, he suggests that such a spectacle might be called 'The Amazing Colossal Man', the title of the film itself. Whether intentional or not, the film thereby examines not only the way in which its own attractions have been sold to the public, but given that the advertising campaign probably predated the film's production, the film also examines the way in which the film itself was conceived and constructed. This concern with spectacle is also continued in the Las Vegas sequences where Manning examines the gigantic objects used to advertise the various hotels and casinos. Initially he stares with fascination at the giant figure which stands on top of the Dunes hotel, then later at a huge crown and slipper. Finally, he directs his aggression at these spectacles, and even fights off his enemies by using the gigantic figure of a cowboy from the Lucky Strike as a weapon.

None the less, the film provides numerous moments of intended or unintended humour: for example, a policeman reacts to the destruction of Las Vegas by asking the army: 'Are you just going to stand by and let him destroy property?' Probably the most ludicrous moment is when the scientists attempt to inject Manning with an anti-growth drug which they have developed. To achieve this end, they use a huge, specially designed hypodermic syringe which results in some truly absurd sequences. Ultimately, however, for all the comic moments, too little time is spent on Manning's own plight and far too much on Manning's fiancée, Carol, and the experimenting scientists, none of whom are particularly interesting or form the basis of a coherent alternative narrative.

This feature is an even greater problem in the sequel, *War of the Colossal Beast*, in which it is revealed that Manning did not die in his fall from the Hoover Dam, but that he is actually down in Mexico where he spends his time capturing trucks which are carrying food-supplies. His sister, Joyce, persuades the military to capture him, but while she wants to help him, they only want to protect society from him. Unfortunately, Manning's brain has been damaged in his fall from Hoover Dam and he has been reduced to little more than an aggressive beast. There is little basis for sympathising with him, though the film does try to evoke some poignant moments such as when the scientists show him pictures of his past and he finds himself struggling unsuccessfully to remember his childhood. The film also manages to evoke some sympathy for him at the end, when Joyce finally gets through to him and persuades him not to harm a bus-load of school children. At this point, Manning recognises the hopelessness of his situation – he has little sense of his own identity and can barely control his aggressive urges – and as a result, he kills himself on some high voltage electric cables.

Attack of the 50 Foot Woman also concerns a character who finds itself growing to gigantic proportions, but in this case it is a woman, Nancy. She is an heiress who is hopelessly emotionally dependent on her abusive husband Harry and, due to his treatment of her, she suffers from alcoholism and psychological trauma. She has even spent time in a private sanatorium. However, Nancy's main problem is that Harry is a louse. He is only interested in her money, and spends most of his time with a young woman, Honey. Indeed, Nancy's time in the sanatorium followed one of Harry's attempts to leave her, an attempt which came to an abrupt end when he found out that he would not get any of her money in a divorce settlement. However, when Harry does return to Nancy, he does not intend his return to be permanent. He simply wants to find another way to get her money. He and Honey even begin to talk about murder as a possible option.

However, before they get the opportunity to develop a plan to kill Nancy, she encounters a 'satellite' in the desert and is attacked by its gigantic, alien occupant. When she manages to escape and returns to town, she hysterically recounts her experiences, but meets with disbelief and derision. Most people believe that it is just a hallucination which is the result of her alcoholism. Increasingly hysterical, Nancy insists that Harry search for the 'satellite' with her, but when they finally do find it, Harry deserts her while she is attacked by the alien giant once more.

Eventually, Nancy reappears, but she is in a coma and suffering from a strange form of radiation which eventually causes her to become the '50 foot woman' of the film's title. Eventually, she regains consciousness, frees herself from the constraints which have been placed upon her and goes on the rampage in a search for Harry. She finds him at a bar with Honey, and as she smashes the place up, Honey is killed and Harry captured in her huge hand. In response to the carnage, the local sheriff calls for the riot gun, but before he is able to shoot and kill her, Nancy manages to crush Harry's tiny body. Finally, as she lies dead, with Harry's broken body in her hands, one character notes that she had 'finally got Harry all to herself'.

This film has become a major cult classic, mainly due to its sensational premise and appalling special effects. The film rarely shows more of the alien or Nancy than a crude, giant hand which seems to be made of plaster, and even when it does the film uses the most awful effects so that the gigantic Nancy and the alien are literally see-through.

However, it is the gender issues involved in the film's sensational premise which have attracted most interest. Indeed, commentary on the film tends to divide into two clear camps. On the one hand, it has been assumed that the film displays a wild male sexual paranoia in which women are portrayed as destructive and monstrous tyrants. In these readings, it is also assumed that Nancy's behaviour is presented in traditional male terms as fundamentally irrational. As Welch Everman argues, for example: 'The movie suggests that, if a woman happens to come by a bit of power, she will use it to destroy the local community and crush her lover to bits – hardly a flattering image but one that still shows up in a lot of more contemporary films.'[7] On the other hand, the film has been seen as a proto-feminist fantasy in which Nancy revenges herself on her abusive husband and rejects the controlling and confining roles which society has imposed upon her. Indeed, while David Pirie refers to the film as a 'delirious pre-feminist horror movie' and claims that its 'psycho-pathology is fascinating',[8] Leonard Wolf claims that it presents 'a quite moving, and startling, image of modern marital distress'.[9]

However, neither position is fully convincing. The first tends to ignore Nancy's abuse by Harry, and the extent to which Harry is presented as a cruel and unsympathetic figure. Indeed, there are few, if any positive male characters within the film who might be used to off-set the image of masculinity presented by the husband. Moreover, it is pointed out that all of Nancy's problems are bound up with Harry's treatment of her, and her analyst emphasises that she was fine until she was married. On the other hand, the film is rarely coherent enough to justify the argument that it is a proto-feminist revenge fantasy. Pirie and Wolf are right in their assessment of the film, but from its start, Nancy is in such a state of hysteria that it is difficult to identify with her. She is simply too frenzied to allow any real sense of interiority to develop.

Indeed, the most interesting feature of the film is its ramshackle incoherence. For example, it never really develops any thematic significance from Nancy's growth. Certainly, if we were to accept certain claims about the film, it could have used Nancy's plight as a way of commenting upon the ways in which her wealth and power dominate and oppress her husband and render him powerless and redundant in the process, but there is no sense in which the film develops this possibility. On the contrary, it is Harry who is clearly the dominating and controlling partner in the relationship, and the difficulty of establishing an identification with Nancy is partly due to her complete sense of worthlessness and dependence. It is she who feels herself to be powerless and redundant.

However, this feature make it difficult to make sense of her growth in size, a problem which is not helped by the preoccupation with the alien 'satellite', a plot-line which is largely an irrelevant and pointless diversion from the central story. Certainly, while it is possible to find pleasure in Nancy's revenge, it can hardly be seen as a reassertion of Nancy's sense of self. Instead, it is presented as a last desperate act which still arises from her sense of hopeless dependence. Indeed, it is an act which is as much self-destructive as it is vengeful.

As a result, while the film cannot be simply dismissed as misogynist and while it does concern the horrors of marital abuse, the film never really goes beyond this to relate its various elements coherently: Nancy and Harry's destructive relationship; the alien satellite and its mysterious radiation; and Nancy's growth. Indeed, unlike other transformation films, it never even explores Nancy's reaction to her changing size. Throughout most of the transformation she is in a coma, and even when she does awake, she does not even suffer the same sense of disorientation and alienation as Colonel Manning in *The Amazing Colossal Man*. While Manning is forced to spend some time in confinement and therefore has time to contemplate his changing relationship to his world, Nancy simply wakes up and goes on the rampage in her search for Harry. There is no pause in the action in which she is given time to consider what she has become and what it might mean to her. If she seems to have been driven mad, it is not her new body which seems to be the cause, but rather her feelings for Harry.

None the less, if Nancy does not really operate as a point of identification within the narrative, she is clearly presented as the
wronged party. She is not only tormented by her husband, but is
also patronised by the police and townspeople, and is even ridiculed
by a news-reporter on her television set. She is an outsider, abused
and controlled by everyone except her faithful butler. Even her analyst, the genial Dr Cushing, has pointedly misled her. His intentions
may well have been good, but it is he who had persuaded Nancy to
take Harry back after their separation, a mistake which even he is
forced to recognise as such during the course of the film.

Teenage monsters

If many of the outsider narratives had offered points of identification for teenagers, *I was a Teenage Werewolf* directly dealt with
teenage problems. It was made in 1957 by Gene Fowler Jnr who
would later direct *I Married a Monster from Outer Space*, and it
remains a classic reference point for many commentators on 1950s
film and culture. Biskind's study of the films of the decade even has
one of the film's publicity photographs on its cover, and many contemporary film-makers refer to it with affection and even reverence.
In fact, it is often used to signify either the best or worst aspects of
the decade, depending upon the preferences of the commentator.

The film also marked a move from the science fiction conventions
of horror in the first part of the decade towards a growing interest
in the gothic during the late 1950s. There is the standard figure of
Pepe, an elderly man from the old country who is able to recognise
the work of a werewolf and remind the audience of the legends and
folklores about this supernatural figure. The police are even visually
presented as a group of angry villagers as they search through the
woods for the werewolf, and use flaming torches rather than battery
operated flashlights. However, these gothic elements had significantly changed in meaning and significance. The film remains
almost entirely secular in its preoccupations, and it is largely unin-
terested in the religious or even ritual conventions associated with
the werewolf as monster. There are no silver bullets, no wolfsbane,
nor even any dependence on the moon. Instead the werewolf is
associated with teenage angst and scientific psychology.

The narrative centres on Tony, a young teenager who is having difficulty staying out of trouble. Tony is bright and does well in class, but he has a short temper and keeps getting into fights. The film actually opens with one fight in which Tony refuses to quit even though his adversary is clearly stronger than him. But failure only makes Tony angrier, and he ends up going too far. He throws dirt in his opponent's eye, and starts swinging a spade about murderously. As he does so he loses the support of his peers who call in support of his opponent, and claim that Tony has been 'asking for it' for a long time. The fight is eventually broken up by the police, who discover that Tony had over-reacted to a 'friendly' tap on the back and insisted on the fight. Tony's only response is to state that he doesn't like to be 'hit from behind by anyone' and that he doesn't 'like to be touched'. It transpires that Tony has been in trouble before, and the sympathetic Officer Donovan claims that he acts as though 'the whole world's [his] enemy'. This provokes a response from Tony who retorts that 'people bug' him. Donovan suggests that Tony needs to learn how to 'adjust' and recommends that the youth visits Dr Brandon, a psychologist who is 'modern' and uses 'hypnosis'.

Tony's fear of being 'hit from behind' suggests a nervousness about his sexuality, though this is not simply homosexual panic. His hatred of being touched is a fear of being feminised, and this fear is directly associated with his refusal to conform. Tony has an 'inner-directed' personality which makes him incapable of doing 'things the other fellow's way'. After the fight, he promises his girlfriend that he will try to do something about his temper, but he insists that he will do it 'my way'. Not only does he resent the intrusion of the police, but he can also see through the hypocrisy of his elders. When his girlfriend's parents insist that he come into their house to pick her up for a date, they begin to criticise him for not having the respectability associated with having a job. But Tony points out the meaninglessness of such 'respectability' by referring to an employee of the local bank who had run off with money from his work and lost it gambling. Tony is also the one who has found a place for the teenagers to meet without the supervision of adults, a place where they can 'do their own thing', rather than conform to the adults' conception of decent and appropriate behaviour. In fact, the adult world's concern with adjustment is best summed up by the school principal who says that she knew that if they could 'really get inside' Tony, he would prove a credit to the school. The notion of 'really getting inside' Tony implies intrusion, control and even brainwashing, an implication which is confirmed by the activities of the psy-chiatrist, Dr Brandon.

But if Tony has problems with adults, he also has problems with his peers. Docherty claims that 'the other teenagers reject him' and that 'Tony is a pariah', but this is not strictly true. He is actually very popular, and even a leader to his friends. He has not only found a meeting place for them, but they value him for doing so. Unfortu-nately Tony's discomfort and anger are not focused enough, and it is too often directed against his friends. As a result, he is in danger of losing their respect, their friendship and of becoming completely isolated. This problem comes to a head at their meeting place where the group amuse themselves by playing pranks on one another. Tony is actually the leader of much of this activity, at least until one of his friends, Vic, decides to play a trick on Tony. Vic sneaks up behind him and blows a trumpet in his friend's ear. At this moment, Tony suddenly loses all control and violently attacks Vic. It is only when he sees that his friends are all looking at him with horror that he realises how inappropriate his response has been. It is at this point that Tony comes to believe that he needs help, and decides to go to Dr Brandon, the psychiatrist recommended by Donovan.

However, the turn to Brandon does not bring Tony any happi-ness. It only leads to further misery and eventually death. Despite the fact that Brandon claims that 'adjustment' is the key to success and happiness in life, he actually uses Tony as a guinea-pig on whom he tries out one of his theories. Brandon believes that 'mankind is on the verge of destroying itself' and that the 'only hope for mankind is to hurl it back into its primitive dawn, to start all over again'. He therefore practises a form of regression therapy on Tony which takes him further and further back into his childhood until Tony finds himself in a cold dark place which he doesn't recognise. At this point, Tony becomes confused and frightened. He begs to be told where he is and Brandon is happy to oblige. The psychiatrist describes a primeval dawn in which happiness is gained through preying upon others.

Later, once he has left Brandon's office, Tony finds himself unable to prevent himself from regressing into a werewolf and attacking his friends and other teenagers. He tries to get help from Brandon, but the latter is too proud of his own success in regressing Tony to help the youth. Initially, Brandon refuses to listen to Tony as the youth pleads for help, and eventually, though he promises to help, he only wants to film another regression. Finally, Tony realises Brandon has betrayed him, regresses into a werewolf and kills the doctor. Unfortunately, as he is doing so, the police rush in to the room and shoot Tony dead.

There are a number of interesting features to this narrative. First, it is made clear that despite Brandon's reference to Tony's 'disturbed emotional background', this is not associated with a dysfunctional family. Tony may have lacked a mother's affection, but both he and his father show genuine affection for one another. Tony's father had even thought about remarrying so that Tony would have a mother, but Tony had recognised that no one could take his mother's place for either his father or himself. Tony's father also stresses that Tony had never needed discipline at home, and would always co-operate: 'you only had to ask him in the right way'. If Tony's family teaches him anything, it is that adjustment or 'doing things the other fellow's way' isn't that appealing. Tony's father asks him to adjust, but is clearly exploited by his foreman and his employer. He is a sad and broken man in a dead-end job. Tony's problems are not a product of his family background, but of the wider social world.

Second, Tony's violence as a werewolf is almost always directed against his peers, at least until Tony realises who is his real enemy and kills Brandon. The first victim is a close friend who is killed while walking home from a party. He has just shown friendship to Tony by recognising that Tony is 'not with it tonight, like you are not yourself'. The second is a girl who Tony sees exercising on the parallel bars, and to whom he is clearly attracted. The scene is actually very touching and tender as Tony watches her in a way that is reminiscent of the creature from the Black Lagoon's first sight of Kay swimming. But this mood is suddenly interrupted by the school bell, a signal of authority which triggers a transformation and results in another killing. This violence against his peers is not only caused by Tony's failure to identify the object of his rage, but also threatens to isolate him from any basis of support. As the police hunt for him in the woods later in the film, the film depicts a series of police interviews with those who care for Tony, such as his friends and his father.

By the end of the film, however, Tony realises that it is Brandon who is his real enemy, despite the fact that the doctor has presented himself as a benevolent figure. Not only has Brandon promised to help Tony, he has presented himself as ideal paternal figure. Brandon requires Tony to place his trust in psychology and suggests that he is guiding Tony on a 'voyage of discovery'. The implicit assumption is that like any good patriarch, Brandon knows what is best for Tony. He even promises that at the end of the 'voyage', Tony 'will no longer be disturbed or troubled because you will be you'. In fact, Brandon is always promising to uncover Tony's 'true self', but when it emerges, it is a self from which Tony feels even more threatened and alienated. It is not Tony's conception of his 'true self', but a projection of the paternal figure's own desires.

In fact, while Brandon believes he has revealed humanity's true primeval nature, there is a strong suggestion that it is not a 'true primitive nature' at all, but rather a construct of Brandon's own fantasies. The regression therapy is conducted under hypnosis, and when Tony has regressed to the cold, dark and alien world before his childhood, he has to ask Brandon where he is. Brandon then supplies his own image of the primitive conditions, one to which the hypnotised Tony is compelled to conform.

In fact, not only does Brandon's paternal figure impose his own image of Tony's true self upon Tony, it is a 'true self' which traps Tony in Brandon's own image of 'immaturity'. For all his attacks on the destructive world of 'mature' adults, Brandon does not recognise youths as having a valid alternative. Instead, he treats them as children. He keeps Tony dependent on him and even regresses him. If Brandon values the primitive, it is only because by regressing humanity to its childhood, he believes that he can shape and control its development. He does not value immaturity for itself, but for the position of paternal power which it will give him. It is in this way that he believes that progress is regression and that regression is progress. By making humans immature primitives, he hopes to make them completely dependent on him and so confirm his ultimate position of expert authority over them. As a result, it is clear that for all his promises, he has no real concern for Tony, but sees him as no more than a guinea-pig to be used and disregarded according to his will. This association with laboratory animals is further emphasised by the fact that it is the sound of the bell which prompts Tony's transformations, just as it prompted the production of saliva in Pavlov's dogs.

If the film does end with the rather trite moral that it is 'not for man to interfere with the ways of God', this last minute religious warning is not tied to any broader moral or theological positions developed within the film. It is simply tagged on and used to ward off criticism from what is a subversive critique of parental authority and its treatment of youth.

This critique is made rather more overtly in AIP's *I was a Teenage Frankenstein* and *How to Make a Monster* which attempted to exploit the success of *I was a Teenage Werewolf*. *I was a Teenage Frankenstein* updates Shelley's original preoccupations with the creator as an abusing father and the creature as an abused child. It concerns an English scientist, Professor Frankenstein, who is in America to explain his research. He takes the idea of transplant surgery one stage further and claims that he can carry 'the principle of selective breeding one step higher' by assembling a creature from the best materials available. To prove his theories, he takes a body from a car crash and transplants two hands and a leg on to it which he has obtained from young athletes who had been the victims of crashed plane.

Once the creature is assembled, Frankenstein brings it to life, but keeps it locked in the cellar. The creature longs to walk among people, but it is horribly disfigured and Frankenstein doesn't want his secret revealed. One night the creature escapes and on its wanderings it sees a young woman to whom it is attracted. But when the woman sees his face, she is terrified and he accidentally kills her as he tries to quieten her. On returning to the laboratory, he is chastised by his creator. However, later, when Frankenstein decides to dispose of his own fiancée, he persuades the creature that she intends to betray them both to the police. The creature is not only convinced that the fiancée must be killed if he is to survive, but is also promised a new face, which would enable him to live among other people, if he will perform the deed. The creature kills the fiancée and obtains his new face, only to discover that Frankenstein is returning to England and intends to dismantle his creation in order to get it through customs. The creature senses betrayal and eventually kills Frankenstein before throwing the scientist's body to the crocodiles which had been used to dispose of the fiancée's body and other unwanted flesh. At this point, the police arrive and rather than accept further captivity and confinement, the creature kills itself.

Despite the rather pedestrian plotting and the plodding direction, the script presents the relationship between the creator and his creation as one between abusive paternal control and a sensitive alienated teenager. When the creature cries at one point, Frankenstein observes that 'we have a very sensitive teenager on our hands'. He also insists on repeatedly calling the creature 'my boy' and orders it to refer to him as 'sir'. The creature is also associated with youth through his sense of alienation from other people. With his face horribly disfigured, he is denied contact with others and is forced to depend on Frankenstein. Most significantly, he finds himself denied contact with the opposite sex who see him as hideously ugly. In this way, the creature is associated with teenage anxieties about sexual rejection, and about dependence on adult authority.

In fact, despite Frankenstein's statements about the value of youth as opposed to age, he is like Brandon in *I was a Teenage Werewolf* to the extent that he does not value youth in itself, but only as something which he believes he can dominate and control. For example, while he claims that he will only use the bodies of the young in his experiments because 'the whole trend [of our society] is towards death' and that 'only in youth is there any hope for the salvation of mankind', he does not value youth as something which can provide new values and new insights. He only values his creation as something which he can 'construct and control'. As he puts it, 'what I create I must control'. As a result, not only does he try to keep the creature in a state of permanent dependence and obedience, but he even insists that it feel pain when he is experimenting on it. His justification for inflicting this torture on his creation is that it will then feel gratitude to him when the pain is relieved. Frankenstein even refuses to see the creature as a person with any rights of its own. He advises his fiancée to 'think of him as a creation of science, like a machine', and at another point, he tells the creature that 'I should destroy you as dangerous evidence'. But the final straw is when he states, 'I assembled him, didn't I; I can disassemble him!' The creature is treated as a mere body or mechanism, not a being with thoughts, feelings and emotions.

The film also contains numerous lines of ludicrous dialogue, the most famous of which is probably when Frankenstein demands of his creature, 'Speak! I know you've got a civil tongue in your head because I sewed it back there.' None the less, the most clearly self-parodic of the AIP teenage cycle is *How to Make a Monster* which brought together both the teenage werewolf and the teenage Frankenstein's monster. However, the film is not really about these characters, but rather the studio which produces their movies. It concerns Pete Drummond, the make-up artist who creates these monsters. Pete loves his work, but one day he is told by the new studio bosses that they are discontinuing horror production in favour of 'escape' pictures: 'musicals, comedies, pretty girls'. Pete is horrified until he hits on the plan of using the monsters which these executives rejected to kill his enemies. Using a foundation cream which causes 'paralysis of the will', Pete makes up the actors playing the werewolf and the Frankenstein's monster, and he tells them that their careers are finished if the studio closes down the production of horror films. He then informs them that they must obey his commands if their careers are to continue, and orders them to kill the two studio executives. All goes relatively well, but the police begin to suspect that Pete is involved in the deaths, and Pete himself starts to appear less as a quaint old man than as an egomaniac. Eventually, he takes the boys back to his house which is filled with models of his previous monstrous creations. Once there, he kills his assistant and seems to be on the verge of literally adding the two teenage boys to his collection, when a fire breaks out and destroys both Pete and his collection. Finally, the police arrive in time to save the two youths.

The studio setting of this film allows it to make numerous jokes and observations about horror production, particularly the types made by AIP. At one point, for example, a movie director tells the werewolf and the Frankenstein's monster, who are appearing in a film together, that the fight which they are just about to stage has 'got to be the greatest fight we've had on the screen, but I've got to get it in one take'. At another point, the werewolf walks past a scriptwriter who is talking with an actor dressed as a pirate. Suddenly the actor has a great idea for a scene. What if, when his character finally climbs on to the ship, he finds that it is not the captain at the helm, but a werewolf. The scriptwriter does not dismiss this ludicrous premise out of hand, but rather relishes its sensational possibilities, at least until he raises the rather awkward question of how the werewolf got on board the ship in the first place, a question which makes them both pause as they try to find a solution.

When not parodying its own conditions of production, the film also refers to more general debates about horror and horror production. On hearing that the studio want to close down horror production because they believe that the horror cycle is over, Pete points out that he had 'heard that 25 years ago', thereby drawing attention to the frequent predictions of the horror film's demise while also undermining these claims at the same time. In fact, later in the film, the director of the werewolf/Frankenstein epic informs Pete that horror production will soon be back, and that even 'one little picture can do it, maybe one of those foreign imports'. The statement has two important aspects. Not only does it stress the continual recreation of the genre from the lower levels of the industry, it also implicitly refers to the impact which Hammer was having on the industry after the success of its gothic horrors. The film even raises broader debates about the horror film. At one point, Pete points out to the studio executives that even psychologists were beginning to see horror as a therapeutic form which helped its audience to deal with childhood fears that were never lost, but merely buried deep within the psyche.

This reference to childhood fears is also important in relation to these films' concern with age and youth. As a moment in the teenage horror cycle, the film clearly presents Pete as a paternal figure who may start out with the appearance of being on the teenagers' side, but is gradually revealed to be a controlling and abusive father figure. Not only is Pete married to his job, he also regards the monsters which he creates as his 'children' or his 'family'. At one point, his assistant overhears him talking to the posters for *I was a Teenage Werewolf* and *I was a Teenage Frankenstein* and asks Pete to whom he had been talking. Pete's response is to claim that 'I was reassuring my children that I won't let them perish'.

Like Brandon and Frankenstein, Pete seems to praise youth, but only as something which he thinks that he can control. He says that he enjoys 'working with teenagers' rather than older actors, and claims that they have 'spirit and confidence'. Unfortunately, he likes working with them because, he claims, 'they put themselves in your hands'. As a result, he uses two tactics to get them to do as he wishes. First, he makes them feel vulnerable and dependent on him, and second, he paralyses their will with the foundation cream. He considers them his 'creations' and therefore his to command and control.

In the process, he fails to distinguish between the teenage actors and the parts for which he has created the make-up. Indeed, by the end of the film, he threatens to reduce the former to the latter entirely by making them part of his collection. When one teenager suggests that Pete sounds as if he wants real heads on his wall, Pete's sinister reply is that he wants heads that are 'as real as I can get them'. Pete is also worried that as actual teenage boys, rather than as objects which he himself has created, the two youths are actually beyond his ultimate control. They have just started to rebel against his attempt to control them, and Pete has come to see them as a threat to him.

In this way, the film clearly draws upon some of the small number of gothic horror films from the early 1950s, most particularly *The Horrors of the Wax Museum* with Vincent Price. Both films portray the artistic act of creation as potentially egomanical and objectifying. In *The Horrors of the Wax Museum*, Price's character wants to use a beautiful young woman as the basis for a work of art. He aims to cover her with boiling wax in order to objectify her as art and so preserve her beauty forever. The fact that this will kill her he sees as incidental to the cause of great art. The similarity to the dominating and controlling scientist seems obvious, and it interestingly suggests that the opposition between science and the ideology of artistic creation which frequently underpins much cultural criticism is not as clear as it initially appears.

The Fly

In 1958, 20th Century Fox, one of the major studios, tried to get back in on the horror phenomenon with their production of *The Fly* based on a story by George Langelaan. The film combines both gothic and science fiction elements through its melodramatic setting which lacks many of the main symbols of modernity, its casting of Vincent Price, and its concern with the 'perils of progress'. The narrative starts with the death of a scientist, André Delambre, who is crushed in a press, apparently by his wife, Hélène. André's brother François, played by Vincent Price, calls the police and they proceed to investigate. Mrs Delambre claims that it was she who killed André, but will give no explanation. Neither François nor the police chief, Charas, feel happy with her story, and are disturbed by her preoccupation with flies. Eventually, François tricks Hélène into telling him the truth in the hope of saving her from being accused of murder, and the story which she tells is one of a happy home which is disrupted by André's obsession with scientific research.

André had been experimenting with teleportation – the transmission of objects through space – and he eventually believed that he had perfected the process and transported himself. Unfortunately, a fly was also in the cabinet with him when he teleported himself, and their bodies become confused. André acquires a fly's head and arm, while his own head and arm become parts of the fly. For some reason, André can still think as himself, for a short period at least, and he persuades his wife that they must find the fly so that he can put things to rights. But before they find the fly, André starts to lose control and the fly portion of his anatomy starts to take over. When this process starts to threaten his wife, he destroys the teleportation machine and insists that his wife crush his head and arm in the press so that his secret will not be revealed. She obligingly performs this task, but continues to search for the fly so that the remaining portion of André need suffer no more.

Unsurprisingly, Charas refuses to accept this story, declares that Hélène is clearly mad and insists that she is committed to an asylum. François's only hope of proving Hélène's story is to find the fly, and he does so just in the nick of time as Charas arrives with the ambulance. Unfortunately, the fly is trapped in a spider's web and just about to be eaten by the spider. The sight of the agonised human headed fly calling for help is so shocking to Charas that he acts on impulse and crushes both the spider and the fly with a rock. The truth of Hélène's story is thereby confirmed, and Charas and François concoct an alternative story to save her from the law without revealing the shameful fate of André.

In an attempt to outdo the cheaper products of AIP and Allied Artists, 20th Century Fox decided to take this production very seriously. They are reported to have invested heavily in the production and they filled it with recognisable character actors such as Vincent Price and Herbert Marshall. The film also featured the up-and-coming Al (David) Henison, who would later play the captain of the *Seaview* in the television series of *Voyage to the Bottom of the Sea*. The director Kurt Neuman is also reported to have hired James Clavell, who was to write *King Rat* and *Shogun*, with the express aim of providing 'realistic' dialogue for what was, after all, a rather fantastic story. Unfortunately, the result is often quite dull and very ponderous, though the film was to become a great success and has continued to have a cult following. Ironically, it is not the classy production which is the best remembered feature of this film, but rather the 'magnificent final scene'[10] in which the fly with André's head lies trapped in the web squealing, 'Help me!' This line was even used as the big moment at the end of the trailer for David Cronenberg's 'remake' of the film (1986), despite the fact that it has nothing to do with Cronenberg's reconceptualisation of the story. The special effects in this sequence are really unconvincingly poor, but this only contributes to the pathos of the scene, and to the audience's affection for the film.

Like other outsider narratives, the film's impact is in its concern with the victimised hero, his original body slowly possessed by the fly and his remaining identity dwarfed and threatened by the spider. None the less, the poor special effects do not distract from the film but only add to its 'surreality'. In fact for many fans of the genre, it is this moment which gives the film its greatness, while the more classy aspects of the Hollywood production become the object of ridicule. Indeed, Leonard Wolf has claimed that

> What is noticeable about this film, besides its magnificent final scene, is the extraordinary cleanliness of everyone in it. Both Vincent Price (François) and Herbert Marshall (Inspector Charas) wear suits that look as if they have just been delivered by a Savile Row tailor. Even Philippe, Hélène and André's son, hasn't a mussed hair in sight.[11]

Notes

1 Thomas Docherty, *Teenagers and Teenpics: The Juvenilization of American Movies in the 1950s* (Boston: Unwin Hyman), 1988, p. 153.
2 *Ibid.*, p. 154.
3 *Ibid.*, p. 155.
4 *Ibid.*, p. 149.
5 *Ibid.*, p. 146–7.
6 *Ibid.*, p. 161.
7 Welch Everman, *Cult Horror Films: From 'Attack of the 50 Foot Woman' to 'Zombies of Mora Tau'* (New York: Citadel, 1993), p. 21.
8 David Pirie in Tom Milne, ed., *The Time Out Film Guide* (London: Penguin, 1989), p. 30.
9 Leonard Wolf, *Horror: A Connoisseur's Gide to Literature and Film* (New York: Facts on File, 1989), p. 16.
10 *Ibid.*, p. 82.
11 *Ibid.*, p. 82.

Part three

Resituating *Psycho*: paranoid horror and the crisis of identity at the end of the decade

A lfred Hitchcock's *Psycho* was released in 1960, and from its opening, the film was a runaway commercial success. The film critics were less charitable, though. Many viciously attacked the film, while others merely dismissed it as an inferior work. However, within a few short years, the film's status had changed. Despite the critical derision which it had received on its release, the film soon became one of the most respected and discussed of all Hollywood films. Indeed, as David Bordwell has claimed, '*Psycho* became the most studied postwar Hitchcock film',[1] Hitchcock being one of the most studied Hollywood directors.

Psycho's acquired status as a great work of cinema was largely due to Hitchcock's established status as a director, but this situation has produced numerous problems for those who have tried to discuss the film's place within the horror genre. It should be emphasised that while Hitchcock has become known as a 'master of terror' within popular culture, *Psycho* was his first real horror film. Earlier films may have had frightening or horrific moments, but they were primarily identified as thrillers both by the studios and by audiences. However, by the time *The Birds* was released in 1963, the poster campaigns were already selling the film as though Hitchcock had a long-running career as a horror director. Indeed, the film was sold as though Hitchcock was *primarily* known as a horror director. As one poster for the film declared, supposedly quoting Hitchcock himself: 'It could be the most frightening motion picture I have ever made!'.

Certainly Hitchcock's new association with horror did have some important and positive effects on the discussion of horror. As Robin Wood has put it, *Psycho* 'conferred on the horror film something of the dignity that *Stagecoach* conferred on the western'.[2] In other words, it gave the genre a level of respectability which it had previously lacked, and so enabled critics and commentators to begin to take the genre seriously as an area for study and discussion.

Unfortunately, Hitchcock's reputation has also resulted in an over-concentration on *Psycho* at the exclusion of other areas of the genre and, most worryingly, it has distorted the genre's history. Too often, *Psycho* is not merely used as an indicator or marker of certain changes within the late 1950s and 1960s, but is seen as the *cause* of those changes. Too often, aspects of the film are identified as Hitchcockian innovations when they were actually the product of more general tendencies and processes within the genre, if not features of Bloch's original novel.

However, Hitchcock's films in general have had an awkward status within the study of film. They have been read as both radical and reactionary, both critiques of patriarchy and deeply misogynist. Even within the work of the same critic one can find these opposed tendencies. For example, in her classic article, 'Visual Pleasure and Narrative Cinema', Laura Mulvey not only uses Hitchcock's films as symptomatic and emblematic of the misogyny of Hollywood cinema in general, but also implies that somehow Hitchcock's films are more interesting and important than others because they make manifest that which is latent elsewhere.[3] As a result, even those who have attacked Hitchcock's films have displayed a fascination with them and end up privileging their supposed misogyny over the more routine forms of misogyny that are claimed to be present within Hollywood film in general. In other words, whether they have been defended or attacked by critics, Hitchcock's films have attributed with greater significance, sophistication, and innovation than popular cinema in general.

As a result, *Psycho* is either read as the key to understanding the horror genre, or as a radical break within its development. In the first case, for example, Stephen Neale and Barbara Creed not only use this film as an example of various different aspects of horror, but often define horror in ways that seem to rely on a reading of *Psycho*, but do not necessarily apply to other less 'worthy' examples.[4] However, it is the second strategy – that of seeing *Psycho* as a break with the genre – which is usually used in more historical accounts of the genre. As Robin Wood argues, for example: 'Since *Psycho*, the Hollywood cinema has implicitly recognised Horror as both American and familial'.[5] Wood's claim is that prior to the 1960s, the horrific or monstrous had been defined as external to American society. The events within horror films were either located in some exotic, foreign landscape, or else were the product of an invasion by forces which were alien to America. *Psycho*, on the other hand, is seen as an innovative and influential film because it supposedly presents its horrors not as the product of forces from outside American society, but as the product of the patriarchal family which is, for Wood, the fundamental institution of American life. Wood's claim is that horror is centrally concerned with the figure of the other which he refers to as 'all that our civilization represses or oppresses'[6] and, he claims, the patriarchal family is the institution through which repression and oppression are internalised within the individual psyche. As a result, while he sees the horror genre as potentially radical because its 'true subject is the struggle for recognition of all that our civilization represses or oppresses',[7] he sees *Psycho* as a groundbreaking, radical and influential text because it does not simply displace that which is repressed on to an alien form, but directly associates it with the family, the central institution of patriarchal, American society. In *Psycho*, it is argued, it is the repressions and tensions within the 'normal' American family which produce the monster, not some alien force. In this way, the film supposedly questioned definitions of normality and abnormality, and so transformed the genre.

As should be clear, this position is strongly contested by other critics. As Barbara Creed's work suggests, Norman Bates's murderous impulses are not presented as the product of a 'normal', patriarchal family, but rather of a family in which the father is absent and the mother has become an overbearing and dominating presence. As a result, she reads the film as a re-affirmation of the patriarchal family, not as a critique of it.

Creed claims that the film revolves around patriarchal fears of women, and of the mother in particular. The absence of the patriarchal father, it is argued, is presented as a problem in that the mother has not been kept in her 'proper' place and has so prevented Norman from breaking the pre-Oedipal bond with her. Norman has failed to perform the separation from, and repression of, the mother which is essential to the male entrance into patriarchal culture. As a result, it has been argued that within *Psycho* the patriarchal family is presented as a model of health and normality, and families in which mothers are dominant are presented as dangerous and abnormal.[8]

A similar position is presented by Peter Biskind in his study of 1950s cinema. While Biskind sees 1950s cinema as essentially conservative, he sees *Psycho* as deepening the decade's reactionary tendencies, not breaking with them. As he puts it: 'No film revealed the centre's shift to the right better than Alfred Hitchcock's *Psycho*, released in 1960, at the end of one decade and the beginning of another.'[9] The film is seen as a wholesale attack on new models of masculinity and femininity in which Norman is supposed to conform to the definition of the 'normal, well-adjusted, sensitive,

American boy' as advocated by Dr Benjamin Spock and his sup-
porters. Biskind claims this film is a part of a reactionary backlash
in the post-Sputnik era in which:

> sexual fluidity had to be repudiated, and cross-dressing could only be
> disturbing, sinister and pathological, as it was in *Psycho*. By the begin-
> ning of the sixties, feminized men were the psychos tough guys were
> earlier. Feminization was regarded as castration, not humanization.[10]

In this way, it is claimed, the film presents a conservative moral
lesson about gender roles in which the strong male is healthy and
normal, and the new sensitive male is a disturbed figure who suffers
from gender confusion.

If Biskind sees the film as an attack on 'feminized men', he also
argues that it is an attack on 'strong women'. For Biskind, the film
presents Marion as a woman who is 'altogether too independent
and domineering for her own good', and it punishes her, through
Norman, 'for her sexual attractiveness and the power it exercises
over men'.[11] In this way, it is implied, the film condones the killing
of Marion which is simply presented as the 'just deserts' for her
crime. But this crime is not simply that she has stolen money from
her employer; it is that she is an independent woman whose sexuality is a threat to men. As a result, critics have often claimed, using
this kind of argument, that women are both the monsters and the
victims within the film. They are not only a sexual threat who need
to be punished, but also the domineering mother, Mrs Bates, who
destroys her son. As Biskind puts it:

> The trouble with Norman is that he grew up in a matriarchal family.
> Norman is a momma's boy, dominated by a bad (overprotective)
> mom, not a bad dad, as in an orthodox corporate liberal film.[12]

Another sign of the film's conservatism, for Biskind, is its presentation of experts. The psychologist may explain everything at the end,
but neither 'the cops nor the docs can do the job' of solving the
crime: 'The cops are too dumb, and although the psychiatrist may
understand Norman's crime, he can't act'.[13] As a result, *Psycho*
'relies on Sam and Lila, do-it-yourselfers independent of both the
cops and the docs', to solve the mystery of Marion's disappearance.
Biskind does acknowledge that it 'would be a mistake to call Sam
and Lila vigilantes', but none the less, he claims that this is 'the
direction *Psycho* ... was taking'.[14]

However, Biskind's position has several problems though, not least that it contradicts other arguments within his book. If he criticises *Psycho* for its supposed attack on non-traditional gender roles, he is just as critical of those 1950s films, such as *Giant*, which had 'encouraged boys and girls to exchange roles'.[15] These other films are dismissed as glibly as *Psycho* through a simple and automatic association with the new values of therapeutic liberalism which urged social conformity and consensus.

It is also ironic that while Sam and Lila have to rely on their own feelings and resources to catch Norman, and have to ignore the wisdom of experts, Biskind sees these very features as a sign of the film's conservatism. Elsewhere he had criticised 1950s horror exactly because people were told to rely on experts and not to act on their own initiative.

The reference to 'mom' is also significant within Biskind's discussion of the film and it is an allusion to the ideas of Philip Wylie whose critique of 'momism' is often referred to in studies of 1950s culture. For Wylie, in his bestseller *A Generation of Vipers* (1942), it was 'Mom' who bred conformity in the American population. It was women who had a hold on American culture, and were raising dependent and conformist men. It was the pampering of children by mom which emasculated men.[16] However, if Norman is a 'momma's boy', it is difficult to see Mrs Bates (at least as Norman imagines her) as the representative of the kinds of liberal, Spockian child-rearing practices to which Wylie and others objected. Mrs Bates, as Norman recalls her, is a tyrannical, dominating conservative who refuses to indulge her son's childish curiosity or pamper him. She refuses to tolerate his sexual curiosity and continually taunts him for not being enough of a man. If anything, it is Norman that doesn't want to grow up, who doesn't want to break with his mother, and who eventually kills her for 'getting a life' which is not centred around his childish demands.

Indeed, as Tania Modleski has pointed out, one of the problems with the debates around Hitchcock's films is that critics have tended to pigeon-hole them unconvincingly. As Modleski puts it:

> what I want to argue is *neither* that Hitchcock is utterly misogynistic *nor* that he is largely sympathetic to women and their plight in patriarchy, but that his work is characterised by a thoroughgoing ambivalence about femininity – which explains why it has been possible for

critics to argue with some plausibility on either side of the issue. It also, of course, explains why the issue can never be resolved and why, when one is reading criticism defending or attacking Hitchcock's treatment of women, one continually experiences a feeling of 'yes, but ...'[17]

Unfortunately, Modleski seems to end up in a position which is not dissimilar from those that see Hitchcock's work as purely misogynistic. Drawing on recent work on masculinity, she acknowledges Hitchcock's preoccupations with male masochism and his 'ambivalent' attitudes towards women, but she ultimately argues that his films simply allow men to 'simultaneously experience and deny an identification with passive, victimised female characters'. For Modleski, 'the male finds it necessary to repress certain "feminine" aspects of himself and to project these exclusively onto the woman, who does the suffering for both of them'.[18] This position, which is also very similar to Carol Clover's work on the slasher films which followed *Psycho*, not only concentrates almost exclusively on the pleasures which these films offer to men, but also tends to reaffirm the notion that these pleasures must ultimately reproduce patriarchal notions of masculinity. This latter feature is less true of Carol Clover's work which seems, despite its theoretical claims, to be far more fascinated by, and sympathetic to, the films which she discusses, but Clover's work still reveals some of the perplexing contradictions inherent in this approach.

At the opening of her book, *Men, Women and Chainsaws*, Clover discusses Brian De Palma's *Carrie* (1976), and asks, 'to whom does this tale appeal?' Her answer is interesting in so far as it reverses some of the assumptions in psychoanalytic feminist criticism. Usually it has been argued that male viewers cannot identify with women in films, but only with the male protagonist. However, Clover argues, *Carrie* appeals to men because the boys who go through the ritual humiliations of adolescence will recognise themselves 'in a girl who finds herself bleeding from the crotch in the gym shower, pelted with tampons, and sloshed with pig's blood at the senior prom'.[19] The awareness of such cross-gender identification is an important contribution to the analysis of film, and horror in particular, but strangely, Clover still seems to suggest that the pleasures of horror can *only* appeal to the masculine viewer. If Clover argues that boys can identify with the figure of *Carrie* because they suffer from victimisation, she oddly claims that *only* they suffer in this way; forms of victimisation, it is suggested, are 'things boys do to each other not by and large things girls do to each other or that boys do to girls'.[20] This seems a very surprising statement, even if she has set up specific forms of victimisation as threats of castration. Indeed, while she argues that boys will identify with *Carrie* because she is a victim, *Carrie* is a victim of the viciousness of other girls. To claim that girls do not taunt, bully or humiliate one another in school seems to be very special pleading. Indeed, Stephen King's original novel has been very popular with female readers for exactly this reason, and as Don Herron claims in a discussion of a radio survey about books and authors, 'most of the call-ins came from teenage girls, and the majority of them voted for ... King himself [as] unquestionably the greatest writer to ever live'.[21]

Clover also makes the rather odd claim that the gender constructions within horror are a hangover from earlier stages of human history in which men and women were not seen as 'opposites', but simply 'inversions' of the same sex. As Clover puts it, horror

> stories ... stem from the one-sex era, and for all their updating, they still carry with them, to a greater or lesser degree, a premodern sense of sexual difference. Horror may in fact be the premier repository of one-sex reasoning in our time (science fiction running a close second).[22]

It seems odd to claim that the complex gender roles of the contemporary horror film from *Psycho* onwards are simply a throwback to an earlier era, rather than the product of changing gender relations within contemporary society.

Indeed, Andrew Tudor has argued that these features need to be understood within a far broader social and historical context. One of the problems with many of the accounts discussed previously is their reliance on various forms of psychoanalysis and their consequent emphasis on gender and the family. This is not to suggest that such issues are unimportant, but simply to take issue with the implications of critics such as Wood who define the family as the central and fundamental institution of American society.

Indeed Tudor challenges Wood's claims concerning the emergence of 'family horror' from *Psycho* onwards, and he argues that it is impossible to see a homogeneous depiction of the family within contemporary horror. As he points out, just as often as the family is presented as the source of problems, it is also presented as an image of community which is used as a 'convenient and powerful focus of audience identification'.[23] Nor are such films necessarily conservative, as Wood seems to imply. In such cases, it is always necessary to examine how such positive families are defined and to which forces they act as an opposition or a defence. Indeed, in many of these films and novels, even the families which are in the process of dissolution are under threat not simply from their own internal psychic tensions, but due to the ways in which the family itself works in relationship to, and is in part a product of, a wide array of different institutions: the state, industry, consumerism, etc. Indeed, Tudor argues that so-called 'family horror' needs to be 'seen in perspective as one strand in the modern genre's reformulation of the horror movie universe'.[24]

Tudor describes this reformulation as a shift from secure to paranoid horror. Like Wood, he sees this shift as a process which, in part, relocates the horror more directly within the landscape of naturalistic, everyday settings, but he argues that it is not simply a crisis of confidence in the family. Instead, it involves a whole array of practices and institutions. For Tudor, the key feature of paranoid horror is therefore 'self-doubt', whether on a global or personal level. In secure horror, while social practices or institutions may have caused the problems in the first place, it is claimed, there was still a faith in society's ability to resolve matters. But in paranoid horror, 'the nature and the course of the threat are out of human control'.[25] Experts are not only a common source of the problems, but prove routinely ineffective in providing any adequate solution.

For this reason, the focus of horror narratives shift from the figure of the expert to the victim or the monster, and as a result, women become increasing central to the genre. Tudor does suggest that this latter development may be more apparent than real, and this may not be the place to resolve such arguments, but in 'a period of victim centrality' in which experts have become threatening or redundant, it is unsurprising that female characters have become increasingly central to horror narratives, and that they are required to rely on their own resources rather than a male hero. If the monster and the victim become the primary foci of horror narratives, Tudor also points out that these figures are frequently blurred or combined. Many central characters are both monster and victim, and this is related to one of the key characteristics of paranoid horror. The crisis of faith in paranoid horror not only leads to doubts about society's institutions, but also about personal identity. The distinction between order and disorder becomes blurred and uncertain, and the abnormal or monstrous frequently erupts from *within* the normal, rather than invading it from *without*.

It is not simply that, as we have seen, the threat may be the result of existing institutions and practices, but even a feature of our own intimate and personal selves. As Tudor puts it:

> Threats emerge without warning from the disordered psyche or from disease, possessing us and destroying our very humanity. Lacking control of our inner selves, we have no means of resisting, and there is a certain inevitability to humanity's final defeat.[26]

As a result, *Psycho* needs to be seen within this context. Its concerns are as much with general crisis of identity within contemporary society as they are with the family, whether patriarchal or matriarchal in character.

These claims lead Tudor to make a distinction between madness and psychosis, the former being more closely associated with secure horror and the latter being more closely associated with paranoid horror. His claim is that while madness is 'framed within an essentially melodramatic context' and its victims are usually 'grandiloquently off their heads', psychosis brings the problem much closer to home. It is placed within the everyday and is depicted in far more naturalistic terms. Hence the problem with psychosis is that it is '*potentially* present within all of us', and worse than that, as with Norman Bates in *Psycho*, we may be completely unaware of it. As Tudor puts it:

> while those suffering from 'madness' are invariably seen to be living in a different world from the rest of us, a world of heightened perceptions, those suffering from 'psychosis' are placed firmly within the same conceptual domain as the sane. Insanity, here, is an emergent feature of the prosaic everyday.[27]

While Tudor emphasises that these distinctions are 'ideal types' or tendencies, and that specific films will usually occupy the middle ground between them, there are still several problems with these formulations.

Most significant is the issue of explanation. Again Tudor is careful to point out that the important feature within contemporary depictions of psychosis is not whether the explanations offered by the films are actually convincing as psychological explanations, 'but the fact that these films conceptualise insanity as caused at all'.[28] However, not only is it the case that, as Tudor himself notes, many of the films which followed *Psycho* conformed to the more melo-dramatic portrayals which he refers to as madness, but also that in contemporary culture, the serial killer is usually overtly presented as defying rational explanation. Psychiatry cannot deal with Michael Myers in *Halloween* (1978), nor can it deal with Hannibal Lecter or the other serial killers in the novels of Thomas Harris and their film versions. Indeed, in *The Silence of the Lambs* (1988), Lecter pointedly mocks the FBI's attempt to analyse him:

> Nothing happened to me, Officer Starling. I happened. You can't reduce me to a set of influences. You've given up good and evil for behaviourism, Officer Starling. You've got everyone in moral dignity pants – nothing is ever anybody's fault. Look at me, Officer Starling. Can you stand to say I'm evil. Am I evil, Officer Starling?[29]

Tudor is right that the threat seems to be internal and can unpre-dictably erupt within anyone, but it is this very feature which makes explanation relatively redundant and useless. In *Psycho*, the film may present the psychiatrist's explanation for Norman's psychosis, but it still doesn't really help. Audiences are still left with the ques-tion, 'Why him?' Why, of all the young men with overbearing moth-ers or fathers, does one become a bizarre killer? It is this problem which makes the psychopathic killer so fascinating and frightening. It could be anyone.

It is this problem which leads Robin Wood and others into some strange, contradictory arguments. Wood criticises the slasher films which follow *Halloween* because, he claims, unlike *Psycho*, they do not give a social explanation for their killers. They simply present them as evil and other, rather than the product of American society itself. In this way, it is argued they do not imply a critique of Amer-ican society and its institutions, and hence do not require society to change the ways in which it is organised. However, when he actu-ally discusses *Psycho* in detail, he is profoundly embarrassed by the explanation at the end of the film, and actually argues that it is used as a trick to give the audience a temporary and ultimately unsatisfy-ing sense of security:

> The psychiatrist's 'explanation' has been much criticised, but it has its

function. It crystallizes for us our tendency to evade the implications of the film, by converting Norman into a mere 'case,' hence something we can easily put from us. The psychiatrist, glib and complacent, reassures us. But Hitchcock crystallizes this for us merely to force us to reject it. We shall see on reflection that the 'explanation' ignores as much as it explains (the murder as symbolic rape, for example). But we are not allowed to wait for a chance to reflect: our vague feelings of dissatisfaction are promptly brought to consciousness by our final confrontation with Norman ...[30]

In this way, even Wood ultimately rejects the desire for an explanation of the killer's actions.

Indeed, as Tudor makes clear, the 'uncharacterised psychotic' may fit into the world of paranoid horror far more neatly than the 'characterised psychotic':

> In 'uncharacterised psychosis', however, insanity is no longer subject to reason, either as understanding or control. It is now something 'other', something strictly inexplicable, and the once-intelligible psychotic has metamorphosed into an irresistible boogey man lurking within our homes, our nightmares, and our selves.[31]

In this situation, the traditional forces of order and control become ineffective and redundant. Psychology cannot deal with Michael Myers or Thomas Harris's serial killers, and all that is left is for Myers' psychologist to shoot to kill, and for Will Graham and Clarice Starling to use their imaginations so that they can think like the killer or his victims. Rational procedures get one nowhere, and all that is left is our own irrational resources.

But this raises another problem with Tudor's account. For Tudor, the threat of psychosis is 'brought forth by the sleep of reason, not its attractions'.[32] It is the product of 'the dangerous excesses of human passion' harboured within the psyche.[33] However, this seems to miss an important point within his own work and within the texts themselves. If paranoid horror is founded on a blurring of distinctions between the normal and the abnormal, order and chaos, it is also based on a blurring of distinctions between the rational and the irrational, the conscious and the unconscious. Many, if not most, of the killers which come after *Psycho* (and *Psycho* itself is not an exception here) are not driven by 'excesses of passion', but are presented as blank, mechanistic automatons. They do not seek to satisfy sexual lusts, but murderously to deny and repress them. Indeed 'excesses of passion' would seem to characterise the madman not the psychotic.

However, Tudor's study does offer an alternative way of approaching the crisis of identity and the psychotic killer's relationship to it. As he argues:

> by the late fifties most capitalist cultures were already accelerating away from post-war repression and towards a market and commodity driven concern with sexuality and personal gratification. The vision of insanity embedded in *Psycho* and *Peeping Tom* is, on this account, no more than the dark side of that development, the new 'price of progress' in a genre world where mad science had ceased to play that role.[34]

While this account still emphasises issues of sexuality and personal gratification in a manner that returns Tudor to his claims about the psychotic's 'excesses or passion', it can be read in a quite different way.

In the early 1950s, as has been argued in part one, there seemed to be a clear distinction between the rational and the irrational. In films such as *The Thing from Another World*, characters could resist conformity and rationalisation through the irrationality of desire and emotion. Desire and emotion within this period were seen as a potential threat to the project of scientific-technical rationality. However, by the late 1950s, it became increasingly common for critics of contemporary society to claim that sexuality and emotion were no longer simply a threat to rationalisation, but that they were actually increasingly organised and controlled through the new consumer culture. The study which most immediately comes to mind in this context is, of course, Vance Packard's *The Hidden Persuaders*.[35]

However, if manipulation and control were now seen as more deeply internalised, this situation presented problems for earlier formulations about the nature of resistance. If one's unconscious desires were now shaped by consumer culture, it became difficult to find a point of resistance to rationality and control. Rationality and control now ordered and controlled the irrational, and as a result, it became difficult to identify a secure point of resistance. Indeed, in resisting one might actually be doing exactly what the system wanted one to do. In this way, neither the conscious nor the unconscious mind was trustworthy. The self had been so thoroughly penetrated that it was virtually impossible to distinguish the self from the other, one's own desires from those which had been implanted by consumer culture.

This problem has become the subject of a whole series of texts. In *Rosemary's Baby* (1968), for example, Rosemary believes that she is resisting the Satanic coven by protecting her baby. She thinks that they want to sacrifice it as a part of their rituals. But at the end, Rosemary discovers that her child is actually the anti-Christ and that in fighting to protect it, she is performing the very role for which the coven has chosen her. Another example might be *Total Recall* (1990) in which Doug Quaid believes that he is a secret agent who has defected to the rebels. Unfortunately for the rebels, at the end of the film, Quaid discovers that this identity is simply a memory-implant and that while he believed he was resisting the tyranny on Mars, he was actually performing a role programmed by the dictator of Mars, a role which has enabled the forces of tyranny to crush the revolution.

In *Psycho*, Norman faces similar problems. He too is a victim of internalised forces that he does not comprehend and therefore cannot resist. Like Rosemary and Quaid, the enemy is no longer simply external, but is now fully internalised; and like these other two characters, his best intentions only threaten to bring about death, destruction and disaster for both himself and others.

However, Tudor still sees *Psycho* as the originator of these new tendencies within horror and, as with other accounts, this is largely due to his concentration on film, and his lack of interest in other forms of horror fiction. Indeed, when one examines the forerunners and contemporaries of *Psycho*, the text not only looks less original and innovative than is often claimed, but other aspects of the horror film, such as Roger Corman's Poe cycle, begin to look a lot closer to *Psycho* than Tudor and others have suggested.

Notes

1 David Bordwell, *Making Meaning: Inference and Rhetoric in the Interpretation of Cinema* (Cambridge, Mass.: Harvard University Press, 1989), p. 235.
2 Robin Wood, *Hollywood from Vietnam to Reagan* (New York: Columbia University Press, 1986), p. 77.
3 Laura Mulvey, 'Visual Pleasure and Narrative Cinema' in Bill Nichols,

ed., *Movies and Methods, Vol. II* (Berkeley: University of California Press, 1985).

4 Stephen Neale, *Genre* (London: BFI, 1980); and Barbara Creed, *The Monstrous-Feminine: Film, Feminism, Psychoanalysis* (London: Routledge, 1993).

5 Wood, *Hollywood from Vietnam to Reagan*, p. 87.

6 *Ibid.*, p. 75.

7 *Ibid.*

8 Creed, *The Monstrous-Feminine*.

9 Peter Biskind, *Seeing is Believing: How Hollywood Taught Us to Stop Worrying and Love the Fifties* (London: Pluto, 1983), p. 338.

10 *Ibid.*, p. 341.

11 *Ibid.*

12 *Ibid.*, p. 340.

13 *Ibid.*, p. 341.

14 *Ibid.*

15 *Ibid.*, p. 340.

16 Philip Wylie, *Generation of Vipers* (New York: Rinehart and Co., 1946).

17 Tania Modleski, *The Woman Who Knew Too Much: Hitchcock and Feminist Theory* (New York: Methuen, 1988), p. 3.

18 *Ibid.*, p. 13.

19 Carol J. Clover, *Men, Women and Chainsaws: Gender in the Modern Horror Film* (London: British Film Institute, 1992), p. 5.

20 *Ibid.*, p. 4.

21 Don Herron, 'King: The Good, the Bad and the Academic', in Tim Underwood and Chuck Miller, eds, *Kingdom of Fear: The World of Stephen King* (London: New English Library, 1986), p. 135.

22 Clover, *Men, Women and Chainsaws*, p. 15.

23 Andrew Tudor, *Monsters and Mad Scientists: A Cultural History of the Horror Movie* (Oxford: Blackwell, 1987), p. 75.

24 *Ibid.*, p. 129.

25 *Ibid.*, p. 103.

26 *Ibid.*, p. 103.

27 *Ibid.*, p. 187.

28 *Ibid.*, p. 57.

29 Thomas Harris, *The Silence of the Lambs* (London: William Heinemann, 1988), p. 16.

30 Robin Wood, *Hitchcock's Films Revisited* (New York: Columbia University Press, 1989), p. 149.

31 Tudor, *Monsters and Mad Scientists*, p. 207.

32 *Ibid.*, p. 184.

33 *Ibid.*

34 *Ibid.*, p. 192.
35 Vance Packard, *The Hidden Persuaders* (Harmondsworth: Penguin, 1960).

Norman Bates: monster or victim in the film version of Robert Bloch's novel *Psycho* (1959).

Chapter 7

Self-division, compulsion and murder:
the fiction of Robert Bloch

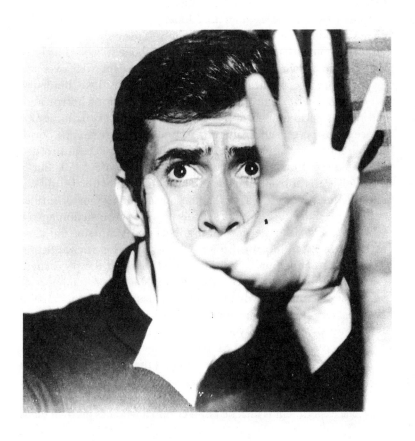

f, as was discussed in part two, Matheson was writing stories concerning a crisis of identity in the late 1950s, even *Psycho*'s concern with gender confusion was predated by Matheson's close friend and associate, Charles Beaumont, whose story, 'Miss Gentilbelle' was published in 1955. It concerns a young boy whose mother raises him as a girl and denies him any knowledge of sexual difference. Confused and uncertain about sexual difference, the boy is also confused and uncertain about his own identity, but his mother prevents him from pursuing his curiosity. She kills and tortures small animals in front of him whenever she feels that he is becoming too inquisitive, and uses the trauma of these acts to dissuade him from asking any more questions. Eventually, the child is driven to insanity. He brutally murders his mother and is reduced to babbling incoherence in which any sense of identity is lost.

Whether these stories influenced Bloch, or were themselves influenced by him, is unclear, and probably ultimately unimportant. However, Bloch had been writing stories about split personalities and people driven by murderous compulsions for well over ten years before the publication of *Psycho* in 1959. Like Bradbury, Bloch began writing in the Lovecraftian tradition of horror and, during this period, his fiction was generally set in exotic locations, concerned strange, supernatural forces, and was written in a florid, melodramatic style.[1] Also like Bradbury, Bloch had begun to distance himself from this type of writing well before 1950. But if much of 1950s horror came out of a hybridisation of horror and science fiction, Bloch's was influential through his horror/thriller hybrids. He did write science fiction and science fiction/horror which was similar to the work of Bradbury and Matheson, but most of his novels were horror/thriller hybrids. Even his science fiction and science fiction/horror writing shared many of the preoccupations of his other fiction. For example, while he wrote a number of stories about robots in which distinctions between the human and the non-human were questioned, these stories revealed a far greater interest in psychology, psychiatry and psychoanalysis than can be found in either Bradbury or Matheson.

'Almost Human' (1943), for example, is the story of a robot who has been designed so that it will not simply follow programming but will learn like a human child and so develop its own identity. However, the experiment is hijacked by a criminal who has his own plans for the robot, plans which go horribly wrong by the end of the story. In this way the story is about the struggles over the robot's psychological development, and its responses to its 'family' environment.[2]

In 'Dead End Doctor' (1956), on the other hand, the last psychoanalyst finds himself in a world that appears to have rendered him redundant. People take drugs to control their emotional states, and many of the old causes of psychological problems have been dealt with. In this world, robots have taken over most forms of manual labour and the world seems rational and harmonious. However, all is not as orderly as it appears, and the psychoanalyst is able to build a new career for himself when he discovers that it is now robots, the functionaries of the new rational order, who are going psychotic.[3]

None the less, Bloch's most influential stories were those which concentrated on the psychology of criminals, particularly murderers, while developing the horrific and gothic aspects of the crime thriller. Indeed, Bloch's most respected and influential story prior to *Psycho* was 'Yours Truly, Jack the Ripper' (1943) which combined horror elements, such as a murderer who kills in order to prolong his own life, with Bloch's long-running fascination with mass murderers and sadistic, serial killers.[4] (Indeed, Jack the Ripper is not only discussed in several other stories by Bloch, but in 1984, he returned to this figure in *The Night of the Ripper*, though this later version discards the supernatural elements of the earlier story and emphasises the psychology of the killer.)[5] While 'Yours Truly, Jack the Ripper' does not play up the psychological angle found in other examples of Bloch's work, much of his fiction is concerned with characters who are uncontrollably compelled to kill.

In his first novel, *The Scarf* (1947), for example, the main character, Dan Morley, tries to stop himself from killing, but finds that he is incapable of doing so. He knows that he does not kill for money, or any other rational motivation. Instead, he claims that 'It's like having someone else inside of you, taking over.'[6] His killing is an unconscious compulsion which he cannot consciously control, a form of compulsion which reduces him to a mere mechanism which is controlled by forces which he cannot even comprehend. At one point, the gesture of drawing out the scarf with which he kills victims is described as 'automatic' by Dan, a term which implies mechanistic behaviour.

Even in cases where the killer seems to be merely killing as part of some broader criminal scheme, the suggestion is that this scheme only operates as an excuse for the killings; that the killer is simply rationalising a psychological compulsion which cannot be controlled. This is made clear in *The Kidnapper* (1954), a novel which Bloch considers to be amongst his best work. In this story, the kidnapper's scheme and his later murders seem to be merely motivated by a desire for easy money, but it gradually becomes clear that it is actually the product of psychological complexes produced by his family and his broader social context. The killer is actually in pursuit of 'social recognition', and the money is simply an excuse for a crime which is unconsciously designed to attract public notoriety and give the kidnapper a feeling of power and importance.[7] The same can be seen in Bloch's fictionalised account of the exploits of H. H. Holmes, *American Gothic*, where the killer believes that he is merely killing for money, but obviously gains a sadistic satisfaction from his grisly activities.[8]

All of these killers have a problem with their sense of self. Selfhood is often associated with the conscious perceptions of one's own identity and actions, but these perceptions are constantly shown to be precarious, unstable and problematic. Bloch's characters are not only prone to unconscious compulsions of which they may not even be aware, but many of these characters even perform acts which they attribute to another identity entirely. Indeed Bloch's preoccupations with multiple personalities goes back at least twenty-four years before *Psycho*. For example, in 'The Suicide in the Study' (1935), one of Bloch's Lovecraftian contributions, a man believes that he can divide his good self from his bad self, a belief that is ultimately confirmed but results in hideous self-destruction.[9] His bad self turns out to be a giant, unreasoning brute intent on his destruction while his good self is only a puny weakling which cannot defend itself. This story clearly draws on Stephenson's *The Strange Case of Dr Jekyll and Mr Hyde*,[10] and its split personality is at least aware that the other is actually only an aspect of the self.

However, in 'Lucy comes to Stay' (1952), Bloch prefigured the main concerns of *Psycho*. The story involves a woman, Vi, who feels imprisoned by her husband and nurse. Her only friend is Lucy, the only figure that Vi believes that she can trust. But in helping Vi to escape her husband, Lucy deliberately kills Vi's husband, a crime of which Vi is entirely unaware, at least until she is finally caught and it is revealed that Lucy doesn't really exist except as one half of Vi's split personality.[11] A similar situation is also present in 'The Real Bad Friend' (1957). In this story, the main character, George, has a best friend called Roderick who plots to destroy George's wife. George keeps trying to stop Roderick, but again it is finally revealed that Roderick does not really exist except as an aspect of George's own divided mind.[12]

Indeed the instability of identity is constantly emphasised within Bloch's fiction. In *The Scarf*, Dan may know that he is the killer, but he still complains that there is no access to reality except through words, and that even 'you' is a word. One only has a sense of a private self through the public medium of language, and whatever other identity one might possess remains entirely inaccessible to others and even to one's own conscious mind. As Dan puts it:

> Your a big word yourself.
> Only deep inside there's a 'you' who doesn't need words, can't use them. A 'you' that cannot talk to others, has no communication. And you try so hard to get through to the others, but its no use ...[13]

This passage is particularly interesting given that it is taken from Dan's own secret diary, 'The Black Notebooks', in which he is trying to analyse and understand himself, and as such it reveals the deep-seated problems of self-division, even in a character such as Dan who is not menaced by a clearly separate identity such as Vi's 'Lucy', George's 'Roderick' or Norman's 'Mother'. In this passage, Dan is writing to himself while trying to identify himself. As a result, there are essentially three Dans: the Dan who writes; the Dan who is addressed by the writing; and the Dan who is written about. This is doubly emphasised by the use of the term 'you' to describe the Dan which is written about, rather than the term 'I'. The Dan that writes is trying to identify the Dan which is written about for the Dan who is addressed, and in this situation, the self is not identified with the self which writes (I) but with the self that is addressed (you).

Even when the term 'I' is invoked, Bloch emphasises issues of self-division. In *The Will to Kill* (1954), for example, the main character is Tom Kendall, a man who is prone to blackouts in which he continues to function, but is later unable to remember what he has done or what has happened to him. At one point, describing one such blackout, he states:

> Then, without any warning, the roof fell in, the curtain came down, and I was lost. 'I' was lost. Not the person that walked, talked, ate,

drank, functioned on the surface level. I'm talking about the real 'I' –
the observed Observer.[14]

Here there is no sense of self without self-division. The self is identified as that which is conscious of itself, and hence both the subject
and the object of consciousness; both that which observes and that
which is observed.

Indeed, the problems of the self's existence as both the subject
and the object of action, whether conscious or physical, is essential
to Bloch's concerns with psychology. The individual's relationship
to the outer world is entirely problematic and can be experienced
either as one in which the individual acts upon, directs and controls
circumstance, or as one in which the individual is acted upon,
directed and controlled. In this way, the individual is caught
between feelings of omnipotence and the fear of utter powerlessness, and it is this situation which frequently troubles Bloch's characters. However, it is a situation which is further intensified by the
individual's realisation of his or her own psychological construction. Either that construction can be seen as that which is unique
and individual – the true self – or else as a force which constrains
and even undermines one's conscious decisions; as a force which
determines one's self from within and so threatens one's sense of
identity. As a result, Bloch's fiction often features characters driven
to prove their own omnipotence through violence and domination,
but, ironically, these very drives are often unconscious impulses
which threaten and even destroy the conscious individual's sense of
control and sense of self.

In *The Scarf*, for example, Dan complains that freedom is an illusion:

> Looking back, looking back and trying to figure what made you that
> way, several things stand out in your mind. There may have been more
> than several. Maybe there were a hundred. Maybe a thousand. Small
> events, little episodes, all pointing you in the same direction, so you
> might think you had free will when you wobbled from side to side on
> the track, but there were no switches for you to throw, no turnings to
> choose.[15]

Dan's psychology is shaped by events over which he has little or no
control, but he is also at the mercy of that psychological construction. It is his unconscious hatred of women, and his need to assert

his power and control of them, which defies his conscious control and eventually results in his own destruction.

For this reason, Steve Collins, the main character of *The Kidnapper*, is continually telling himself that he must control himself. He must survey and dominate his own emotions in order rationally to control the outer world, but his own destruction is ensured by his failure to understand that his conscious attempts at rational control are themselves the products of unconscious emotional desires of which he is entirely unaware and ultimately unable to control.

These concerns with control are also related to the recurring preoccupation with the activity of collecting within Bloch's fiction. Indeed, while Tudor claims that the psychotic killer of contemporary horror is driven by 'excesses of passion', most of Bloch's killers are presented as extremely analytical in their procedures. Their frequent preoccupation with collections is an attempt to order and control their world. Indeed it is often an attempt to convert the animate into the inanimate; to convert those beings which might act upon the self into mere things that the self can order and control. For example, while G. G. Gregg in *American Gothic* (1974) believes that he is merely killing for profit, this belief is revealed to be a self-delusion through his obsessive dissection of his victims whose body parts he preserves and labels as part of a grisly collection. Indeed there is a strong connection made between collecting and sadism within Bloch's stories. In *The Will to Kill*, for example, the sadist, Mingo, is an obsessive collector of materials which relate to his obsession with torture and murder, and in *The Scarf*, these issues are made still clearer through Dan's writing.

He too is a collector, but he collects through the act of writing. Each of his novels is based upon a particular female associate whose life he details before finally killing them. As the psychologist, Ruppert, explains, both his need to write and his need to kill are part of an unconscious desire to dominate and control women, a desire which is itself motivated by an unconscious fear and hatred of women. However, Ruppert detects this hatred through the analytic detailing of the female characters within Dan's fiction. As Ruppert puts it:

> Its there, in the book. More than detachment, cynicism, objectivity –
> I can sense pure hatred in your descriptions and the attitudes behind
> them. Actually, you don't describe. You dissect. Sadistically.[16]

Indeed, while many critics have seen the story of *Psycho* as an unconscious attempt to dominate and control women, *The Scarf* is directly and self-consciously about this process. Dan writes about women in order to give himself a feeling of control over them. He converts them into things which he can study, detail and analyse. But once he has finished a novel, he no longer sees the woman concerned as a real person but simply as a thing, a thing that he must finally kill in order to complete the process. As Ruppert puts it: 'You write about women to exorcise them – and completed the exorcism with the scarf.'[17]

However, the characteristics of the killer and of the other characters within Bloch's novels are not very different. While Dan's murderous impulses are connected with the analytical detailing of his female characters, the same features are also associated with the psychologist, Ruppert. Dan tells Pat, the woman whom he loves, that Ruppert cannot understand feelings, but can only label things. As a result, Ruppert is associated with a compulsive need to dominate and control the world, and Dan claims that he is incapable of relating to women as equals, but only knows how to adopt a paternalistic role in relation to them. In *The Will to Kill*, on the other hand, while Mingo's sadism is associated with his status as a collector, the hero, Tom, is also associated with collecting. He runs a shop for collectors and even catalogues the collectors who frequent his shop. As Tom claims:

> Sherlock Holmes would have loved my business. Dealing as I did in stamps, coins, magazines and second-hand books, I got an odd assortment of customers. After a time, I was able to size them up and make a pretty reasonable snap judgement. One look usually told me what the newcomer was seeking. I could even refine it down to categories within categories.[18]

Indeed while Tom is not the killer in the novel, he too is prone to unconscious processes which he cannot control, processes that are responsible for his blackouts.

The same is true of most, if not all, of Bloch's characters. Indeed, in a passage which he has used in a number of different contexts, he claims:

> There is no place in this modern world for ogres or bogey men. We are well aware that we deal with nothing more alarming than sadists, psychopaths, paranoiacs, schizophrenics, manic-depressives, necro-

philes, zooerasts, pyromaniacs and other deviants and borderline neu-
rotics whose combined total is probably less than one-third of the
entire population.[19]

This passage is typical of Bloch's cynical humour. The estimate that
one third of the population are actually dangerously disturbed is
undercut by the 'probably less' which also suggests the alternative:
'possibly more'. But even then this third are only the most disturbed
manifestations, and the strong suggestion throughout Bloch's career
has been that normal everyday life in the modern world has created
a disturbed population of which the criminally insane are only the
tip of the iceberg.

Indeed most of Bloch's fiction emphasises that the disturbed
killers of his stories are merely the most sensational manifestations
of the more mundane horrors of everyday life in the modern world.
Steve Collins in *The Kidnapper*, for example, points out that the rich
are little different from the criminals, except that the former never
got caught. Even when the child that he has kidnapped dies, it is
claimed:

> The worst part about finding the body is that they know the kid is
> dead, and the heat is really turned on. Everybody goes crazy: parents,
> police, the FBI, and the whole damn country. The way the papers play
> it up, you'd think kids weren't getting killed every day by reckless dri-
> vers and stuff.[20]

The media only concentrates on certain horrors and so repress the
more mundane horrors of everyday life.

Nor is this position simply the killer's justification for his own
actions. In *The Couch* (1962), the psychologist muses about the fact
that despite the publicity given to the serial killer who is lose in the
city, no-one complains about the army's violence,[21] and in latter
novels, such as *Night-World* (1974), *The Night of the Ripper* (1984)
and *The Jekyll Legacy* (1990), Bloch himself emphasises the forgotten inequalities and horrors whose scale dwarfs his killer's actions.[22]

As a result, Bloch places his killer's compulsions within the broad
context of social life, rather than simply concentrating on the context of the family. These compulsions are the product of many different types of traumatic experiences, and in this context, *Psycho*'s
use of the mother is, as with Matheson's work, only one cause
among many. *Psycho*'s concern with the crisis of identity may use
the figure of the mother, but it does not simply emerge out of anx-

ieties about 'momism' or the matriarchal family. While the killer in
The Scarf is compelled by attitudes towards sex which are associated
with his relationship to his mother, the killer in *The Kidnapper* is
motivated by his relationship to his father. The same is also true of
the killer in *The Couch* whose killings are the product of a deep-
seated hatred of father figures.

Indeed, Bloch has been highly sympathetic to matriarchal societies as is illustrated by his science fiction novel, *Ladies Day* (1968).
In this novel, a man from the twentieth century, Harry Collins,
wakes up to find himself nearly two hundred years in the future, and
in a society which is now dominated by women. Harry is initially
horrified and bemused by this new order, and the novel plays upon
the expectation that it will obey the science fiction conventions of
the period; that he will join the resistance and overthrow the 'un-
natural' and 'totalitarian' order. However, at the end of the narrative, he actually accepts that the new order may have something to
offer, and works to protect it, even though this action will consign
him to the role of his partner's supportive helper and objectified
playmate. But as he concludes at the end of the novel:

> Maybe it would feel funny wearing ermine-trimmed slacks at first. But
> it was worth a trial. Men had had their chance – thousands of chances
> – and they'd made a mess of things. Now why not let them take it easy
> and play a subordinate role for a while and see if women could do any
> better. At least go slow until they could swing the pendulum back and
> try to find a permanent equality near the middle of the road.[23]

Indeed, Harry is persuaded by some very pertinent critiques of masculinity, particularly a critique of the 'warrior concept'. Although it
is pointed out that this concept may well have been useful in the
early stages of human development, it is argued that it became a
problem as 'civilization advanced and circumstances changed'.

Men were still raised to be 'manly' and 'brave', and came to see
all aspects of life as a competition or struggle for mastery. As Doctor
Lee, a high-ranking member of the new order and Harry's later
partner, puts it:

> Men lived in a world where it was possible to bring peace and plenty
> to all, except for one fact: they persisted in dramatizing every aspect
> of their lives as a competitive struggle. My team against your team, my
> city against your city, my nation against your nation. And even the
> relationship between men and women was commonly called 'the

battle of the sexes' – wasn't it? ... You lived in a world where men 'conquered' and women 'surrendered,' where relations between the sexes were looked upon as a game or a contest of wills.[24]

This 'warrior concept' not only hindered the relations between people in society, but actually led to the threat of global destruction through nuclear warfare.

A similar position can also be found in Bloch's essay, 'Imagination and Social Criticism', which was based on a lecture delivered to the University of Chicago in 1957. The essay starts out by claiming that after World War II, mainstream literature changed so that instead of taking a critical stand in relation to their society and culture, 'Writers suddenly woke up to reality and forgot all this stupid criticism.'[25] But while it is argued that 'modern social criticism seems just about dead', it is also claimed that science fiction is 'one place where you're still likely to run into it'.[26] However, Bloch is still critical of much of the science fiction writing of his period, and he argues that for all its concern with the totalitarian tendencies of the present, the 'ultimate assumption ... is simply that THE FUTURE HOLDS LITTLE BASIC CHANGE'.[27]

In one sense, Bloch's point is ironic: the totalitarian societies of the future which are envisioned by science fiction are actually little different from modern America, a position which is a critique of the existing *status quo*. But Bloch does have other more genuine criticisms. In a discussion of Heinlein, for example, Bloch argues that despite all the supposed sophistication of Heinlein's discussions of genetic engineering, he 'still subscribes to a rather naive theory – you can't change human nature'.[28] This criticism is mostly directed against Heinlein's preoccupation with competitive masculinity, particularly Heinlein's suggestion that in the future, 'the fighting spirit [will be] preserved because it is biologically useful'.[29]

In response to this position, Bloch claims that Heinlein's position is 'a complete rationalisation', and that 'the fighting spirit' may not only be a particular social manifestation rather than an 'eternal human nature', but also that it may not be desirable at all. As Bloch claims, Heinlein's

> concept of human nature, his concept of desirable attributes, seems to include pugnacity, sensuality and sentimentality in extremis. A survey of anthropology and ethnology might help him to revise his perspective, for human nature is not a constant, or even a clearly-demarcated

concept, and human behaviour can and does alter. Whole civilizations
and cultures can exist and have existed without war or drug-addiction,
and with every variant of patriarchal and matriarchal control. There
is no more reason for supposing that 'Anglish' modes are either superior or better fitted to survive than for one to believe that such well-
established folk-ways as human sacrifice, public execution, slavery,
religious prostitution, group suicide and marriage by capture are
enduring manifestations of human nature. These phenomena have
existed over the world at various times throughout recorded history,
and have played as important a part in the lives of millions of people
as any of the social customs Heinlein chooses as desirable.[30]

Indeed one of Bloch's complaints about much of 1950s science fiction is that its heroes do not have very striking alternatives to offer
in place of the totalitarian orders which they oppose. These heroes
basically fight against tyranny, but only to restore 'the "normal" culture and value-standards of the mass-minds of the twentieth-century'. Bloch is somewhat overstating his case for dramatic affect, but
he is right to claim that there do not seem to be any heroes 'fighting
in defense of incest, homosexuality, free love, nihilism, the Single
Tax, abolition of individual property-rights, euthanasia or the castration of the tonsils of Elvis Presley'.[31]

As a result, Bloch has been a strong critic of those who see human
nature as fixed, and patriarchal society as either natural or positive.
Mrs Bates is not part of a wholesale attack on the changing gender
roles, at least not in Bloch's version of the story. Indeed, within
Bloch's tales, his killer's compulsions are at least as often associated
with general tendencies within modern American society as they are
with their family backgrounds. Indeed, the killer is often seen as a
product of modernity, rather than maternity.

This feature is emphasised at the end of *The Night of the Ripper*
where the young American hero states: 'I'm going back to the
States. At least we have less violence to fear there.' But as his friend
stresses, 'America is young yet … Wait and See.'[32] Indeed these
prophetic remarks are reaffirmed by the last lines of the novel which
suggest that the horrors may not have ended, but only really started.
After all, Bloch's previous novel but one had been *American Gothic*,
the story of an American serial killer, which is set during the
Chicago World's Fair of 1893, only five years after the events in
London referred to in *The Night of the Ripper*.

This association of the killer with modernity may seem to be at odds with other features of the stories. In *The Night of the Ripper*, most chapters begin with an account of some grisly incident in human history from 2300 BC up until the period in which the novel is set, and *American Gothic* ends up with the cynical suggestion that the present is no more 'enlightened' than the 1890s. However, Bloch's cynicism about the process of enlightenment is actually directly related to his association between his serial killers and modernity.

For Bloch, the modern world has not necessarily increased human beings' understanding of their world, but only changed the labels through which it attempts to order and control that world. However, the change from magical or religious account of the world to an essentially rational one is seen as having worrying implications. While Bloch rarely subscribes to magical explanations in his stories, he continually suggests that with the advent of rational and scientific accounts of the world the concept of 'evil' has lost its meaning along with many other aspects of human existence. As Dan stresses, in *The Scarf*, the act of simply labelling him 'crazy doesn't solve anything';[33] it does not explain why he kills. He also refers to Jack the Ripper and other killers, and claims that he likes to think of them as figures 'who dare[d] to dramatize death – give it meaning'.[34] As a result, while Bloch does not accept supernatural explanations for his killer's behaviour, it is frequently implied that rationality may have much to learn from the concept of evil.

Indeed, as with many other figures, Bloch relates his killers' motivations to a more general loss of meaning within the modern world. Often, as has been suggested, his killers are presented as opponents to the hypocracy of modern life, figures who recognise the mundane everyday horrors of the modern world, and refuse to accept them. As the killer in *Night-World* points out, society condones killing and even compels people to kill in times of war, and he vows that he will kill, but not because he has been ordered by others or 'because of something that happened between me and my mother, father, sister, brother, wife'. Instead he will kill because 'it is the nature of man to be free, to resent confinement. It is the nature of man to oppose hypocracy and injustice.'[35] His killings may still be horrific and monstrous within the novel, but he kills because he refuses to be constrained by the meaningless hypocracies of the modern world. Most of Bloch's other killers are less self-conscious and articulate about their actions, but in most cases the killers are still associated with aspects of modernity.

Indeed the serial killer is often associated with the loss of com-munity, and the vast urban landscapes where most people are strangers. In *The Couch*, for example, the detective tracking the killer discusses the problems of finding the 'impulse killer' when all you know about him is that he is an impulse killer, a killer who has had no previous relationship with his victims, and is therefore as difficult to find as a needle in a haystack. However, it is also stressed throughout Bloch's work that even those nearest to one are often strangers now, figures about whom one actually knows very little. Indeed the killer in *The Couch* is not suspected by his landlady who is too busy collecting cuttings about the killings from the newspa-pers, nor even by his own psychoanalyst.

If it is implied that, in the modern world, people are strangers to one another, it is also suggested that their lack of communal ties removes any firm sense of their own identity. Bloch's killers are often drifters of one sort or another; wanderers who have rejected or lost contact with their pasts and are in search of new identities to acquire or construct. This feature is even true of Norman Bates even though he rarely leaves the home in which he was raised as a child and remains tied to his 'Mother'. After all, Norman's problems began when he felt that he was losing his mother, and decided to kill her for abandoning him. Like other characters, Norman has lost his connection to the past, even though the identities which he attempts to construct are ones that will recreate that connection.

Indeed, *American Gothic* directly associates its killer with the spectacles of modernity which draw people away from their old lives and towards the novelties of the new. But this modern world of spectacular novelty is also continually presented as a world of 'make-believe' in which features of the past and of other cultures are decontextualised and reassembled so that they lose their origi-nal meanings and significances. The killer, Gregg, has built a medieval castle in the centre of urban life, but he is also a performer who creates identities for himself in order to attract the attentions of his victims. He is even described as 'very much the boule-vardier',[36] a figure discussed by Poe, Baudelaire and Benjamin[37] who lives in the eyes of the public, but can also remain anonymous for that very reason.

Indeed most of Bloch's killers are associated with masks, whether literal or metaphorical. They are performers who present a mask to the world which disguises aspects of their identities from others and even from themselves. However, Gregg is not the only person who engages in masquerade within *American Gothic*. Almost all the characters are caught up in some form of deception or pretence, and even Crystal, the main character, is a journalist who poses as a secretary in order to investigate Gregg's activities. Crystal also emphasises the double nature of modernity within Bloch's fiction. She is a new woman who has rejected the traditional roles for women within society, and is seeking to create a public space outside the home for both herself and other women. However, this aspect of modernity is not presented negatively. Bloch clearly sympathises with aspects of the feminist cause, and hence his critique of modernity is not simply a conservative call for traditional values.

In his fiction, the dangers of modernity are associated with the ways in which the detached and isolated people who compose modern society become prey to new forms of control, particularly through the media and technology. Again and again, within his fiction, he attacks television and advertising, in both of which he had worked at various stages of his career. In *The Scarf*, for example, Dan is motivated by a desire to enter the in-crowd, the people who 'tell us all how to live and how to work and what to think and worship'.[38] To this end, Dan joins an advertising firm, becomes a popular fiction writer, and finally goes to Hollywood to work on a screenplay.

In *The Kidnapper*, on the other hand, Mr Ranklin, a criminologist discusses the crime of kidnapping with Steve, and claims that it is 'an American crime'. For Ranklin, the professional criminal is no longer motivated primarily by the pursuit of money, but by a desire for status which they have internalised from the media:

> It is no longer enough to be a good husband, a good father, a good crafts-man. If you do not have a Cadillac in the garage, you are a failure. That is the message of modern advertising, that is the new standard of values we accept.[39]

If, for Bloch, advertising internalises a desire for consumer goods as symbols of status, he also claims that it has other effects on people's motivations and sense of identity.

In *The Dead Beat* (1959), for example, one of the characters, Jim Whittacker, is writing a study of the 'youth-fetish'. He claims that in the twentieth century there has been a gradual shift from the status given to age and wisdom to a privileging of youth. However, it is not simply age that is important, but the way in which consumer culture places an emphasis on the values of novelty and newness and has 'debunked the past' in the process. As Jim puts it:

> Gradually advertising and the arts became spokesmen for the youth fetish. The basic appeal was directed to the young – in fashions, cosmetics, products for women. One was youthful if one bought a new car, a new radio, a new refrigerator – owning such products was desirable, and the advertisers did their damnedest to make folks think that the *owners* would become desirable too.[40]

However, Whittacker's claims do not go unchallenged in the book. As Larry Fox, the killer who is also presented as representative of the dangerous aspects of the new generation, points out, there are actually very good reasons why the young no longer respect their elders.

However, if the desire for status and success is internalised through the media, the media also becomes the main way of achieving them. In the end of *Psycho House* (1990), it becomes clear that the killer has been killing in order to attract the media attention which is necessary for his 'material success', while in *The Kidnapper*, Steve's crime is unconsciously motivated by a desire for public notoriety, and he has performed a crime which will create a media sensation.

However, popular media are not the only means through which people's identities are shaped and controlled. Despite his interest in psychoanalysis, Bloch was deeply critical of its methods and its aims. If some of the mysteries in his stories are solved through the use of psychoanalysis, many are actually a result of it. In *Spidersweb* (1954), for example, the main character, Eddie Haines/Judson Roberts, becomes involved in a conspiracy to use psychoanalysis and therapy as a means of dominating and controlling people,[41] and in 'The Screaming People' (1959), the main character discovers that he and other patients have been programmed by his psychoanalyst so that they will unconsciously do the analyst's bidding.[42]

For Bloch, the main problem with psychoanalysis is its aim to adjust people to 'reality', to make them conform. As a result, it is presented as another form of control and domination, but also one which is directly focused on the reorganising of people's psychologies. As the main character in *Firebug* (1961) claims:

lately, some of those head-shrinkers have adopted safe-cracking tactics, boring into the skull with chisels. Nothing's really inviolate anymore. You can't hide anything, they always find out ...[43]

If the ability to 'penetrate' the mysteries of the human mind can prove useful in the detection of the new breed of psychological killer, it can also be the problem, controlling people's psychological processes and creating the very crisis of identity which preoccupies most of Bloch's stories.

As a result, Bloch not only has a very ambivalent attitude to psychoanalysis, but also to adjustment and conformity. At one level, the killer is clearly a menace within his stories, a menace which must be contained and controlled, but they also frequently provide a critique of 'normality' which is both pertinent and convincing. For example, in *The Scarf*, Dan attacks psychoanalysis and argues that the non-adjusted often cope better with life than the supposedly well-adjusted citizen. This claim may be partly undercut by his own agonised inability to control his own murderous impulses, but he still presents a convincing case that the well-adjusted person lives in a world of misery in which 'success' comes before happiness.

In *The Will to Kill*, on the other hand, Tom Kendell is desperately trying to adjust. He no longer wants to be seen as a 'freak', but wants to conform instead. But this pursuit does not bring him happiness either. It is presented as an attempt which requires him to put up with a series of miseries from drinking bad coffee to hanging out in places which he cannot stand. This pursuit is even virtually identified as an attempt to annihilate or repress the self, and this aspect becomes clear when he discusses his habit of frequenting *Swanee's*, one of the places which he hates. As he puts it:

> I'd learned to conform, and when you conform you go to places like Swanee's where the lights are bright and the music loud – so loud you can't hear yourself think.
>
> There must be thousands of places like Swanee's scattered all over the country, and they all have the same atmosphere. When you go in, you can't hear yourself think, and that's the big secret of their success: nobody wants to hear himself think anymore.[44]

As a result, while the representatives of the non-conformist and non-adjusted may be presented as compulsive killers in certain cases, the agents of adjustment and conformity are usually unappealing, too. Ruppert, the psychoanalyst in *The Scarf*, seems cold and unfeeling, and Jim Whittacker in *The Dead Beat* is continually undermined by the novel. He is a self-important prig who, for all his talk about the analysis of youth, cannot understand his own daughter or see what is going on under his own nose.

Another recurring concern within Bloch's fiction is the figure of the military. As has been argued, the killer in *Night-World* despises society's hypocritical attitude towards killing in which it is required in wartime and forbidden in peacetime. It is also the militarism of the American government which Larry Fox, in *The Dead Beat*, uses to illustrate that his elders do not deserve his respect. In many other stories, Bloch also criticises the dangers and horrors of militarism. For example, 'Daybroke' (1958) describes a vast panorama of Americans who lie dead in their homes after a war in which 'millions upon millions' have died. However, at the end of the story, the focus shifts to a surviving general whose face is 'gleeful and exultant' as he ignores the carnage and declares proudly and triumphantly: 'We won!'[45]

Indeed the psychologist in *The Couch* sees 'the real contributors to the cult of violence' in America as

the bored D.I.'s [drill instructors] in the camp down the Coast, barking at the boots: 'Now take that goddam friggin' bayonet and lemme see you stick it in his guts – forget it's a dummy, give it to him –'[46]

This concern is also a feature of *The Will to Kill* in which Tom Kendell's psychological problems go back to his experiences as a soldier during the Korean War, but his problems are not presented as unique or individual. As Mingo claims:

During the past several years [presumably since the Korean War], I've been struck by the number of cases in which ex-soldiers have literally run *amok*, you might say. They all seem to follow the same pattern. Breakdown, confinement, discharge – followed by a period of seemingly normal adjustment to civilian life. Then, suddenly, something snaps. And they kill, in blind berserk fury. Wives, mothers, sweethearts, children, strangers. During one year alone the clippings bureaus have supplied me with over a hundred items.[47]

Within Bloch's fiction, the army not only shows little or no concern for the welfare of the population which it claims to be defending, but actually transforms its own personnel into virtual automatons who are programmed to kill and are sometimes unable to repress the impulse even once they have returned home.

Robert Bloch's *Psycho*

Within this context, Robert Bloch's *Psycho* appears to be less of a radical break within horror than the product of a series of different tendencies within the genre. Indeed, while many have tended to dismiss the novel in favour of Hitchcock's film version of the story, Bloch's novel was a significant contribution. Not only was it well received prior to the film version, but, as Les Daniels has argued:

> it would be ridiculous to deny the brilliance of Hitchcock's work, ... [but] it is equally absurd to suggest, as some commentators have, that the director somehow succeeded in making a silk purse out of a sow's ear. Bloch's novel is an indisputable tour de force, the distillation of twenty-five years of experience and experimentation: it provided not only the plot for the movie, but many of the clever little touches most critics assume are Hitchcock's own.[48]

Despite the introduction of Norman Bates in the first chapter, the novel still presents Mary Crane's story with enough sympathy and detail that her murder comes as a shock and a surprise within the novel. The novel also includes the scene where Mary's car sinks with unsettling slowness into the swamp while Norman watches. It even contains the final scene in which the psychologist's explanation is followed by the image of Norman sitting in his cell after having been finally and utterly overwhelmed by the 'Mother' part of his mind.

The story is now well known. Indeed it has become a part of twentieth-century folklore, and Norman Bates has acquired a familiarity within popular culture denied to all but a couple of other horror monsters: Dracula, Frankenstein's monster and perhaps the wolfman. The story concerns a woman, Mary Crane, who steals money from her employer in the hope that it will enable her to marry her debt-ridden lover, Sam Loomis. She heads off with the money to see Sam, who is unaware of the crime, but stops off at the Bates Motel along the way. There she meets Norman Bates, a man who seems to be dominated by his mother. Mary and Norman talk about their respective problems, and Mary decides that she must return the money. However, before she gets a chance to leave, she is murdered, and Norman, believing that his mother is responsible for the killing, covers up the crime. Sam is unaware of these events, at least until Lila, Mary's sister, turns up at his store and is soon followed by a detective, Arbogast, who is trying to trace the stolen money. The three investigate; Arbogast is killed when he visits the Bates's home in an attempt to speak to Norman's mother; and it is eventually revealed that Norman is a split personality who has murdered Mary and Arbogast while possessed by the identity which he calls 'Mother'. Norman, it turns out, had murdered his mother when he was a child and she had begun to see another man, but he had been unable to acknowledge this crime. As a result, he had kept his mother alive within his own mind, and developed a multiple personality composed of the adult Norman, the child Norman, and 'Mother'. These three identities functioned as relatively discrete identities which were able to talk to one another. As a result, Norman had really believed that it was 'Mother' who had killed Mary, and had covered up the crime under the delusion that he was protecting her.

Like many other Bloch stories, *Psycho* therefore concerns a killer who is driven to kill by unconscious compulsions which he is not only unable to control, but of which he is also unaware. Also like other Bloch tales, Norman's psychological problems are bound up with fantasies of omnipotence and fears of powerlessness. Norman imagines his 'Mother' as a figure of virtual total power while his childhood self is seen as a figure of utter powerlessness. Indeed by making the story about a figure with three different identities, Bloch is able to focus these concerns far more clearly than in much of his other fiction. The adult Norman is therefore placed between the two extremes of mother and child, and desires and fears the positions of both. He is caught in a continual struggle to negotiate a position between the two, between that of complete subject and complete object. Behind the apparent normality of Norman's adult identity are opposed tendencies which threaten to either tear it apart or else engulf it. These dynamics are constantly played out within the narrative in ways that Hitchcock's version does not even begin to touch on. For example, Norman's perceptions of women are constantly shifting between childish awe and adoration in which he feels impotent and powerless, and his 'Mother's' disgust and hatred which gives him some feeling of superiority and control. Indeed, while he is disposing of Mary's body, he finds himself caught between these two positions: that of the 'Mother' and that of the victim. At one point, he begins to fantasise that his mother is going down into the swamp like Mary, but then, suddenly, finds the situation reversed so that he is sinking and 'Mother' is standing on dry land. He fantasises about the first as he begins to identify with Mary, and decides that his mother needs to be put away in an institution, but suddenly this identification with 'the poor, helpless girl'[49] places him in the position of powerlessness and his mother in the position of power over him. It is she who can offer Norman life or death.

Norman is therefore caught in a world of pure oppositions in which he can find no stable, middle ground between omnipotence and powerlessness, and it is this problem which accounts for his misogyny. His hatred of women is bound up with an inability to picture his relationship to them as anything other than dominator or dominated, and his desperate desire to avoid the full implications of the latter.

It is also directly related to his fascination with collecting. His hobby is taxidermy in which he converts animate creatures into inanimate objects in much the same way as his murderous impulses. He converts that which has the ability to act upon him into an object which is his to order and control. However, his collection of books operates somewhat differently for him. By reading them, he can escape from the outside world. As 'Mother' claims:

> You hate *people*. Because, really, you're afraid of them, aren't you? Always have been, ever since you were a little tyke. Rather snuggle up in a chair under the lamp and read. You did it thirty years ago, and you're doing it now. Hiding away under the covers of a book. (p. 16)

But through reading, Norman can also fantasise that he is powerful. He dreams that he is learning to understand, and so control, the universe. As Norman puts it: 'when he read the books he wasn't her little boy any more. He was a grown man, a man who studied the secrets of time and space and mastered the secrets of dimension and being' (p. 117).

However, despite the attacks on Hitchcock's film which claim that it is a critique of 'momism' or the matriarchal family, Bloch's novel is very careful to question whether the real Mrs Bates was actually responsible for Norman's psychological problems. As Sam puts it while paraphrasing the psychologist, Steiner: 'we'll never actually know just how much she was responsible for what he

became' (p. 213). All that Steiner has been able to offer is 'an edu-
cated guess' based on Norman's testimony, a testimony which can
only provide his own interpretation of the relationship between
himself and his mother.

Indeed, 'Mother', the part of Norman's mind that believes that it
is Mrs Bates, suggests that it is Norman who refused to let go of her,
not vice versa. As she claims: 'I don't make you sick. You make yourself sick' (p. 14). She maintains that Norman could have stood up to
her, but that he never really wanted to:

> all you did was whine. And I know why. You never fooled me for an
> instant. It's because you really didn't *want* to move. You've never
> wanted to leave this place, and you never will now, ever. You *can't*
> leave, can you? Any more than you can grow up. (p. 15)

If Norman's 'Mother' is demanding and infantalising, it may not be
because Mrs Bates was actually like this, but because Norman
wanted her to be.

Indeed, as in Hitchcock's film, Norman is not the only character
in the novel who is oppressed by a close relative. Mary is oppressed
by the memory of her mother and Sam is oppressed by the debts left
by his dead father. Indeed, Mary and Norman share much in
common. When her father died, Mary had to take over the role of
mother to both her sister and her mother, and feels that, as a result,
she has never had a life of her own. She is also a split personality,
though not in as extreme a sense as Norman. On the trip to see Sam,
she catches sight of her reflection in the rear view mirror, and it
appears strange and alien. She even imagines that it talks to her and
the experience reminds her of when she 'went to pieces' after her
mother died (p. 32).

She also fears and resents the powerlessness of her social position
which allows men like Cassidy, the customer whose money she
steals, to treat her like an object. Indeed, the stealing of the money
is a rejection of her status as an object as is made clear by the following passage:

> she never forgot that this world belonged to the Tommy Cassidy's.
> They owned the property and they set the prices. Forty thousand to a
> daughter for a wedding gift; a hundred dollars tossed carelessly on the
> desk for three days' rental privileges of the body of Mary Crane.
>   *So I took the forty thousand dollars* – (p. 28)

By stealing the money, she tries to obtain the social power which enables Cassidy to treat her as an object, an inanimate form of property.

Indeed, like Norman, she is also divided in other ways. When Sam discovers about the theft of Cassidy's money, he realises that he really knew very little about Mary. However, it is not just that Mary has kept certain aspects of herself hidden from Sam, but that Sam, like Norman, Cassidy and most other men in the novel, sees women as essentially interchangeable objects. He even mistakes Lila for Mary when he first meets his fiancée's sister.

Mary and Norman are not presented as unique for having hidden aspects of their characters from others. As Sam also notes, there are many examples, even in a small town like Fairvale, of people who have performed actions which have confounded the community's sense of who they were and what they were like. In this way, Bloch also places his novel within the context of the modern world, a world composed of isolated strangers who know little of one another, a world in which other people are unpredictable and hence potential threats.

However, Mary is also like Norman to the extent that she cannot even predict or understand her own actions. She believes that 'she *must* have gone crazy' to have taken the money (p. 47). She comes to see the theft as something alien to her, an impulsive action over which she had little or no conscious control. But it is also an act which is clearly placed within the context of the modern world, within particular systems of economic and gender inequalities. Mary does not just steal the money because of the power which it enables Cassidy to exercise over her, but also because she desperately wants to marry. Within the novel, Mary's fear of being 'left on the shelf' is emphasised much more than in the film. She believes that she has missed out on life, but also that she is nearly past marriageable age. She is already twenty-nine, well past the average age by which women married in the 1950s, and she fears that without marriage she will have no identity or security; that she will be at the mercy of men like Cassidy. Mary's theft is not an attack on patriarchy, but a last desperate attempt to conform, to fulfil the role which she believes her mother and her society would expect of her. Mary's unconscious impulses are the product of internalised social norms to which she feels compelled to conform.

Norman's impulses are somewhat different. They remain strange and largely unexplained. However, Norman is in retreat from the world of 'development': adulthood and modernity. He is caught between a desire for omnipotence and a fear of growing up. This may be partly due to a realisation that with adulthood comes not the assertion of self, but rather conformity to social norms. He is also scared of other people, and frightened of the hostile and impersonal world which exists outside the family circle. It is, after all, the introduction of a stranger into the family home which prompts his first murders and his own psychological problems.

Robert Bloch, television and *Alfred Hitchcock Presents*

As a result, *Psycho* can be seen to emerge out of a series of long-running preoccupations within Bloch's writing. Hitchcock's decision to make a film of the novel was, on the other hand, despite critical hindsight, something of a break with his earlier film career. If promotions for *The Birds* assumed a strong association between Hitchcock and horrific tales of terror, it was not simply due to *Psycho*. Indeed, *Psycho* itself was promoted less as a film by the director of *North By Northwest* (1959), *Vertigo* (1958) or *Rear Window* (1954), and more as a film from 'Alfred Hitchcock', the figure who brought television audiences *Alfred Hitchcock Presents*. The film was not even made with Hitchcock's usual motion picture unit, but with the crew from this series, a choice of personnel which created a greater continuity of visual style with the series than with his film productions. Furthermore, as Thomas Schatz has argued:

> The highlight of the ad campaign was an elaborate movie trailer in which Hitchcock, playing off his TV monologues, conducted a tour of the Bates Motel and the ominous mansion nearby, describing just enough of the story to tantalize the viewer.[50]

These features are significant because, like Bloch's fiction, the series had developed a similar hybrid of thriller and horror in which the sinister and terrifying lurked within the everyday. Indeed between 1955 and 1961, Bloch himself had written a number of scripts for the series. When one re-examines *Psycho* in terms of the series, it begins to look like a fairly predictable development, rather than either a radical break in horror or a simple continuation of Hitchcock's film career. Indeed, the film looks very much like an extended episode of the series, with the exception of the sexually explicit and violent elements which would have had to have been toned down for the small screen.

Notes

1 See, for example, Lin Carter, ed., *The Mysteries of the Worm: All the Cthulhu Mythos Stories of Robert Bloch* (New York: Zebra, 1981).
2 Robert Bloch, 'Almost Human' (1943), in *Final Reckonings: The Complete Stories of Robert Bloch Vol. I* (New York: Citadel, 1987).
3 Robert Bloch, 'Dead-End Doctor', in *Final Reckonings*.
4 Robert Bloch, 'Yours Truly, Jack the Ripper' (1943), in *The Opener of the Way* (Jersey, Channel Islands: Neville Spearman, 1974).
5 Robert Bloch, *Night of the Ripper* (1984) (New York: Tor, 1986).
6 Robert Bloch, *The Scarf* (New York: Dial, 1947), p. 244.
7 Robert Bloch, *The Kidnapper* (1954) (New York: Tor, 1988).
8 Robert Bloch, *American Gothic* (1974) (New York: Tor, 1987).
9 Robert Bloch, 'The Suicide in the Study' (1935), in *Mysteries of the Worm*.
10 Robert Louis Stevenson, *The Strange Case of Dr Jekyll and Mr Hyde* (1886) (Harmondsworth: Penguin, 1979).
11 Robert Bloch, 'Lucy Comes to Stay' (1952), in *Final Reckonings*.
12 Robert Bloch, 'The Real Bad Friend' (1957), in *Bitter Ends: The Complete Stories of Robert Bloch Vol. II* (New York: Citadel, 1990).
13 Bloch, *The Scarf*, p. 120.
14 Robert Bloch, *The Will to Kill* (1954), in *Screams* (Los Angeles: Underwood Miller, 1989), p. 12.
15 Bloch, *The Scarf*, pp. 35–6.
16 *Ibid.*, p. 128.
17 *Ibid.*, p. 244.
18 Bloch, *The Will to Kill*, p. 15.
19 Robert Bloch, 'The Hungry Eye' (1959), in *Bitter Ends*, p. 234.
20 Robert Bloch, *The Kidnapper* (1954) (New York: Tor, 1988), p. 97.
21 Robert Bloch, *The Couch* (London: Fredrick Muller, 1962).
22 Robert Bloch, *Night-World* (1972) (New York: Tor, 1986); *The Night of the Ripper*; and Robert Bloch and Andre Norton, *The Jekyll Legacy* (New York: Tor, 1990).
23 Robert Bloch, *Ladies' Day* (1968) (New York: Belmont Tower, 1974), p. 172.
24 *Ibid.*, p. 140–2.
25 Robert Bloch, 'Imagination and Modern Social Criticism', in Basil Davenport *et al.*, *The Science Fiction Novel: Imagination and Social Criticism* (Chicago: Advent, 1969), p. 100.
26 *Ibid.*, p. 101.

27 *Ibid.*, p. 109.
28 *Ibid.*, p. 112.
29 Robert Heinlein, quoted in Bloch, *Ibid.*, p. 113.
30 Bloch, 'Imagination and Modern Social Criticism', pp. 112–13.
31 *Ibid.*, p. 109.
32 Bloch, *The Night of the Ripper*, p. 284.
33 Bloch, *The Scarf*, p. 175.
34 *Ibid.*, p. 174.
35 Bloch, *Night-World*, p. 14.
36 Bloch, *American Gothic*, p. 191.
37 See, Walter Benjamin, *Charles Baudelaire: A Lyric Poet in the Era of High Capitalism* (London: Verso, 1968).
38 Bloch, *The Scarf*, p. 44.
39 Bloch, *The Kidnapper*, pp. 183–4.
40 Robert Bloch, *The Dead Beat* (1959) (London: Robert Hale, 1961), p. 76.
41 Robert Bloch, *Spidersweb* (New York: Ace, 1954).
42 Robert Bloch, 'The Screaming People' (1959), in *Bitter Ends.*
43 Robert Bloch, *Firebug* (1961) (New York: Tor, 1988), p. 18.
44 Bloch, *The Will to Kill*, p. 18.
45 Robert Bloch, 'Daybroke' (1958), in *Bitter Ends*, p. 128.
46 Bloch, *The Couch*, p. 87.
47 Bloch, *The Will to Kill*, p. 86.
48 Les Daniels, 'Robert Bloch' E. F. Bleiler, ed., in *Supernatural Fiction Writers: Fantasy and Horror* (New York: Scribner's, 1985), p. 904–5.
49 Robert Bloch, *Psycho* (1959) (New York: Tor, 1989), p. 75.
50 Thomas Schatz, *The Genius of the System: Hollywood Film-making in the Studio Era* (New York: Simon & Schuster, 1989), p. 489.

The victim turned victimiser: Vincert Price as Medina in *The Pit and the Pendulum* (1961).

Chapter 8

The crisis of identity and the American gothic revival:
from *Forbidden Planet* to the films of Roger Corman

Science fiction/horror and the crisis of identity

In horror films, the crisis of identity can be traced back at least as far as *Forbidden Planet* (1956). This film may seem an odd place to start. It is a science fiction/horror film of the mid-1950s. However, unlike most other science fiction/horror films of the period, it is neither concerned with alien invaders nor with the figure of the outsider. Instead it involves a space-craft on a routine patrol of colonised planets which arrives at Altair 420 to check up on a party of colonists who had settled on the planet a couple of decades before. On the planet they find Edwin Morbius and his daughter, Alta, to be the only humans still alive. Morbius warns of a dangerous 'planetary force' which had killed all the members of the original party, with the exception of himself and his wife. But none the less, he insists that while there is danger for the crew of the space-craft, he and his daughter are perfectly happy and need no assistance.

The captain is suspicious, however, and maintains that the circumstances require him to remain on the planet until he can get further orders from his superiors. Then, just as Morbius has warned, a strange force begins to attack the ship. One night something enters the vessel unseen and destroys valuable equipment, and later it enters and tears one man limb from limb. Security measures are taken, but they prove routinely useless.

In the process, Morbius becomes increasingly suspect. He is revealed to be hiding secrets not only from the crew, but from humanity itself, and it becomes increasingly clear that behind his guise as a liberal intellectual, he is really an egomanical elitist.

On the planet, he has discovered the remains of an ancient, noble and extinct civilisation, the Krel, and he has been spending his time uncovering their secrets. Thousands of years more advanced than even the human society of this science fiction/horror tale, the Krel had planned and built a vast complex of almost infinite power which was designed to grant them the power of *'pure* creation' or creation by mere thought. Whatever they imagined would gain physical substance. However, for some reason, the Krel had become extinct and Morbius considers their wisdom to be too advanced for ordinary mortals. He has used their machines and one of them has boosted his already colossal intelligence. As a result, he feels qualified to decide what Krel knowledge should be passed on to humanity as a whole and what should be kept from them.

Eventually, the captain and the ship's doctor decide that they must use the brain booster in order to solve the mystery of the monstrous 'planetary force'. Recognising the risks involved, the captain insists that he must use the brain booster on himself, but when he is distracted by Alta, with whom he has fallen in love, the doctor takes the opportunity to accept the risks himself.

When he returns, the doctor is dying, but he has managed to solve the mystery. Morbius has been 'too close' to understand what is going on, and the threat is really 'monsters from the id'. The captain doesn't understand this reference, but Morbius does, at least in part. He explains that the id is 'An obsolete term once used to describe the elementary structure of the subconscious.'

However, his callous disregard for the doctor's death finally allows Alta to resolve her own conflicts. She loves the captain, but is also loyal to her father. But when Morbius shows contempt for the doctor's life, she rejects her father. He reacts angrily and makes vague references to the punishment which she will face, but the threat of punishment comes more swiftly and more menacingly than he has anticipated, and the monstrous 'planetary force' begins to attack their home. The captain tries desperately to make Morbius see that the monster is really himself, a manifestation of his own unconscious rage which has been given shape by the Krel technology with which he has unknowingly connected himself. As the captain puts it, 'That thing out there is you!'

Eventually Morbius recognises the truth of the captain's claims and tries to deny his monstrous, unconscious creation, but such a denial can only logically end in his death. As his unconscious, it can only die if Morbius dies also and, indeed, the film never makes it clear whether Morbius is killed at the hands of his own creation as the conscious and the unconscious literally destroy one another, or whether in willing the death of his own unconscious, the Krel technology fulfils his wish by ending his life.

As a result, the film deals directly with the crisis of identity in so far as the monstrous 'planetary force' is revealed to be a manifestation of Morbius's own unconscious mind and one which he is not only unable to control, but which he doesn't even recognise as himself. Like Norman Bates, he finds that the monster is not external to himself, but a facet of his own internal psychology.

If this film does present the 'monsters from the id' as the natural, pre-civilised and elemental aspects of human ('the beast, the mindless primitive' as Morbius puts it), the film does not, as Biskind claims, suggest that the problem is that people are not rational enough; that 'people are still imperfect, insufficiently machinelike'.[1] Indeed, Biskind is unable to unravel the specific way in which the film presents the problem, and this leads him into several contradictory claims. For example, he argues that Morbius's world is a utopian 'Garden of Eden' in which Alta exists outside culture in a naive, innocent promiscuity. However, it is worth noting that while Alta does exist in harmony with the animals of the natural world, she does not treat the men as a naive innocent. Her behaviour is not defined as inappropriate because it is uncivilised, but because it is entirely too civilised. She treats the men entirely rationally. She describes them as 'specimens' and does not kiss them out of lust (at least initially), but out of a detached, scientific interest. Her problem is that, as her father's child, she has no understanding of the emotions. As the captain puts it at one moment, 'No feelings. No emotions. Nothing human would ever enter your mind.'

Indeed, Morbius's problem is that like the Krel, he regards rationality as the highest virtue and dismisses as 'primitive' those whom he regards as less intelligent than himself. He also admires the Krel for their scientific rationality and sees them as therefore superior to humans. However, like the Krel, his mistake is that he has lost touch with the emotional world of the unconscious and not only does this make him tyrannical and callous, but it also means that he cannot understand or even acknowledge his own feelings, feelings which emerge as monstrous, destructive and other. It is his privileging of the rational and his disavowal of the unconscious which eventually destroys him, just as it had destroyed his precious Krel. In this way, the film at least hints that the unconscious need not be inherently monstrous, but may only become so if it is disavowed and repressed.

Indeed, the film positively endorses the emotions through its love plot in which Alta must learn to stop seeing men and sex in purely scientific terms, and must appreciate the importance of emotional relationships. It is not simply a lesson to be learned by women, nor one which is simply designed to confine them to the domestic sphere. The captain also learns the value of love and the importance of the imagination. When the ship is first entered by the monster, he dismisses the comments of one crew member who has heard the monster in his sleep. In response he barks out an order: 'I'll have less dreaming aboard this ship!'

Indeed dreams are central to the film. The monster attacks the ship while Morbius sleeps, and the doctor describes it as a 'nightmare' long before he realises the literal truth of this remark. Dreams are therefore not irrelevant and unimportant, as the captain seems to believe in the early parts of the film, but they are forces with real power and significance. Indeed, the division between dreams and reality are continually undermined throughout the film. Not only is the Krel's technology one which will literally realise the imagination as material substance, but their own rationality, like that of Morbius, is itself based on a delusion. If, as Morbius claims, the Krel are an 'all but divine race', their mistake (and his) is to accept this position a little too literally. As the captain says at the end of the film, the story of Morbius and the Krel exists to 'remind us that we are, after all, not God'.

However, the issue of religion creates problems within the film. On the one hand, the introduction of religious concerns seems to divert the film from some of its more interesting suggestions. Most particularly, the film seems to end up in a religious compromise between the 'base primitivism' which is the unconscious and the hubris of rationality which threatens to usurp God's rightful authority. If Morbius's worship of rationality has made him lose touch with the unconscious, the captain also claims, 'we're all part monster in our unconscious. That's why we have laws and religion.' However, this statement has awkward implications for the film. It not only suggests that humans must repress the irrational for social survival, but also that God may actually be a human creation designed to achieve this end. But if God is merely a human creation designed to organise the emotions, then humans cannot usurp His power.

Indeed, the threat of hubris is presented quite differently. While the captain and the doctor are shown around the Krel complex, the film tries to elicit a sense of awe at the vast scale of this creation. But it is also a sense of awe which involves a sense of terror and unease. The scale of the complex literally dwarfs the human and while the complex does have a specific, limited size, the film makes it appear to be virtually endless. This is partly conveyed, as Telotte has noted, through the film's continual references to the powers of reproduction, a feature which is also present in the design of the complex.[2] Indeed the energy which is generated by the complex is, as Morbius emphasises, 'raised almost to the power of infinity'. Also when

Morbius reveals the source of this energy, it turns out to be a series of atomic reactors on which the humans cannot look. Instead they must face a mirror, a reference which Morbius makes clear when he states: 'Man does not behold the Gorgon and live.' These issues are still further extended in relation to the brain-booster, a machine which is so powerful that it not only kills the doctor, but has also killed one of the original colonists and even placed Morbius in an extended state of unconsciousness on his first encounter with it. Indeed, when Morbius encounters the doctor's dying body, he alienates his daughter by saying: 'As though his apes brain could contain the wisdom of the Krel.' It is the scale of science which is therefore horrifying. It overwhelms the human body and mind, and induces a sense of sublime terror.

However, if this film does raise the possibility that Morbius's unconscious is only monstrous due to his repression of it, the film does not deal with the sense, found in later films, that the uncon-scious is itself the product of broader social forces which determine the individual. It does provoke anxieties about the crisis of identity in which the monster comes from inside rather than from outside the individual, but it does not provoke anxieties about the ways in which systems of rational control may be manipulating the uncon-scious itself. What is more, later films discarded the film's science fiction trappings, and located the crisis of identity more firmly with the everyday world of 1950s America.

From science fiction to psychological horror

One of the major influences upon this shift was H. G. Clouzot's *Les Diaboliques* (1955), a film which has also been seen as a major influ-ence on Alfred Hitchcock's *Psycho*. The film was based on a novel by Pierre Boileau and Thomas Narcejac who first suggested Hitch-cock as a director for the film version. Hitchcock himself chose not to film it, but he did film another of their novels as *Vertigo*. For a subtitled, foreign-language film, *Les Diaboliques* was hugely suc-cessful and influential in America, and it has received considerable critical acclaim as a horror movie.[3] It concerns a young woman who, with the help of a friend, conspires to kill her husband. Unfortu-nately, the murdered man seems to return from the dead, and in a shock-ending, it is revealed that the murder had been faked by the friend and the husband so that they could scare the wife to death and inherit her wealth. John McCarthy sees both the novel and the film as deeply influential upon *Psycho* and argues:

> The ... oppressive air of Grand Guignol gloom, its chilling surprise ending, and its horrific bathroom murder ... would all be recalled in *Psycho*.[4]

Indeed, the film not only influenced *Psycho* but a whole host of other film-makers, particularly William Castle.

Castle's films also shifted American horror away from its association with science fiction and towards an association with the psychological thriller. Describing the influence of *Les Diaboliques* upon his own work, Castle has claimed:

> I wanted to work for myself. But I had to find something sure, something that was virgin territory. I found it when my wife and I tried to get into a cinema to see the Simon Signoret picture *Les Diaboliques*. There were lines all around the block, and it took us days to get in. I decided then and there that I had a wide-open chance at something special. If a foreign horror picture with English subtitles could draw such a huge crowd, think what an all-English-speaking picture could do![5]

The Castle films which followed were small, cheap, and black and white. In *Macabre* (1958), for example, Dr Barratt's daughter has supposedly been buried alive by a madman and the doctor has only a few hours to save her. However, the film has a shock-ending (like *Les Diaboliques*) in which it is revealed that the whole search was a hoax organised by the doctor who is trying to scare his wealthy father-in-law to death.

Despite its thriller elements this film, and the Castle productions which followed, all clearly defined themselves as horror through their imagery, settings and luridly sensational advertising campaigns. Almost the whole of *Macabre* is set in an undertaker's and a foggy graveyard, and like Hitchcock's *Psycho* which followed two years later, Castle's films managed to combine elements of the psychological thriller with the imagery of gothic horror. The killers in Castle's films are not always victims of unconscious compulsions, like Norman Bates, but none the less, they are presented as cold, heartless psychopaths driven by their own need to dominate, and a callous disregard for human life. Indeed, in some films, like certain of Bloch's stories, there is the suggestion that even the killer's calculated and premeditated plots are merely a rationalisation or an excuse which allows them to satisfy their essentially murderous impulses.

Roger Corman and the American gothic revival

Indeed, the gothic aspects of horror received a widespread revival in the late 1950s due, in part, to both the American success of the films produced by the British studio, Hammer, and the success of the television showings of Universal classics of the 1930s, such as *Dracula, Frankenstein*, and *The Mummy*. The major American rival to Hammer was to become Roger Corman and AIP. In co-ordination, they produced a series of seven gothic horror films from the 1960s onwards, all of which were supposedly based on the works of Edgar Allen Poe.

Despite his reputation as probably the pre-eminent cult director, the writing on Corman remains strangely disappointing, and it can be divided into three main categories. First, there is a kind of 'gee-whizz' biographical approach in which anecdotes about his film-making are recited. Often based on interviews with Corman and his associates, or on fan mythology, this kind of writing usually recounts the ways in which Corman made his films on small budgets and used his ingenuity to overcome specific difficulties. There are already at least four books that provide this kind of material,[6] and they often involve an *auteurist* praise of Corman as a director who achieved greatness by struggling within specific restrictions. However, this approach is often at odds with another tendency within this writing which praises Corman for existing outside the established studio system. Hence, these studies imply that Corman was a heroic outsider who refused the standards of mainstream film and courted imperfection, just as mass culture critics had argued was the case with avant-garde films. Indeed, Corman did not just struggle against the restrictions of his small budgets, but actually chose to make his films in particular ways. He seems very proud of his economy, and in the case of *Bucket of Blood* (1959) and *Little Shop of Horrors* (1960), for example, he has said that if the films 'look like they were made on a bet, they pretty much were'.[7] In fact, he made *Little Shop of Horrors* in two days, just to see if it could be done.

Under this gloss of cultural legitimation is also another aspect of this writing; a fascination with Corman's technical wizardry, or his ability to make things work, to invent and improvise. If, in Corman's case, this feature seems to be often bound up with a cynicism about aesthetics, and while it has been claimed that he talks more about how cheaply he made a specific film than about how good it might be, there is none the less the sense that he loves the *craft* of movie-making, and it is this quality which makes these studies enjoyable and informative. When they work, they succeed by conveying Corman's sense of pleasure and humour.

The second main body of writing concentrates on Corman's long-standing role as a man who has found, encouraged and taught several generations of new talent within Hollywood.[8] The list of the so-called 'Roger Corman Alumni' is certainly impressive and includes: James Cameron (*The Terminator*), Francis Ford Coppola (*The Godfather*), Joe Dante (*Gremlins*), Jonathan Demme (*The Silence of Lambs*), Robert De Niro (*Raging Bull*), Gale Anne Hurd (*Aliens*), Amy Jones (*Love Letters*), Jonathan Kaplan (*The Accused*), Jack Nicholson (*One Flew Over the Cuckoo's Nest*), John Sayles (*Matewan*), Martin Scorsese (*Taxi Driver*), Robert Towne (*China-town*), and many others. However, like the first category of writing, this category remains largely anecdotal and provides little real analysis of Corman's films.

Much the same could also be said of the final type of writing on Corman, the largely academic studies of his work. This category falls into two main subsections: those studies produced out of *auteur*-structuralism and those studies produced out of genre criticism. The problem with the former is largely due to its particular theoretical position. In this kind of criticism, Corman's films are seen as working in relation to mythical processes so universal that the critic finds it hard to say anything concrete about the films themselves. The most significant example of this approach to Corman is Paul Willeman's 'Roger Corman The Millenic Vision' which tries to discuss Corman's films in terms of mythologies of time, and examines the ways in which opposition between 'sacred' and 'profane' time operate within his 'oeuvre'. Unfortunately, the generality of this framework provides problems for its application to the work of a specific film-maker (to say nothing of specific films) and as a result, Willeman seems to do little more than spend his time unconvincingly dividing up the films into various categories and subcategories as if he were merely cataloguing an archive, rather than using it for study.

Indeed, the project is further undermined by his own admission that Corman's gangster films present a problem for this approach:

> Corman's gangster films retain less of the mythical qualities which characterise his work in other genres. This is due, in part, to the very precise iconography required by the gangster film, which allows for comments on sociology, psychology and existential philosophy, but leaves little room for paradisiac myths, and even less for the Myth of the Eternal Return.[9]

On the one hand, this admission undermines the supposed universality of the specific myth under discussion and on the other, it undermines its usefulness as a way of categorising Corman's films.

The second subcategory of academic work is largely concerned with Corman's adaptations of Poe. It is this approach which is usually taken in discussions of Corman's place within the horror genre, whether these discussions are primarily concerned with the horror genre in literature or film. Indeed, Corman's reputation as a director (at least, that is, outside of cult audiences) is largely dependent on these films, and even fan writing often uses these films as a way of legitimating him. This situation has created two problems. First, it has meant that his other films have largely been ignored by critics and are only really discussed within fan writing; and second, it means that Corman's status is judged according to his fidelity to the literature of Poe, rather than as a body of work with its own preoccupations and merits. David Punter does try to take a slightly different tack and claims:

> To criticise Corman as an exploiter of Poe seems to me to beside the point: Corman's cycle is surely very much a self-consistent set of horror films, with their own detailed and impressive *mise en scene*, within which elements of Poe are embedded.[10]

None the less, he still tries to place Corman's work within the context of eighteenth- and nineteenth-century gothic literature, rather than twentieth-century popular culture.

Indeed, Corman's Poe adaptations need to be seen as a complex attempt to deal with Poe's different readerships. At one level, it is clear that Corman used Poe, at least in part, because of its literary status. Corman had turned out a number of quick and cheap films throughout the mid to late 1950s, but by 1960, he wanted to spend more time and money on his productions. However, he was also

aware, along with others at AIP, that Poe's literary status could produce a problem, and as Corman has commentated, 'Jim [Nicholson]
wondered if a youth market was there for a film based on required
reading in school.'[11] However, Corman's answer was that 'kids
loved Poe. I had'. He explicitly acknowledged that Poe had at least
two readerships: a cultural establishment for whom Poe was a major
American writer; and a popular readership for whom Poe was a
torrid and sensational horror writer. What is more, it was as a
member of this latter readership that Corman himself had first come
into contact with Poe while he was still studying science in high
school. If Corman wanted to gain credibility through his adaptations of Poe, he was also well aware that he was making films for a
popular audience, and that it was as a member of this audience that
he himself had first been inspired by Poe.

Another problem with writing on Corman is the concentration
on *The Masque of the Red Death* (1964). The film is usually seen as
the best of the series by critics but is largely untypical of Corman's
Poe films. Not only is the central character, Prince Prospero, a figure
of 'promethean defiance' rather than the usual 'doom laden and
enfeebled aristocrat',[12] but the film presents three figures who represent the positive virtues of Christian love and innocence, figures
and values which are almost entirely absent from Corman's other
Poe adaptations. As a result, critics have tended to ignore or dismiss
the more typical concerns of the series and have concentrated
instead on the exception.

Indeed, the majority of Corman's Poe films are directly concerned
with crises of identity. Their central figures (usually played by Vincent Price) are, in Tudor's terms, melodramatic madmen. They live
'in a different world from the rest of us, a world of heightened perceptions',[13] and yet they do so precisely because they are morbidly
aware of their own psychic vulnerability. Indeed, they are not only
aware of their vulnerability, but often seem to actually desire their
own destruction. Products of corrupt families, they seem simply to
lie in wait for the fulfilment of their worst fears, fears that they will
be engulfed by the past; that they will be condemned to repeat the
histories of their forebears.

In *The House of Usher* (1960), for example, Roderick Usher
believes that his family line is tainted and that he and his sister,
Madeline, are doomed to perpetuate its corruption. As a result,
when Madeline insists that she should be allowed to marry her

suitor, Winthrop, and claims that her life is her own, Roderick pointedly asks, 'is it?'. In *The Pit and the Pendulum* (1961) and *The Haunted Palace* (1963), on the other hand, the main characters are possessed by the personality of an ancestor. In the former, Nicholas Medina is possessed by the personality of his brutal and oppressive father, Sebastian Medina; and in the latter, Charles Dexter Ward is possessed by his great-great-grandfather, Joseph Curwen. In other films, characters are also dominated through various forms of mind control. Scarabus uses magic to control both Dr Craven's servant and Dr Bedlo's son, Rexford; and in 'The Facts in the Case of Mr Valdemar' (the third section of *Tales of Terror* (1961)) and in *The Tomb of Liegia* (1964), hypnosis is used to control Valdemar and Verdon Fell respectively.

Indeed, these films have strong similarities to Hitchcock's concerns, even if their handling of them is strikingly different. They seem to be obsessed with male masochism, and like many Hitchcock films, such as *Rebecca* (1940), *Vertigo* and even *Psycho*, there is a recurrent preoccupation with a dead woman whose memory haunts the main protagonists, but who also threatens to return and destroy these men. Indeed, as David Pirie has pointed out, both 'Morella' (the first section of *Tales of Terror*) and *The Tomb of Liegia* have striking similarities to *Vertigo*.[14]

In all three films, the main protagonist is obsessed by a woman whom he believes to be dead, but whom he consciously or unconsciously wishes would return. In *Vertigo*, Scotty (James Stewart) restyles one woman so that she becomes a replica of another (both played by Kim Novak), but in 'Morella', Locke's wife possesses the daughter whom she believes to be responsible for her death and switches places with her. The daughter becomes a desiccated corpse as Morella had been before, while her mother becomes vibrantly alive. Even more striking is the similarity between *Vertigo* and *The Tomb of Liegia* in which Verdon Fell (Price) thinks that he will escape from his obsession with his dead wife, Liegia, by marrying Lady Rowena. But as the casting of Elizabeth Shepherd for both female roles suggests, Fell is actually still trapped by his obsessions. His new wife is chosen for her similarity to Liegia, but is also unconsciously hated because she can never actually be Liegia herself.

However, as Pirie also points out, the handling of these issues is very different. If Hitchcock's films are essentially suspense stories with clear, linear narratives, Corman's treatment is, in Pirie's words, 'spatial'.[15] The films are largely atmospheric rather than narrative in their emphasis, and they concentrate on subtle shifts in a fixed structure of relationships between a limited number of characters. For Pirie, these relationships are essentially all aspects of the main protagonist's personality, but it might be more accurate to argue that the main protagonist's personality is rather a function of these relationships. In Corman's Poe films, the main protagonists are not coherent and autonomous beings which exist independently of others, but are rather internally shaped and constructed by their relationships.

As a result, while these protagonists are threatened by the return of the past, they most commonly fear the ways in which the past has been internalised within themselves. These characters fear a loss of control over their own 'inner selves', and often dread the fact that they may already have lost control without even knowing it. It is for this reason that they seem so sensitive, introvert and inert. Filled with guilt and desires for punishment, they cannot trust themselves enough to act, and long for death. As Nicholas Medina puts it in *The Pit and the Pendulum*, 'I must accept whatever vengeance Elizabeth chooses to inflict upon me.' Nor are their fears groundless. Again and again, their minds are possessed by the past, and they die in a battle with elements in their own 'inner selves'. In *The Pit and the Pendulum*, Nicholas Medina not only fears that he might have unknowingly buried his wife alive, just as his father had consciously done to Nicholas's mother. But still worse is his uncertainty about the various signs that she may have returned from the dead to punish him. However, he is most horrified by the possibility that he may be acting unconsciously, that his own 'inner mind', as he puts it, may be trying to punish himself.

However, while it is often these characters' families which are responsible for their fragile sense of identity and for the powerful forces within their psyches which threaten to destroy them, the films do not place the blame on mothers. The problems are at least as often associated with oppressive father figures. There a number of films that do feature evil and manipulative women, but just as many involve cruel and dominating males. Indeed while Willeman has claimed that the 'motif of the female who assumes a dominating role recurs in almost every film which Corman has made',[16] it would be wrong to see this simply as a sign of his unconscious fears of women. Many of these dominating females are positive rather than negative figures within the films.

In his first film, *Monster From the Ocean Floor* (1954), the dominating female is a woman who is seeking to solve the mystery of a sea monster which preys on a particular village. She is ridiculed by her scientist boyfriend, but when she finally solves the mystery and proves the existence of the creature, he is finally forced to acknowledge that he has been ignorant and condescending towards her. In *It Conquered the World* (1956), Clare Anderson tries to persuade her husband to stop helping an alien being which is intent on dominating the world, but when she fails to teach her husband about the importance of human emotions, she decides to take action herself and goes after the creature with a rifle. While she dies in the attempt, she remains the most developed and sympathetic figure in the film. In *Viking Women vs the Sea Serpent* (1957), on the other hand, a whole tribe of women set sail to rescue their males and display bravery and intelligence along the way. Indeed, Corman's films are filled with active female characters who are often presented positively.

Even those dominating women who are presented negatively are often, like the male protagonists, caught within certain psychological complexes which derive from their situation. In *The House of Usher*, Madeline is sympathetic and powerless like Roderick until she is buried alive by her brother. When she finally escapes from her tomb and is possessed by the Usher madness, her first action is to destroy the family crypt. She has been buried elsewhere and her action is therefore not simply one of random violence. She, like Roderick, is at war with the family which will not allow her a life of her own. Her final attack on Roderick, rather than Winthrop, is also motivated by a similar impulse. In attacking Roderick, she fulfils the logic of both her own and Roderick's desires to escape the family, an escape which both believe can only be achieved through the annihilation of that family. As she attacks Roderick, the House of Usher is both literally and metaphorically destroyed so that it is 'as if it had never been'.

In *The Pit and the Pendulum*, Elizabeth Medina's actions are similar. She is far more of an aggressor than Madeline. She has been plotting with Dr Leone to drive Nicholas mad, but none the less, her actions are telling. At one point, she destroys her old room which Nicholas has carefully preserved so that it is just as she had left it, and most significantly, she slashes a portrait which Nicholas has painted of her. She also chooses to fake her death by pretending that she has died of shock while accidentally trapped within an iron maiden, one of Sebastian Medina's instruments of torture. She can therefore be seen as revolting against the confines of her role as Nicholas's wife and this can also be seen in the flashback sequences in which Nicholas describes their lives together as husband and wife. While she is initially a perfect, fetishised wife, she later appears petulantly irritated by Nicholas's attempts to look after her. Nicholas's problem is not that he dominates her in a straightforward manner, but rather that he idealises her and dotes upon her. He panders to her whims and wishes, and describes how he spent great time and money on the arrangement of her room.

Elizabeth can therefore be seen as reacting against her position of powerless dependence, and she does so by shifting to the opposite position of the dominating and brutal cruelty which is associated with Sebastian Medina. She becomes fascinated with his torture chamber and even when she finally succeeds in driving Nicholas mad, she inflicts indignities and cruelties upon him which, as even Dr Leone points out, have no purpose or function within their overall plan. Indeed, Nicholas also follows a similar course. When he is finally driven mad, he also shifts from his position as a powerless victim to adopt the role of dominating torturer under the belief that he is actually Sebastian and that Elizabeth and Leone are actually his adulterous mother and uncle. Both Nicholas and Elizabeth are trapped within the world of the house in which the legacy of Sebastian Medina only seems to offer them the position of victim or victimiser. Indeed, as David Pirie has pointed out, both are shown at the end of the film to be still alive, but trapped and immobilised within the world of the torture chamber. Nicholas lies immobile at the bottom of the pit and Elizabeth is locked within the iron maiden which she had previously used in order to fake her own death.[17]

Furthermore, while Pirie has seen Corman's Poe films as exhibiting the same unconscious ambivalence about the figure of the mother as Poe's fiction in which, it is claimed, the mother is seen as both an object of love and fear, Corman was fully aware of these psychoanalytic themes within his material. Corman was deeply interested in psychoanalysis at the time of making the films and has even discussed them in psychoanalytic terms more recently. For example, he has claimed:

Horror can be a reenactment of some long-suppressed fear that may have seized a child, even a baby. A dream. A taboo. A fear gets locked in the subconscious. In dealing with suspense at a later stage of development the house can be seen as a woman's body with its openings – windows, doors, arches. The corridor becomes a woman's vagina. The deeper you go into the dark hallways, then, the deeper you are delving into, say, an adolescent boy's first sexual stirring. There are contradictory urges – an irresistible attraction and desire for sex and the fear of the unknown and illicit. The very ambivalence builds tension.[18]

However, while this might suggest a simple male point of view within the films, Corman has also commented upon his interest in female characters and their struggles against male dominated society.

For example, in a discussion of *Dragnet Highway*, he has commented upon the central female character, a racing driver who has been 'barred from the race because she is a woman' and who teams up with a man that is on the run from the police. As Corman puts it:

Its a story about two outsiders. Even then, I was attracted to stories about outcasts, misfits, or antiheroes on the run or on the fringe of society. That theme would recur time and again throughout my directing career.[19]

Indeed Corman has frequently stated his support for the feminist movement, and is well known for the support which he has given to women working within the film industry. As Gale Anne Hurd has commented:

One extraordinary aspect to Roger is that he is and has always been, without question, a great champion to women in film, 100 percent … When I left Roger, I thought all of Hollywood was going to be like that, that women would be given the opportunities and even considered better candidates for the job than men. I think Roger prefers to work with women. I never even realised sexism *existed* in Hollywood until I got outside New World [Roger Corman's film company]. Roger had no problem, continues to have no problem, hiring women directors, women editors, women art directors, producers, writers. Through my experiences at New World, Roger gave me a naive idealism that this was an industry with no barriers to sex or age.[20]

In both his films and his production practices, Corman has created spaces for women.

Indeed Corman has often been seen as a left of centre film-maker. Describing his own formula as a director and producer, he describes his films as 'contemporary dramas with liberal to left-wing viewpoint and some R-rated sex and humour'.[21] However, the precise nature of this 'liberal to left-wing viewpoint' is difficult to define, partly because, as Corman has repeatedly claimed, he has avoided overtly 'socially committed film-making'. Corman often associates this avoidance with his experience of making *The Intruder* (1961), a film about racial prejudice in small town America which was based on a novel by Charles Beaumont who was to write several of the screenplays for Corman's Poe adaptations. The film was Corman's first commercial failure, but he claims to have learned a lesson from this setback:

> I was devastated. I decided, then and there, that I would never again make a movie that would be so obviously a personal statement. From that point onward, I would never go to the audience directly with my feelings. I would make only films that functioned on two levels. On the surface they would be entertaining, and any personal statement or feeling I wanted to express would be on a subtextual level. That way the audience would, first and foremost, be entertained. The film's message would be left as an afterthought.[22]

Corman may have made this decision consciously after the failure of *The Intruder*, but it was a policy which he had been following at some intuitive level throughout his previous career.

Indeed Corman's politics seems to be less a matter of commitment to specific social problems or agendas than a more general philosophical attitude. As has been previously argued, Corman has always been drawn to outsider figures who are isolated from, and misunderstood by, those around them. Perhaps the most obvious examples are Walter Paisley and Seymour Krelbourne in *Bucket of Blood* and *Little Shop of Horrors* respectively, but these outsiders also include a wide variety of figures and groups such as teenagers, criminals and overreaching scientists.

In *The Man with X-Ray Eyes* (1963), Corman emphasises another aspect of these preoccupations. Dr Xavier (Ray Milland) is a scientist who finds a way to extend the normal range of human vision, but it not only allows him to see more, it also makes him see differently. Like many of the protagonists in the Poe films, Xavier acquires a heightened awareness of the world, an awareness that

displaces him from the everyday world and renders him vulnerable
and powerless. He is not only constantly assaulted by the world of
sensation, but he no longer sees the world in the same way as others.
Other people become unrecognisable when he sees beyond their
skin to their organs and skeletons, and the city around him appears
as no more than 'girders without stone … its flesh dissolved in an
acid of light'.

At the beginning of the film, he believes that his new vision will
give him power over life and death, but it actually renders him powerless. He cannot even sleep at night because his eyelids no longer
give him protection from light. As a result, he retreats from the
world and resorts to wearing sunglasses indoors. Paul Willeman
refers to Corman's constant use of eyes as a 'metaphor for consciousness' and to the use of sunglasses as an aspect of this
metaphor. However, he makes a rather unconvincing opposition
between figures with 'extraordinary visual powers' and those who
wear sunglasses:

> The extraordinary visual powers of Paul Johnson in *Not of this Earth*
> [1956] and Dr. Xavier in *The Man with X-Ray Eyes* represent intense
> awareness, while poor vision or the use of sunglasses signifies either a
> decreasing degree of consciousness or a desire to ignore certain
> aspects of 'reality'…[23]

However, both Paul Johnson and Dr Xavier wear sunglasses to protect themselves as do numerous other characters. Indeed it is usually those figures with the most acute sensory powers who are
condemned to use sunglasses as a way of cutting themselves off
from the sensory assaults which the world makes upon them and
hence as a means of controlling their environment. The glasses also
usually highlight their distance and difference from others.

In the process, these characters become outsiders, figures who
have different perceptions of the world to other characters and are
therefore also misunderstood. In this way, these characters are used
to highlight the ignorance and repression upon which supposedly
'normal' life is based. Indeed Corman has claimed that the aim of
most of his films is to 'show that much reality is unreal';[24] that reality is as much a product of *how* we perceive as it is something *which*
we perceive. As a result, Corman often uses his outsider figures as a
way of challenging notions of 'normality'. Indeed, Corman's
'heroes' are often objects of ridicule within his films, figures whose

intervention provoke crises rather than solving them. If the melodramatic madmen are acutely aware of their world, the heroes are
usually blind to that which surrounds them. Indeed these heroes are
usually presented as arrogant, insensitive and incapable of comprehending the world around them. They usually remain strictly committed to a rational view of the world which is, more often than not,
contradicted by the evidence before them.

For example, it is Winthrop's intrusion into the House of Usher
which precipitates the crisis within it. He not only fails to understand the forces at work within the house and tries to force Madeline to leave with him in order to accept the dubious pleasures of
bourgeois domesticity, but he continually fails to take account of
Roderick's acute senses, and constantly causes him pain as a result.
Indeed, as Roderick tries to explain, Winthrop's 'logical mind' is
incapable of comprehending either Roderick's or Madeline's situation or the meanings of their actions. Indeed, Winthrop hardly
offers a very appealing alternative to Roderick. If the story is largely
about the two men's struggle over Madeline, it is made quite clear
that marriage to Winthrop is a quite unattractive option. He continually bullies and invalidates Madeline. He dismisses her fears as
'nonsense' and even in one sequence tries to feed her as though she
were a child. When she refuses to eat, he is angered and tells her,
'I'll have no scrawny women in my house'. Against this mundane
tyranny, the perverse relationship between Madeline and Roderick
looks positively desirable.

Many of the same problems are shared by Elizabeth Medina's
brother, Francis Barnard, in *The Pit and the Pendulum*. His attempt
to investigate the death of his sister, and his suspicions about
Nicholas, place greater and greater pressures upon Nicholas who is
the innocent victim of the narrative, rather than the guilty party.
This feature is taken to hilarious extremes in *Little Shop of Horrors*
which parodies the television series *Dragnet* through its two detec-
tives, Joe Fink and Frank Stoolie. These two figures not only fail to
solve anything, but discuss everything in a cold, mechanically dead-
pan way:

Joe Fink: How's the wife, Frank?
Frank Stoolie: Not bad, Joe.
Fink: Glad to hear it. The kids?
Stoolie: Lost one yesterday.

Fink:　　Lost one, eh? How did that happen?
Stoolie:　Playing with matches.
Fink:　　Well, them's the breaks.

Even the death of a child fails to break these two out of their blank, mindless behaviour.

Indeed, rationality is a recurring problem within Corman's films, and scientists are often presented as arrogant, dominating and destructive figures. In *The Day the World Ended* (1955), for example, they are responsible for the destruction of humanity, and in *The Undead* (1956), the scientist views his female subject as an almost subhuman species who exists only as an object for his research.

However, in *It Conquered the World*, Corman focuses his attack on science. It concerns Tom Anderson, a scientist whose brilliant but outrageous theories have made him an outcast from the scientific community. As a result, when he makes contact with beings from another world, he is easily convinced that the world needs a saviour which will put an end to its 'sickness' and bring rationality and vision to the earth. Unfortunately, the alien is less benign than Tom is led to believe, but Tom fails to see this until the creature kills his own wife. Tom's problem is that he sees human emotions as a sign of weakness and yearns for rational leadership.

In response, both his wife and his best friend, Paul Nelson, try to illustrate the importance of emotions. Clare Anderson points out that his attachment to her is not strictly rational, that he could go out and hire a women who will fit all his 'fetishes' and that there is something more to their relationship, something which is based on emotions rather than rationality. Paul, on the other hand, argues that without emotions there can be no values, that rationality cannot provide the basis for a fully developed life. Rationality cannot provide the values necessary for communal life, but only for the domination of others. As Paul puts it: 'Pure logic works only for the individual. There's no group feeling. No patriotism. No co-operation of any kind.'

None of this persuades Tom, and it is only when Clare is killed that he realises the folly of his ways and sacrifices his own life in order to kill the creature. At this point, Paul makes an impassioned speech which not only privileges the irrational over the rational, but also challenges the values of films such as *The Day the Earth Stood*

Still in which human salvation can only be achieved through discipline from above:

> He learned almost too late that man is a feeling creature. And because of it the greatest in the universe. He learned too late for himself that men have to find their own way, to make their own mistakes. There can't be any gift of perfection from outside ourselves. And when men seek such perfection they find only death, fire, loss, disillusionment, the end of everything that's gone forward. Men have always sought an end to toil and misery. It can't be given. It has to be achieved. There is hope. But it has to come from inside, from man himself.

Unfortunately, Paul is a scientist himself and one who is tied to definitions of 'normality'. None the less, the emotional centre of the film is not Paul, but Tom and Clare. It is these two, rather than Paul, who represent the moral struggles which Paul's speech values. Indeed, Paul is a deeply troubling figure who is so sure of, and committed to, specific institutional and ideological systems that he seems to have little difficulty in killing his own wife when she is taken over by the alien. Ironically, it is Tom whose feelings for his wife are so strong that her death finally makes him see the error of his ways.

Indeed as David Punter has pointed out, Corman's approach means that 'any kind of bourgeois moralism' is 'totally absent' from his films.[25] Those who try to impose abstract systems upon the world routinely fail, and it is those who are willing to struggle in their dealings with the world who are presented sympathetically, whatever the consequences of their actions. Indeed, unlike Hammer's gothic films of the period, religion is usually completely absent from Corman's world. There may be talk of evil, but this is rarely defined within religious terms.

As a result, in *The Masque of the Red Death*, despite the figure of the Red Death within the film, Propero's mistake is to believe in religious frameworks, even if he rejects God. His belief that it is the devil and not God who is the ruler of the universe is finally shown to be as deceptive as the reverse. As the Red Death informs Prospero: 'Each man creates his own God for himself, his own heaven and his own hell.' Even the symbolic figures of death are not determined by some larger moral scheme. They take the worthy and the unworthy, the young and the old. They are merely forces of nature whose actions are entirely arbitrary and lack either meaning or purpose. In this way, Corman can be seen as a liberal humanist for whom values come from humanity itself and are not laid down by some external being such as God. If be does believe in good and evil, the first is equated with tolerance and altruism and the second with prejudice and domination.

However, it would be wrong to give the impression that Corman's films are anything but sensationalist exploitation movies, but as with other areas of exploitation cinema, it is their very disregard for conventional notions of 'good taste' which often attracts cult audiences. If in some cases cult films achieve their notoriety through their ineptness, Corman has probably become one of the most celebrated cult directors because he seems so well aware of the cult medium. His films often revel in vulgarity. His monsters usually look like cheaply made props; the dialogue is often ludicrous; and particularly in his Poe adaptations, his use of colour is wildly excessive. However, all of these elements seem to be carefully managed so that the films appear intentionally camp, and as Punter has argued, it is this quality which makes them cult films.[26] These films require audiences which recognise the conventions being used, and so create a sense of community between the film-maker and such audiences. Both acknowledge the other's awareness of the generic conventions, and so share a common position of distance from, and involvement with, the material. Indeed, as the Poe series progressed, Corman pushed these elements further and further until the production of *The Raven* (1963), an outrightly comic Poe adaptation, after which he returned to a more even mix of humour and horror.

Indeed Corman has often commented on the similarity between horror and comedy. He has claimed that they both operate though a process of mounting tension before they eventually reach a climax and release. However, he might also have commented upon how this process is also related to their uses of the vulgar and grotesque. His films' humour is also related to other aspects of the films, particularly the melodramatic figures played by Vincent Price. Price works so well in these films exactly because he can achieve the right sense of knowing excess in his performances, and it is this quality which partly differentiates his characters from the films' nominal heroes. While Price's ludicrous excesses can create a bond with the audience in which both share the joke, the humour which revolves around the more conventional heroes seems to be almost entirely at the heroes' expense. While Price can play both knowing under-statement and knowing excess to comic effect, the humour of the heroes is almost entirely produced out of the mundane inappropri-ateness of their reactions. In *The House of Usher*, for example, Winthrop comments on the fissure that is threatening to split the house in two, a fissure which is one of the central symbols in both Poe's original story and Corman's film version, and he says, without the slightest touch of irony, 'Don't you think that crack in the wall should be repaired?' Like many of the other heroes in the Poe adap-tations, Winthrop's character provides humour because he is so ludicrously unaware of the environment within which he appears.

Notes

1 Peter Biskind, *Seeing is Believing: How Hollywood Taught Us to Stop Worrying and Love the Fifties* (London: Pluto, 1983), p. 110.

2 J. P. Telotte, 'Science Fiction in Double Focus: *Forbidden Planet*', in *Film Criticism* 13:3 (1989), pp. 25–36.

3 See, for example, Ivan Butler, *Horror in the Cinema* (New York: Paper-back Library, 1970).

4 John McCarthy, *Movie Psychos and Madmen: Film Psychopaths from Jekyll and Hyde to Hannibal Lecter* (New York: Citadel Press, 1993), p. 86.

5 William Castle, quoted in McCarthy, *Movie Psychos and Madmen*, p. 92. See also William Castle, *Step Right Up: I'm Gonna Scare the Pants Off America* (New York: Pharos, 1976).

6 Roger Corman and Jim Kerome, *How I Made a Hundred Movies in Hollywood and Never Lost a Dime* (London: Muller, 1990); J. Philip di Franco, ed., *The World of Roger Corman* (New York: Chelsea House, 1979); Mark Thomas McGee, *Roger Corman: The Best of the Cheap Acts* (Jefferson: McFarland and Co., 1988); and Ed Naha, *The Films of Roger Corman: Brilliance on a Budget* (New York: Arco, 1982).

7 Corman and Kerome, *How I Made a Hundred Movies in Hollywood and Never Lost a Dime*, p. 62.

8 See, for example, Kim Newman, 'The Roger Corman Alumni Associa-tion', in *The Monthly Film Bulletin*, Vol. 52, 622 (November 1985) and Vol. 52, 623 (December 1985).

9 Paul Willemen, 'Roger Corman: The Millenic Vision', in David Will and Paul Willeman, eds, *Roger Corman: The Millenic Vision* (Edin-burgh: Edinburgh Film Festival, 1970), p. 18.

10 David Punter, *The Literature of Terror: A History of Gothic Fictions from 1765 to the Present Day* (London: Longman, 1980), p. 356.

11 Corman, *How I made a Hundred Movies in Hollywood and Never Lost a Dime*, p. 78.
12 Punter, *Literature of Terror*, p. 357.
13 Andrew Tudor, *Monsters and Mad Scientists: A Cultural History of the Horror Movie* (Oxford: Blackwell, 1987), p. 187.
14 David Pirie, 'Roger Corman's Descent into the Maelstrom', in Will and Willeman, *Roger Corman: The Millenic Vision*, p. 66.
15 Pirie, 'Roger Corman's Descent into the Maelstrom', p. 66.
16 Willemen, 'Roger Corman: The Millenic Vision', p. 10.
17 Pirie, 'Roger Corman's Descent into the Maelstrom', p. 54.
18 Corman, *How I Made a Hundred Movies in Hollywood and Never Lost a Dime*, p. 80.
19 *Ibid.*, p. 24.
20 *Ibid.*, p. 235–6.
21 *Ibid.*, p. 181.
22 Roger Corman, quoted in Naha, *The Films of Roger Corman*, pp. 51–2.
23 Willemen, 'Roger Corman: The Millenic Vision', p. 26.
24 Roger Corman, quoted in Pirie, 'Roger Corman's Descent into the Maelstrom', p. 56.
25 Punter, *Literature of Terror*, p. 358.
26 *Ibid.*, pp. 358–9.

The past is no refuge: the now famous Psycho-house in Alfred Hitchcock's *Psycho* (1960).

Chapter 9

Mothers and children:
maternal dominance and childhood trauma in *The Haunting of Hill House* and Hitchcock's *Psycho*

f, as has been argued, many of the texts concerned with crises of identity do not revolve around the figure of the mother or even the family, even those stories which feature a failed separation from the mother, and relate this feature to its main character's psychological problems, need not necessarily be read as misogynist. For example, in 1959, the year before the release of *Psycho*, Shirley Jackson's *The Haunting of Hill House* was published. This novel has become a classic within the genre and has earned considerable respect from critics with no investment in the genre. It concerns a young woman, Eleanor, whose life has been consumed by the demands of her mother, and whose attempt to establish an independent identity fails, propelling her into insanity and death.

However, rather than being read as a misogynist attack on the figure of the mother, the novel has usually been seen as an important example of 'women's writing' which examines the dilemmas of female identity. For example, Judie Newman uses Nancy Chodorow's psychoanalytic account of the construction of female identity to discuss the novel, an account which is frequently cited within feminist cultural studies, and Newman does so to claim that the problem of Eleanor's identity is bound up with her relationship to her mother. For Chodorow and many other psychoanalytic theorists, while the presence of the father disrupts the male child's pre-Oedipal bond with the mother, the female child cannot take the father as an image of identification. As a result, she cannot separate from, and so repress her desire for, the mother. Instead, she must remain attached to the mother and learn to identify with her.

For Newman, it is this situation which accounts for 'the male fear of women [which] may originate as terror of maternal omnipotence ... since [separation from the mother] is tied up with the assertion of gender'.[1] However, while males define their identities through separation and difference from their mothers, females define their identities through their similarity to their mothers. The identities of males and females are therefore supposed to develop through very different relationships to the mother, a situation which produces a very different sense of identity in each. As Newman puts it:

> Girls therefore learn to see themselves as partially continuous with their mothers, whereas boys learn very early about difference and separateness. Male development therefore entails more emphatic individuation, and more defensive firming of experienced ego boundaries,

whereas women persist in defining themselves relationally, creating fluid, permeable ego boundaries, and locating their sense of self in the ability to make and maintain affiliations.[2]

However, Newman does point out that women may also yearn for independence and separation, too.

It may be the case that separation can also produce severe anxiety, and that women 'may form close personal relationships with other women to recapture some aspect of the fractured mother-daughter bond' or else 'reproduce the primary attachment [to the mother], by themselves bearing children'.[3] None the less, it would be quite wrong to suggest that fantasies of separation and independence are simply patriarchal and masculine in character, or that women do not have access to them. As Newman points out, Jackson's novel, along with many other examples of women's writing, ends in the death of the main female character, and this feature is part of a refusal 'to accept an adulthood which denies female desires and values'.[4]

However, Eleanor's problems are not produced by enforced separation, but rather she is unable to resolve her contradictory desires for dependence on, and continuity with, others, on the one hand, and independence and identity on the other. As Newman puts it:

the source of both the pleasures and the terrors of the text springs from the dynamics of the mother-daughter relation with its attendant motifs of psychic annihilation, reabsorption by the mother, vexed individuation, dissolution of individual ego boundaries, terror of separation and the attempted reproduction of the symbiotic bond through close friendship.[5]

Eleanor's problem is her contradictory desires for independence and identity and her fear of being isolated and alone. She yearns to be recognised and acknowledged, but is terrified of being exposed. When, due to the psychic manifestations of the house, the words 'HELP ELEANOR COME HOME' appear on the walls, she reacts with horror and says, 'It knows my name, doesn't it? It knows *my* name.'[6]

Also, as Newman points out, Chodorow's work implies that women's identities involve 'a double identification ... in which they take both parts of the pre-Oedipal relation, as mother and child'.[7] Eleanor not only desires independence and identity, but also longs both to be mothered and to mother others. However, she also reacts violently against these roles due to a fear of being both dependent and depended on. Given these contradictions, it is hardly surprising that Eleanor's identity and desires are doomed to frustration and failure, and that she eventually ends her life in madness and death.

Indeed, if *Psycho* has been accused of being a defence of the patriarchal family which presents the absence of the father as ultimately responsible for Norman's problems, this criticism is actually far more appropriate to *The Haunting of Hill House*. This is not to argue that either story is inherently patriarchal, but only that if the argument can be made in relation to *Psycho*, there is far more evidence for it in relation to Jackson's novel. Eleanor is invited to Hill House because she already has an association with psychic phenomena. After the death of her father, the home in which her mother lived with her two young daughters – the twelve-year-old Eleanor and her eighteen-year-old sister – had been showered with stones for three days, an event which, it is suggested, was an unconscious psychic manifestation of Eleanor's grief at her father's absence. Indeed, later in the novel, Eleanor's happy memories of childhood are associated with her father, not her mother:

> It was the first genuinely shining day of summer, a time of year which brought Eleanor always to aching memories of her early childhood, when it had seemed to be summer all the time; she could not remember a winter before her father's death on a cold wet day. (p. 15)

Indeed, her nostalgia for her father is directly related to her desires for separation from her mother. As Newman argues, girls often idealise 'the father as their most available ally' in their 'struggle to free themselves' from the fears of 'material omnipotence', fears that can result from the close identification between mother and daughter.[8]

Indeed, Eleanor is very similar to figures such as Norman Bates and Corman's protagonists. She too is consumed with guilt about her mother's death. She has desired independence so much that she has wished her mother dead, and when her mother's death finally came, she convinced herself that she was responsible; that she probably ignored her mother's calls for help and indulged herself by going back to sleep. As a result, like these other figures, Eleanor cannot escape her mother who continues to haunt her. Her mother does not return as a ghost, but rather continues to exist as part of Eleanor's own psyche, a psyche which has internalised her mother's opinions to such an extent that she can never be free of them.

For example, while she is packing her clothes for the journey to Hill House, Eleanor suffers guilt over her choice of clothes:

> Mother would be furious, she had thought, packing the slacks down at the bottom of her suitcase so that she need not take them out, need never let anyone know she had them, in case she lost her courage. (p. 41)

Indeed so deeply internalised are her mother's opinions that Eleanor is often uncertain of her own opinions and desires, and consequently, she continually swings between pleasure and horror at her actions and responses.

Like *Psycho*, the novel also begins with a theft. In order to get to Hill House, Eleanor 'steals' a car which she jointly owns with her sister. However, despite this supposedly shared ownership, Eleanor still sees the act of taking the car as one of theft because her sister has insisted that she needs it for her family and that Eleanor will have to do without it.

Once she has taken the car, and begun her journey to Hill House, Eleanor displays other highly contradictory responses. At one level, she is elated by the trip and sees it as one of independence and escape. But at another, she suffers severe feelings of guilt. At one point, she misreads a sign which says 'DAREDEVIL', and believes that it says 'DARE EVIL'. This misreading is clearly presented as a product of her own feelings of guilt, not simply about having taken the car, but about pursuing her own desires. She believes that her act of daring is really evil.

Also, as she journeys along, she fantasises about the sights which she sees along the way. But most of these fantasies are not about escape at all. Instead they are about finding a home and settling down. In this way, the novel already suggests the failures which are to come. Despite her desire for escape, Eleanor cannot imagine independence, and constantly fantasises about belonging. One of these fantasies also draws upon fairy-tales. She sees a square of oleander trees and dreams that if she were to go towards them, she would break a magic spell and discover that she is really a long lost princess who had returned home. She images the Queen, who has been awaiting her return, welcoming her home 'because the enchantment is ended and the palace is itself again. And we shall live happily ever after' (p. 20). This sequence is significant in a number of ways. Not only does its illustrate Eleanor's desire to belong and be mothered, it is also important that she frames this fantasy in terms of a fairy story. Although she also frequently repeats the line 'Journeys end in lovers meeting', she hates 'love stories' partly because her mother had forced Eleanor to read them to her. While Eleanor continually fantasises about being loved and belonging to someone, and while these are often couched in romantic terms, Eleanor uses the childhood narratives of fairy-tales to frame them, rather than the more adult subject matter of romantic fiction.

Indeed, the fantasy of the long-lost relative returns again and again throughout the novel. This fantasy is a common one for children. It allows the child to reject their real parents in favour of ideal parents which enable the child to fantasise an alternative and idealised identity for themselves. A similar pattern is repeated when Eleanor finally gets to Hill House. On her arrival, she finds that she is the first of the group to turn up and she begins to feel isolated and vulnerable. Her fantasies of escape quickly vanish, and she immediately attaches herself to Theodora, the next member of the group to arrive.

Theodora and Eleanor are soon pretending to be long-lost relatives, but their relationship is a tortuous and strained one. Initially, Theodora is an image of independence and freedom to Eleanor who wants to be like her. But this desire is fraught with problems. First, Eleanor's response is to attach herself to Theodora, rather than achieve independence itself, but the problems are still more deepseated. By taking Theodora as an image of independence, Eleanor cannot become herself, but only a mirror image of Theodora, an imitation which is ultimately dependent on its original. This produces yet more problems. Not only does Theodora's presence infantalise Eleanor, but Eleanor is also plagued by her mother's judgements. When Theodora paints Eleanor's toenails, for example, Eleanor is initially excited, but then suddenly horrified and disgusted. Indeed, Theodora also tries to reassert her own independence and resorts to teasing and humiliating Eleanor who is becoming too demanding and dependent. Theodora even emphasises many of these problems when she suggests that Eleanor is behaving like a schoolgirl with a crush.

In an attempt to resolve matters, Eleanor briefly turns her attention to Luke in an attempt to establish something like a conventional heterosexual relationship. Again this ends in failure. Believing that she is 'learning the pathways of the heart', Eleanor tries to elicit an intimacy from Luke, something which only they will share. But Luke's response is simply to tell her that he never had a mother. This response horrifies and disgusts Eleanor who asks herself: 'Is *that* all he thinks of me, his estimate of what I want to hear from him; will I enlarge this into a confidence making me worthy of great confidences?' (p. 166). Her comments imply two related aspects. First, she implies that the confidence offered by Luke is not special or intimate enough, but her response would seem somewhat excessive if it were not for the second aspect. She feels that he wants her to mother him, and that he believes that this is what she wants to do for him. This aspect is made still clearer by Luke's claim that the absence of a mother has left him 'entirely selfish' and that he has always been 'hoping that someone will … make me grow up' (p. 167). Eleanor's response is to reject him by asking, 'Why don't you grow up by yourself?' (p. 167). But, of course, this is also Eleanor's problem: like Luke, she does not know how to grow up by herself.

Finally, Eleanor turns back to Theodora in the hope of returning home with her after their time at Hill House, but Theodora rejects her and so destroys Eleanor's last hope of establishing a stable identity. She begins to lose her tenuous hold on reality. Throughout the novel, there is a confusion in Eleanor's mind between the house, her mother and herself. When one of the psychic manifestations starts, she is asleep and as she wakes, she initially thinks that it is her mother calling for help. At other points, the house sends messages which call her home as if it were her mother calling to her.

However, it is also suggested that these manifestations may not be the product of supernatural forces within the house, but rather that they are projections of Eleanor's own unconscious fears and desires. Just as it is implied that the shower of stones which fell on her house as a child were an unconscious expression of her grief over her father's death, so the events in Hill House may be caused by a psychic ability of which she is entirely unaware. This feature further complicates the questions of identity found elsewhere in the novel. It emphasises the confusion between the outside world and Eleanor's inner self which lie at the heart of her insecurities.

Indeed, Eleanor is trapped in the condition of narcissism, but narcissism is not, as is commonly supposed, a love of self. Rather it is an inability to distinguish the self from the world. As Christopher Lasch claims, the narcissicistic self 'is a self uncertain of its own outlines, longing either to remake the world in its own image or to merge into its environment in blissful union'.[9] Indeed Eleanor not only feels that she is in danger of being engulfed by the world around her, but sometimes fantasises that the outside world is simply a product of her own imagination. Indeed the morning after the first major paranormal event of the novel, Eleanor not only claims that the house 'wanted to consume us, take us into itself, make us a part of the house' (p. 139), but also tells the other guests: 'I could say, … "All three of you are in my imagination; none of this is real"' (p. 140).

As the novel progresses, Eleanor's hold on reality becomes more and more tenuous. After another manifestation, Eleanor becomes frightened and claims that she is losing contact with the world:

> When I *am* afraid, I can see perfectly the sensible, beautiful not-afraid side of the world, I can see chairs and tables and windows staying the same, not affected in the least, and I can see things like the careful woven texture of the carpet, not even moving. But when I am afraid I no longer exist in any relation to things. I suppose because things are *not* afraid. (p. 159)

The 'sensible' side of the world – the world of reason and empirical reality – seems disconnected from her, and her sense of dislocation, isolation and homelessness only increases. But it is after Theodora's rejection of her that Eleanor really finds her relation to reality in crisis.

Earlier Eleanor had expressed a fear of being engulfed by the house and of losing her identity. For example, just after she expresses her fear of losing contact with the 'sensible' side of the world, she says:

> There's only one of me, and its all I've got. I *hate* seeing myself dissolve and slip and separate so that I'm living in one half, my mind, and I see the other half of me helpless and frantic and I can't stop it, but I know I'm really going to be hurt and yet time is so long and even a second goes on and on and I could stand any of it if I could only surrender – (p. 160)

But after Theodora rejects her, Eleanor does surrender. She seems to give up any hope of finding independence or of preventing herself from 'disappearing inch by inch into this house' (p. 201).

Finally, she gives in to the demands which she believes the house is making on her:

No; its over for me. It is too much, she thought, I will relinquish my possession of this self of mine, abdicate, give over willingly what I never wanted at all; whatever it wants of me it can have. (p. 204)

After this moment, she becomes fully infantalised. She plays nursery games with the voice of a ghostly child, and rises in the night to follow a voice which she calls 'Mother'. However, this state is no longer terrifying to her. She now finds the house pleasant and welcoming. She enters the nursery which had previously frightened her, and when she hears the other guests, she runs into the library for protection, a place that had also filled her with dread in the past.

There she remembers the sights which she had seen on her journey to Hill House, particularly the square of oleanders, but she now transfers the fairy-tale fantasy to the house: 'I have broken the spell of Hill House and come inside' (p. 232). Being inside the house is no longer accompanied by a fear of engulfment, but is rather seen as a state of blissful and protective unity. She even begins to imagine that she can feel the others moving around the house, just as she had previously believed that the house could sense her movements within it. She and the house are now one, and it is the others whom she fears, the others who may try and separate her from the house.

However, this bonding with the house is also associated with suicide and self-annihilation. She climbs the dangerous spiral stairway which leads to a tower where a previous occupant had hanged themselves. Eleanor has already commented on this death by playing on the word 'attached' in a manner which associates affection and intimacy with death. Finally, when the other guests manage to coax her down, and decide that she must leave Hill House, she rejects the suggestion and chooses instead to drive her car into a tree, so killing herself. As she speeds towards the tree, she is almost ecstatic: 'I am really doing it, I am doing this all by myself, now, at last; this is me, I am really really really doing it by myself' (p. 245). It is as if she is finally affirming her own identity and independence, but in the last instant before the car collides with the tree, she asks: 'Why am I doing this? Why am I doing this? Why don't they stop me?' (p. 246). In the final instance she is still unsure which desires are her own, and desires to be protected and looked after.

In this way, Eleanor's story comes around full circle from feelings of non-identity, through a struggle to define an independent self, to failure and death. Indeed the novel is filled with circle motifs. The

house is built on a design in which concentric circles of rooms are
built around one another. The library contains a spiral staircase, and
all the main characters end up where they started: Eleanor goes to
Hill House in the hope of defining an independent identity, but only
finds death and non-existence; Theodora comes to the house to get
away from her partner only to return to this partner at the end of
the novel; Dr Montague hopes that his study of Hill House will
enhance his scholarly reputation, but the article which he publishes
about his experiences receives only a 'cool, almost contemptuous
reception'; and Luke, who was sent to Hill House by his aunt in the
hope that it would teach him responsibility and bring an end to his
dissolute lifestyle, finally takes off for Paris, 'where his aunt fer-
vently hoped he would stay for a while' (p. 246). Even the novel
itself is in some sense circular, its last lines being identical to its
opening.

However, the novel does not simply privilege reality over fantasy.
Eleanor's tragedy is not simply that she loses touch with reality.
Indeed, the opening of the novel reverses certain assumptions about
the relationship between sanity and reality. For example, it is stated:

> No live organism can continue for long to exist sanely under condi-
> tions of absolute reality; even larks and katydids are supposed, by
> some, to dream. (p. 3)

Indeed if Hill House is actually malevolent or 'not sane', it is
because it exists in 'conditions of absolute reality' and rationality
with its doors 'sensibly shut'. Insanity and evil are, in this novel, not
simply products of the unconscious, but of some dislocation
between the conscious and the unconscious. A world of absolute
reality and rationality is itself problematic.

As a result, the novel has an ambivalent attitude towards conformity. On the one hand, it is shown to be dangerous and cruel, and
this is no clearer than in the case of Mrs Montague's friend, Arthur,
a schoolmaster whose definitions of masculinity are stern, callous
and unthinking, particular with regards the pupils whom he labels
'crybabies'. Indeed, Jackson was famous for her jaundiced view of
'conformity' which is illustrated by her most famous short story,
'The Lottery' (1948) in which a small town calmly holds a yearly
lottery in order to decide who will be the object of a public ston-
ing.[10] In the novel which followed *The Haunting of Hill House*, *We
Have Always Lived in the Castle* (1962), on the other hand, she

gives a sympathetic portrayal of Merricat, a young woman who has poisoned almost her entire family before virtually cutting herself off from the rest of the world. Indeed, in contrast to the appealing deranged Merricat is her cousin, Charles, a materialistic and unimaginative man, who nearly destroys Merricat and her world.[11]

In *The Haunting of Hill House*, these issues are focused when Eleanor watches a child refuse her milk because it is not in her own special cup:

> Don't do it, Eleanor told the little girl; insist on your cup of stars; once they have trapped you into being like everyone else you will never see your cup of stars again; don't do it; and the little girl glanced at her, and smiled a little subtle, dimpling, wholly comprehending smile, and shook her head stubbornly at the glass. Brave girl, Eleanor thought; wise, brave girl. (p. 22)

However, in *The Haunting of Hill House*, non-conformity is not entirely unproblematic. Hugh Crain, the original owner of Hill House, had built the house according to an eccentric design in which every angle is just a fraction off. As Dr Montague comments: 'Hugh Crain must have detested other people and their sensible, squared-away houses, because he made his house to suit his mind' (p. 105).

However the result is a monstrous object which 'suggests evil'. As Jackson writes:

> somehow a manic juxtaposition, a badly turned angle, some chance meeting of roof and sky, turned Hill House into a place of despair, more frightening because the face of the house seemed awake ... (p. 34)

Eleanor's problem is not simply that she cannot control her unconscious desires, or that she is strictly rational, but that despite her wishes for independence and identity, both her conscious and her unconscious minds have been thoroughly shaped by others, a situation which produces inherently contradictory desires and makes her fundamentally uncertain of what she really wants.

Hitchcock's *Psycho*

Within the context described in this section, *Psycho*'s preoccupation with an infantalised adult who is prey to contradictory desires and unconscious compulsions seems less original than is commonly claimed. It also suggests that the film need not necessarily be seen as an inherently patriarchal attack upon the matriarchal family. Indeed few families are presented positively within the film, and it is not just mothers who dominate and constrain their children's identities. Sam Loomis is unable to marry Marion not only because of his ex-wife's demands upon his income, but also because he is forced to pay off his dead father's debts. Like Norman, he is not simply oppressed by other people, but by people who are no longer present and yet continue to determine his life. As Sam complains to Marion at the start of the film, 'I'm tired of sweating for people who aren't even there.' But like Norman, he is also unable to get out from under the weight of his past, unable to reject the demands of his absent father.

Mr Cassidy is also a case in point. Marion's crime is initiated when Cassidy comes into her office to buy a house. He claims that he is buying it as a wedding present for his daughter who is 'getting married away from me'. However, the gesture is not entirely altruistic. As his reference to her marriage implies, he resents his daughter leaving him for another man and is using his money so that he can continue to exercise control over her life. He will continue to dominate his child's life, even once she is married. Indeed Cassidy also emphasises the shallowness of 'family values'. While he intends to perpetuate his parental control, he is also prepared to indulge his own desires in an extra-marital affair. Despite the remarks by Marion's fellow secretary, who claims that Cassidy must have flirted with Marion because he had seen her own wedding ring, it is made quite clear that the wedding ring was irrelevant. His flirtations were not influenced by any regard for such considerations. If Marion had been wearing the ring, it would probably have made little difference.

Indeed the only family which is presented at all positively within the film is that of the sheriff and his wife. But even their family would be 'dysfunctional' according to traditional definitions of the family. They do not have children, and this point is significant. Not only does it dissociate them from the dominant definition of the 'normal' American family which pervaded America during the late 1950s and early 1960s, it is also essential to their placing within the film. Any association with children and child-rearing would only have raised problems for their presentation as positive and likeable figures. However, their positiveness should not be overemphasised. They may be likeable but they are entirely ineffective. They completely fail to see what is going on at the Bates Motel, and seem altogether too bland and inert to operate as any model of appropriate behaviour. Instead they are, like many other figures within the film, simply pleasant, but uncomprehending, conformists who fail to see the disturbing unpredictability which lies beneath the familiar and everyday.

Nor is it the case that Marion is presented as a threat to patriarchy who is therefore 'evil', or even 'guilty' and in need of punishment. Indeed rather than being 'too independent and domineering for her own good',[12] her actions are entirely motivated by traditional, and largely family, values. She wants marriage and respectability. She wants Sam to perform his traditional role as a man and marry her. She wants him to take on the role of patriarch in relation to her, and so enable their relationship to become one of which her mother would have approved. Indeed, it is not just Norman who feels the pressure of the maternal gaze, but Marion, too. She wants a relationship where they can keep her mother's picture on the wall, and it is only in an attempt to achieve this goal that she decides to steal the money in the first place.

However, the forces of surveillance are not simply associated with the mother, as Creed tends to suggest, but with almost all aspects of society.[13] One of the disturbing features of Marion's workplace is the large front windows which put her on display before the entire street. She is also vulnerable before the gaze of Cassidy whose position as a man and as a potential client enables him to assume the right to treat her as an object for his own amusement. After she steals the money and begins her journey to Fairvale, Marion feels herself under surveillance from the police, used-car salesmen, and even, when she reaches the Bates Motel, Norman himself. Nor are such issues of surveillance simply external. Marion has internalised the gaze of surveillance within her own mind. Her mother is not present, but Marion still feels the need to behave in ways in which her mother would approve, and on the long journey with the money, she continually imagines the voices of other characters commenting on her actions and passing judgement upon her.

Nor is it the case that the film endorses Marion's murder, covertly or otherwise. The readings of the film which make this sequence a misogynist attack on women on the part of the film itself, miss certain crucial features. First, as is often pointed out, the first third of the film is at great pains to elicit the audience's identification with Marion. Indeed even the theft of Cassidy's money is legitimated to some extent by his admission that it is the profits of undeclared earnings. Cassidy himself has no more right to the money than Marion. Furthermore, as Marion imagines the voices of others passing judgement over her, one of them is Cassidy's who promises to retrieve the money or take 'it out of her fine, soft flesh'. It is difficult to see the film as actually trying to position Cassidy's comment as the model of moral judgement.

Indeed, Marion has already decided to return the money when she is killed, and she is in the act of cleansing herself both literally and metaphorically when she is attacked. Nor can her crime simply be associated with her sexuality. As has already been pointed out, her motives are not a threat to patriarchy, but result from an over-investment in its values. She does not even flirt with Norman, or exploit her sexuality in relation to him. To read her killing as a punishment for her sexuality is to claim that women are responsible for men's sexual violence towards them, a position which is never encouraged by the film itself. It is Norman who is attracted to her, not she who encourages his attraction. When she undresses and excites his desire, she is blissfully unaware of his voyeuristic gaze. Indeed, for this reason, there are considerable grounds for the claims of Telotte and others that the film is actually a critique of certain ways of relating to people. For Telotte, the film encourages an identification with Norman's voyeurism (a claim that is questionable) only to highlight the logical implications of the voyeuristic gaze; that by turning people into objects, one effectively denies their humanity. As a result, it is only a short step, it is argued, from Norman's act of objectification to the violent murder which finally denies Marion's right to an independent existence. Indeed, for Telotte, the audience is implicated in this process both by the organisation of the sequence and the final image of Marion's dead eye staring back at the audience.[14] This is not to imply that the film is an unproblematic critique of patriarchy along the lines of Wood and others, but it is only to deny that it is simply misogynist either.

Indeed the death of Marion was not only a shock to its original audiences, who had built up an identification with Marion and did not expect the main star of the film to die at such an early stage, but even on repeated viewings, it is difficult really to believe in this death as final and definitive. Whatever one may know about the narrative, there is still a sense of disbelief and an expectation that Marion will somehow return from the dead.

However, with Marion's death, the narrative shifts to Norman who is not presented as a monstrous figure, but rather as a deeply sympathetic character. Indeed, even once one knows that Norman is actually the killer, he is still a deeply affecting persona. Whether or not audiences know he is the killer, he is still the victim as much as the monster, a figure who is as much at the mercy of destructive forces as any of his victims. Whether he is read as a figure who is terrorised by his mother, or a man who is unaware of the murderous impulses within his own psyche, he is still at the mercy of forces which he cannot control, a tragic and pathetic figure who elicits our sympathy.

Indeed although the entrance of Lila Crane, Marion's sister, shifts the narrative away from Norman to a large extent and towards the investigation into Marion's death, neither Sam Loomis, Lila Crane or Arbogast really operate as points of identification to any significant extent. Indeed, as David Bordwell has claimed of critical responses to the film:

> despite the divergences and struggles for novelty, the interpretations
> of *Psycho* display a high degree of consensus. All critics treat Marion
> and Norman as the primary characters ...[15]

Most accounts whether in popular or academic writing almost completely ignore the later parts of the film up until the psycharist's explanation. The investigative narrative may be important to the structure of the narrative as a whole, but it doesn't seem to be the section in which people invest or even really remember. It is certainly not the section which people tend to discuss in any great detail.

This response is relatively unsurprising. Sam, Lila and Arbogast are all basically two-dimensional characters who are given little or no sense of interiority. Despite the fact that Lila has lost her sister, she rarely becomes a point of sympathy. Indeed the only sequences in which any real sense of identification is ever established are the shockers in which Arbogast, and later Lila, secretively attempt to visit Mrs Bates. The first sequence only really develops a point of identification in order to enhance its shock-ending in which Arbogast is killed, and in the second, Lila only really operates as a surrogate for the audience's supposed desire for an explanation of the mystery. Neither sequence develops its characters or gives any more sense of their interiority.

Much has been made of the ending in which the psychologist explains Norman's split personality and in which Norman is shown, now completely taken over by 'mother', but it is important to note that all these elements are present in Bloch's original novel. However, as with Bloch's original novel, it is also important to remember that despite criticisms of the film, which claim that it is an attack on matriarchy and motherhood, no real evidence is given that substantiates the claim that Mrs Bates is actually to blame for anything. All that is seen of Norman's mother are his perceptions and interpretations of her. Indeed once Norman has been captured and accused of the killings, 'the mother half of Norman's mind' changes. Her voice becomes softer, frailer and kindly. She now sees herself as the victim of her murderous son's behaviour. In Norman Bates's mind, blame has now shifted from 'mother' to 'son'. 'Mother' is not the real Mrs Bates, but rather a function of Norman's psyche. She is a personality that exists in its relation to other aspects of his mind, and shifts in character when Norman is identified as the killer. Like the novel, the film therefore makes it almost impossible to extricate the 'truth' of Mrs Bates from the evidence which Norman supplies. It would have been easy, were the film really an unambiguous condemnation of motherhood, for it to have provided some degree of authorised evidence about Mrs Bates, but none is given except for the psychiatrist's explanation, an explanation that no critic seems to find satisfying or convincing.

However, the issues of childhood and development are also related to other aspects of the film. Norman's motel is a failing business because, as he repeatedly informs people, the highway has moved away and left the motel on a now largely disused road. Indeed, the film makes a great play of issues of modernisation and development. It starts in a large, impersonal city which dwarfs the people within it, before gradually closing in on one small room in which Sam and Marion are stealing a brief moment of intimacy from their working day. Both characters are trapped within their mundane existences. They are faceless people within a vast, impersonal world. However, Marion's escape from the city into the world of rural America proves no more appealing. It is important to bear in mind that while the 'psycho house' now looks terrifying and sinister, it is merely a typical example of an old, traditional American mansion. In this film though, as in many later horror films such as *Deliverance* and *The Texas Chainsaw Massacre*, the old world of the American past is no longer simply a refuge from the impersonality of modern American life, but has become corrupt and degenerate. Isolated from the impersonal world of modern America, it is not a repository of positive values, but rather an introvert and decaying world arrested in an unsustainable past. As Lila looks around Norman's room, it seems to be the room of a child. It is filled with toys and has a small bed in the corner, but this room is not a child's room. The objects within it are worn and decaying. It signifies age and decay, not youth and life. In this film, the past is no escape from the present or future, but simply a decaying realm that has been forgotten by the impersonality of progress.

Notes

1 Judie Newman, 'Shirley Jackson and the Reproduction of Mothering: *The Haunting of Hill House*', in Brian Docherty, ed., *American Horror Fiction* (London: Macmillan, 1990), pp. 121–22.

2 *Ibid.*, p. 122.

3 *Ibid.*

4 *Ibid.*

5 *Ibid.*, p. 123.

6 Shirley Jackson, *The Haunting of Hill House* (1959) (London: Robinson, 1987), p. 147.

7 Newman, 'Shirley Jackson and the Reproduction of Mothering', p. 122.

8 *Ibid.*

9 Christopher Lasch, *The Minimal Self: Psychic Survival in Troubled Times* (London: Picador, 1984), p. 19.

10 Shirley Jackson, 'The Lottery', in *The Lottery: Adventures of the Demon Lover* (New York: Avon, 1949).

11 Shirley Jackson, *We Have Always Lived in the Castle* (1962) (London: Robinson, 1987).

12 Peter Biskind, *Seeing is Believing: How Hollywood Taught Us to Stop Worrying and Love the Fifties* (London: Pluto, 1983), p. 341.

13 Barbara Creed, *The Monstrous-Feminine: Film Feminism, Psychoanalysis* (London: Routledge, 1993).

14 J. P. Telotte, 'Faith and Idolatry in the Horror Film', in Barry K. Grant,

ed., *Planks of Reason: Essays on the Horror Film* (Metuchen: Scarecrow, 1984).

15 David Bordwell, *Making Meaning: Inference and Rhetoric in the Interpretation of Cinema* (Cambridge, Mass.: Harvard University Press, 1989), p. 247.

Conclusion

A bel Ferrara's *Body Snatchers* (1993) is only the latest in a long line of 'remakes' of the 1950s horror classics. Indeed, not only is Ferarra's film actually the second 'remake' of the 1950s classic, but numerous other films have been remade: *Attack of the 50 Foot Woman*, *The Blob*, *The Fly*, *Invaders from Mars*, *Little Shop of Horrors* and *The Thing*. In addition to these movies, many contemporary films self-consciously draw imagery or ideas from 1950s horror: *Aliens* (1986) borrows heavily from *Them!*; *The Stepford Wives* (1974) replicates elements of *The Body Snatchers*; *Jaws* takes visual images from *Creature from the Black Lagoon*; and the opening of *It Came from Outer Space* reappears in *Starman* (1984) and a host of other films.

Indeed, 1950s horror does not seem to have disappeared, but is being constantly reworked and reshown within the present. It continues to have an important place within contemporary popular culture. Not only do 'cult' channels, such as *Bravo* in Britain, frequently reshow the films, but one of the major television successes of recent years, *The X-Files*, continually and self-consciously reworks the narratives of this period.

As a result, it is important to note that while the contemporary horror genre has changed since the 1950s, it has not simply broken with its past. Indeed, the continual attempts to identify breaks within the development of genres has very severe problems. As was shown in the case of *Psycho*, these attempts not only tend to ignore the processes which culminated in specific transformations, but also tend to ignore the ways in which earlier periods are are constantly available for reworking and reinterpretation, and are not simply dispensed with, or rendered redundant.

Indeed, the importance of 1950s horror is that it established many of the preoccupations which are central to contemporary horror. It was 1950s horror, for example, which moved the genre away from its concern with exotic locations and began to place it firmly within the context of modern American society.

However, 1950s horror also continues to be important because of the central and formative role which it had for the writers and film-makers who grew up in the 1950s and 1960s. As has been argued, figures such as Stephen King and Stephen Speilberg continually refer to the horror of this period and regard it as the most vivid and influential example of 1950s popular culture. Indeed, younger audiences often share similar memories, having watched these films on television at an early age.

As a result, while this book has tried to re-examine these films within the context of their original production, there is also a pressing need to examine the contemporary significance of these film, as the case of both *Bravo* and *The X-Files* makes clear. Unlike many other areas of 1950s popular culture, 1950s horror has occupied a central place within the development of 'cult' or 'trash' audiences, an important and well-established section of contemporary popular culture.

Indeed, one figure who may seem strangely absent from this account of 1950s horror is Edward D. Wood, the subject of a recent biopic which was directed by Tim Burton.[1] This absence is largely due to Wood's 'eccentricity'. His films do not really conform to the dominant tendencies within the period, although he does draw upon certain elements of 1950s horror. Indeed, Wood's contemporary importance is not a product of his significance within the 1950s, but of the specific strategies of interpretation which contemporary 'cult' audiences have brought to the period. His significance is a product of the ways in which the period has been reinterpreted within the present.

As a result, while this book has re-examined these films within the context of their original production, there is still a pressing need to study the ways in which they are read by contemporary audiences, and the ways in which the reading strategies of contemporary 'cult' audiences are the product of the differential distribution of cultural capital and the struggles between different taste formations.[2]

Notes

1 For information on Edward D. Wood, see Randolph Grey, *Nightmare of Ecstasy: The Life and Art of Edward D. Wood, Jr.* (Los Angeles: Feral House, 1992).

2 See Pierre Bourdieu, *Distinction: A Social Critique of the Judgement of Taste* (London: Routledge, 1984).

Chronology

1935
Robert Bloch, 'The Suicide in the Study'

1938
John Campbell, 'Who Goes There?'

1943
Robert Bloch, 'Almost Human'
Robert Bloch, 'Yours Truly, Jack the Ripper'

1945
Ray Bradbury, 'The Big Black and White Game'

1947
Robert Bloch, The Scarf
Ray Bradbury, 'The Meadow'
Ray Bradbury, 'Zero Hour'

1948
Ray Bradbury, 'The Earth Men'
Ray Bradbury, '–And the Moon Be Still As Bright'

1949
Ray Bradbury, 'The Concrete Mixer'
Ray Bradbury, 'Marionettes, Inc.'
Shirley Jackson, The Lottery: Adventures of the Demon Lover

1950
Ray Bradbury, The Martian Chronicles, also published as The Silver Locusts
Ray Bradbury, 'The Exiles'
Ray Bradbury, 'The Fox and the Forest'
Ray Bradbury, 'The Long Years'
Ray Bradbury, 'The Taxpayer'
Ray Bradbury, 'The Third Expedition'
Ray Bradbury, 'Usher II'
Ray Bradbury, 'The Veldt'
Ray Bradbury, 'Way in the Middle of the Air'
Richard Matheson, 'Born of Man and Woman'
Richard Matheson, 'Third from the Sun'
Richard Matheson, 'When the Waker Sleeps', published as 'The Waker Dreams'

1951
Ray Bradbury, The Illustrated Man
Ray Bradbury, 'The Fire Balloons
Ray Bradbury, 'The Other Foot'
Ray Bradbury, 'The Pedestrian'
Ray Bradbury, 'The Rocket Man'
The Day the Earth Stood Still dir. Robert Wise
Richard Matheson, 'Blood Son', originally published as 'Drink My Blood'
Richard Matheson, 'Clothes Make

the Man'
Richard Matheson, 'F——',
  published as 'The Foodlegger'
Richard Matheson, 'The Thing'
  The Thing from Another World
  dir. Christian Nyby

1952
Robert Bloch, 'Lucy Comes to Stay'
Ray Bradbury, *The Golden Apples
  of the Sun*
Ray Bradbury, 'The Murderer'
Richard Matheson, 'Brother to the
  Machine'
Richard Matheson, 'Lover When
  Your Near Me'
Richard Matheson, 'SLR AD'
Richard Matheson, 'To Fit the
  Crime'

1953
The Beast from 20,000 Fathoms
  dir. Eugene Lourie
Ray Bradbury, *Fahrenheit 451*
House of Wax
  dir. Andre de Toth
Invaders from Mars
  dir. William Cameron Menzies
It Came from Outer Space
  dir. Jack Arnold
Richard Matheson, 'Clothes Make
  the Man'
Richard Matheson, 'Death Ship'
Richard Matheson, 'Disappearing
  Act'
Richard Matheson, 'Full Circle'
Richard Matheson, 'The Last Day'
Richard Matheson, 'Lazarus II'
Richard Matheson, 'Legion of
  Plotters'
Richard Matheson, 'Shipshape
  Home'
Richard Matheson, 'Trespass',

published as 'Mother By Protest'
War of the Worlds
  dir. Byron Haskin

1954
Robert Bloch, *The Kidnapper*
Robert Bloch, *Spidersweb*
Robert Bloch, *The Will to Kill*
*The Creature from the Black
  Lagoon*
  dir. Jack Arnold
The Fast and the Furious
  dir. Edward Samson and John
  Ireland
Jack Finney, *The Body Snatchers*,
  published in *Collier's Magazine*
The Mad Magician
  dir. John Brahm
Richard Matheson, *I Am Legend*
Richard Matheson, 'Being'
Richard Matheson, 'The
  Conqueror'
Richard Matheson, 'The Curious
  Child'
Richard Matheson, 'The Day is
  Dun'
Richard Matheson, 'Descent'
Richard Matheson, 'The Doll that
  Does Everything'
Richard Matheson, 'The Test'
Monster from the Ocean Floor
  dir. Wyott Ordung
Them!
  dir. Gorden Douglas

1955
Apache Woman
  dir. Roger Corman
Charles Beaumont, 'Miss
  Gentilbelle'
Ray Bradbury, *The October
  Country*
The Day the World Ended

dir. Roger Corman
Jack Finney, *The Body Snatchers*
Five Guns West
   dir. Roger Corman
It Came from Beneath the Sea
   dir. Robert Gordon
Richard Matheson, *Third from the Sun*
Richard Matheson, 'Miss Stardust'
Revenge of the Creature
   dir. Jack Arnold
Tarantula
   dir. Jack Arnold

1956

Attack of the Crab Monsters
   dir. Roger Corman
Robert Bloch, 'Dead-End Doctor'
Earth versus the Flying Saucers
   dir. Fred F. Sears
Forbidden Planet
   dir. Fred M. Wilcox
Invasion of the Body Snatchers
   dir. Don Siegel
It Conquered the World
   dir. Roger Corman
Richard Matheson, *The Shrinking Man*
Richard Matheson, 'A Flourish of Strumpets'
Not of this Earth
   dir. Roger Corman
Plan 9 from Outer Space
   dir. Edward D. Wood Jnr
The Undead
   dir. Roger Corman

1957

The Amazing Colossal Man
   dir. Bert I. Gordon
Charles Beaumont, *The Intruder*
Robert Bloch, 'The Real Bad Friend'

Jack Finney, *The Third Level*
I Was a Teenage Werewolf
   dir. Gene Fowler Jnr
The Incredible Shrinking Man
   dir. Jack Arnold
Richard Matheson, *The Shores of Space*
Richard Matheson, 'The Holiday Man'
Viking Women Versus the Sea Serpent
   dir. Roger Corman

1958

Attack of the 50 Foot Woman
   dir. Nathan Hertz (Juran)
The Blob
   dir. Irvin S. Yeaworth Jnr
Robert Bloch, *Shooting Star*
Robert Bloch, 'Daybroke'
The Fly
   dir. Kurt Neumann
How to Make a Monster
   dir. Herbert L. Strock
I Married a Monster from Outer Space
   dir. Gene Fowler Jnr.
I Was a Teenage Frankenstein
   dir. Herbert L. Stock
Macabre
   dir. William Castle
Richard Matheson, 'The Edge'
Teenage Caveman
   dir. Roger Corman
War of the Colossal Beast
   dir. Bert I Gordon
War of the Satellites
   dir. Roger Corman

1959

Robert Bloch, *Psycho*
Robert Bloch, 'The Hungry Eye'
Robert Bloch, 'The Screaming People'

Ray Bradbury, *The Day it Rained Forever*
Ray Bradbury, 'Dark They Were and Golden Eyed'
Ray Bradbury, 'Here There Be Tygres'
Ray Bradbury, 'Perchance to Dream'
Ray Bradbury, 'Referent'
Ray Bradbury, 'The Rock Cried Out'
Ray Bradbury, 'A Scent of Sarsparilla'
Ray Bradbury, 'The Strawberry Window'
A Bucket of Blood
    dir. Roger Corman
The House on Haunted Hill
    dir. William Castle
Shirley Jackson, *The Haunting of Hill House*
Richard Matheson, 'Advance Notice'
Richard Matheson, 'The Creeping Terror', originally published as 'A Touch of Grapefruits'
Richard Matheson, 'Mantage'
Richard Matheson, 'No Such thing as a Vampire'
The Return of the Fly
    dir. Edward L. Bernds
The Tingler
    dir. William Castle

1960

Robert Bloch, *The Dead Beat*
The House of Usher
    dir. Roger Corman
Little Shop of Horrors
    dir. Roger Corman
Richard Matheson, 'From Shadowed Places'
Richard Matheson, 'Graveyard

Shift' originally published as 'The Faces'
Psycho
    dir. Alfred Hitchcock
The Wasp Woman
    dir. Roger Corman

1961

Robert Bloch, *Firebug*
Homicidal
    dir. William Castle
Richard Matheson, *Shock!*
Richard Matheson, 'Mute'
Richard Matheson, 'Nightmare at 20,000 Feet'
The Intruder
    dir. Roger Corman
The Pit and the Pendulum
    dir. Roger Corman
The Premature Burial
    dir. Roger Corman
Tales of Terror
    dir. Roger Corman

1962

Robert Bloch, *The Couch*
Robert Bloch, *Terror*
Ray Bradbury, *Something Wicked This Way Comes*
Shirley Jackson, *We Have Always Lived in the Castle*
Richard Matheson, 'The Likeness of Julie', originally published under the pseudonym Logan Swanson

1963

The Birds
    dir. Alfred Hitchcock
Ray Bradbury, *Something Wicked this Way Comes*
The Haunted Palace
    dir. Roger Corman

The Man with X-Ray Eyes
  dir. Roger Corman
Richard Matheson, 'Deus Ex
  Machina'
Richard Matheson, 'Girl of My
  Dreams'
Richard Matheson, 'Shock Wave'
The Raven
  dir. Roger Corman
The Terror
  dir. Roger Corman

1964

The Masque of the Red Death
  dir. Roger Corman
Richard Matheson, *Shock 2*
Strait-Jacket
  dir. William Castle
The Tomb of Ligeia
  dir. Roger Corman

1966

Richard Matheson, *Shock 3*

1968

Robert Bloch, *Ladies' Day*
Robert Bloch, *The Star Stalker*
Rosemary's Baby
  dir. Roman Polanski

1969

Robert Bloch, *The Todd Dossier*
Richard Matheson, 'Therese'

1970

Jack Finney, *Time and Again*
Richard Matheson, *Shock 4*

1971

Richard Matheson, *Hell House*

1972

Robert Bloch, *Night-World*

Night of the Lepus
  dir. William Claxton

1974

Robert Bloch, *American Gothic*
The Stepford Wives
  dir. Bryan Forbes

1975

Jaws
  dir. Steven Spielberg
Richard Matheson, *Bid Time
  Return*

1978

Halloween
  dir. John Carpenter
Invasion of the Body Snatchers
  dir. Philip Kaufman
Richard Matheson, *What Dreams
  May Come*

1979

Robert Bloch, *There is a Serpent in
  Eden*

1982

Robert Bloch, *Psycho II*
Richard Matheson, *Earthbound*
The Thing
  dir. John Carpenter

1983

The Twilight Zone: The Movie
  dir. John Landis/Steven
  Spielberg/Joe Dante/George
  Miller

1984

Robert Bloch, *Night of the Ripper*
Star Man
  dir. John Carpenter

1986

Aliens

dir. James Cameron
The Fly
  dir. David Cronenberg
Invaders from Mars
  dir. Tobe Hooper
Little Shop of Horrors
  dir. Frank Oz

1988
The Blob
  dir. Chuck Russell
Thomas Harris, *The Silence of the Lambs*

1989
Robert Bloch, *Lori*

1990
Robert Bloch, *Psycho House*
Robert Bloch and Andre Norton, *The Jekyll Legacy*
Total Recall
  dir. Paul Verhoeven

1992
Charles Beaumont, *The Howling Man*

1993
Body Snatchers
  dir. Abel Ferarra

Bibliography

Primary sources

Beaumont, C., *The Intruder* (New York: Fawcett, 1957).

Beaumont, C., *The Howling Man*, ed. R. Anker (New York: Tor, 1992).

Bloch, R., *The Scarf* (New York: Dial, 1947).

Bloch, R., *The Kidnapper* (1954) (New York: Tor, 1988).

Bloch, R., *Spidersweb* (New York: Ace, 1954).

Bloch, R., *The Will to Kill* (1954), in *Screams* (Los Angeles: Underwood Miller, 1989).

Bloch, R., *Shooting Star* (New York: Ace, 1958).

Bloch, R., *Psycho* (1959) (New York: Tor, 1989).

Bloch, R., *The Dead Beat* (1960) (London: Robert Hale, 1961).

Bloch, R., *Firebug* (1961) (New York: Tor, 1988).

Bloch, R., *The Couch* (London: Fredrick Muller, 1962).

Bloch, R., *Terror* (New York: Belmont, 1962).

Bloch, R., *The Star Stalker* (New York: Pyramid, 1968).

Bloch, R., *Ladies' Day* (1968) (New York: Belmont, 1974).

Bloch, R., *The Todd Dossier* (as Collier Young) (New York: Delacorte, 1969).

Bloch, R., *Night-World* (1972) (New York: Tor, 1986).

Bloch, R., *American Gothic* (1974) (New York: Tor, 1987).

Bloch, R., *There is a Serpent in Eden* (also published as *The Cunning*) (New York: Zebra, 1979).

Bloch, R., *Psycho II* (1982) (New York: Tor, 1989).

Bloch, R., *Night of the Ripper* (1984) (New York: Tor, 1986).

Bloch, R., *Lori* (New York: Tor, 1989).

Bloch, R., *The Jekyll Legacy*, with Andre Norton (New York: Tor, 1990).

Bloch, R., *Psycho House* (1990) (New York: Tor, 1991).

Bloch, R., *The Opener of the Way* (Jersey, Channel Islands: Neville Spearman, 1974).

Bloch, R., *Atoms and Evil* (London: Corgi, 1977).

Bloch, R., *The Mysteries of the Worm: All the Cthulhu Mythos Stories of Robert Bloch*, ed. Lin Carter (New York: Zebra, 1981).

Bloch, R., *Final Reckonings: The Complete Stories of Robert Bloch Vol. I* (New York: Citadel, 1987).

Bloch, R., *Bitter Ends: The Complete Stories of Robert Bloch Vol. II* (New York: Citadel, 1990).

Bloch, R., *Last Rites: The Complete Stories of Robert Bloch Vol. III* (New York: Citadel, 1991).

Bloch, R., 'Imagination and Modern Social Criticism', in Basil Davenport *et al.*, eds, *The Science Fiction Novel: Imagination and Modern Social Criticism* (Chicago: Advent, 1969).

Bradbury, R., *The Martian Chronicles* (1950) (London: Corgi, 1956).

Bradbury, R., *The Illustrated Man* (1951) (London: Corgi, 1955).

Bradbury, R., *The Golden Apples of the Sun* (1952) (London: Corgi, 1956).

Bradbury, R., *Fahrenheit 451* (1953) (London: Corgi, 1957).

Bradbury, R., *The October Country* (New York: Ballantine, 1955).

Bradbury, R., *The Day it Rained Forever* (1959) (Harmondsworth: Penguin, 1963).

Bradbury, R., *Something Wicked This Way Comes* (1962) (London: Corgi, 1965).

Campbell, J. W., 'Who Goes There?' (1938), in *The Mammoth Book of Classic Science Fiction* (New York: Carroll and Graf, 1988).

Finney, J., *The Body Snatchers* (New York: Dell, 1955).

Finney, J., *Time and Again* (New York: Simon and Schuster, 1970).

Finney, J., *The Third Level* (New York: Rinehart, 1957).

Harris, T., *The Silence of the Lambs* (London: Heinemann, 1988).

Jackson, S., *The Lottery: Adventures of the Demon Lover* (New York: Avon, 1949).

Jackson, S., *The Haunting of Hill House* (1959) (London: Robinson, 1987).

Jackson, S., *We Have Always Lived in the Castle* (1962) (London: Robinson, 1987).

Matheson, R., *I Am Legend* (1954) (London: Corgi, 1956).

Matheson, R., *The Shrinking Man* (1956) (London: Sphere, 1988).

Matheson, R., *Hell House* (New York: Viking, 1971).

Matheson, R., *Bid Time Return* (New York: Viking, 1975).

Matheson, R., *What Dreams May Come* (New York: Putnam, 1978).

Matheson, R., *Earthbound* (1982) (London: Robinson, 1989).

Matheson, R., *Third from the Sun* (New York: Bantam, 1955).

Matheson, R., *The Shores of Space* (1957) (London: Corgi, 1958).

Matheson, R., *Shock!* (1961) (London: Corgi, 1962).

Matheson, R., *Shock 2* (1964) (London: Corgi, 1965).

Matheson, R., *Shock 3* (1966) (London: Corgi, 1967).

Matheson, R., *Shock 4* (1970) (London: Sphere, 1980).

Shelley, M., *Frankenstein: or the Modern Prometheus* (1818) (Oxford: Oxford University Press, 1969).

Stevenson, R. L., *The Strange Case of Dr Jekyll and Mr Hyde* (1986 (Harmondsworth: Penguin, 1979).

Secondary sources

Adorno, T. W. and M. Horkheimer, *The Dialectic of Enlightenment* (London: Verso, 1979).

Aldiss, B., ed., *The Penguin Omnibus of Science Fiction* (Harmondsworth: Penguin, 1973).

Barker, M., *A Haunt of Fears: The Strange History of the British Horror Comics Campaign* (London: Pluto, 1984).

Bell, D., *The End of Ideology: On the Exhaustion of Political Ideas in the Fifties* (Cambridge, Mass.: Harvard University Press, revised edition, 1988).

Bell, D., *The Cultural Contradictions of Capitalism* (London: Heinemann, 1979).

Benjamin, W., *Charles Baudelaire: A Lyric Poet in the Era of High Capitalism* (London: Verso, 1968).

Biskind, P., *Seeing is Believing: How Hollywood Taught Us to Stop Worrying and Love the Fifties* (London: Pluto, 1983).

Bleiler, E. F., ed., *Supernatural Fiction Writers: Fantasy and Horror* (New York: Scribner's, 1985).

Boorstin, D., *The Image: Or What Happened to the American Dream* (Harmondsworth: Penguin, 1963).

Bordwell, D., *Making Meaning: Inference and Rhetoric in the Interpretation of Cinema* (Cambridge, Mass.: Harvard University Press, 1989).

Bourdieu, P., *Distinction: A Social Critique of the Judgement of Taste* (London: Routledge, 1984).

Brookeman, C., *American Culture and Society Since the 1930s* (London: Macmillan, 1984).

Butler, I., *Horror in the Cinema* (New York: Paperback Library, 1970).

Carrol, N., *The Philosophy of Horror: Or Paradoxes of the Heart* (New York: Routledge, 1990).

Castle, W., *Step Right Up: I'm Gonna Scare the Pants Off America* (New York: Pharos, 1976).

Caughie, J., ed., *Theories of Authorship* (London: Routledge, 1981).

Clarens, C., *Horror Movies: An Illustrated Survey* (London: Secker and Warburg, 1967).

Clover, C. J., *Men, Women and Chainsaws: Gender in the Modern Horror Film* (London: BFI, 1992).

Collins, J. *et al.*, eds, *Film Theory Goes to the Movies* (New York: Routledge, 1993).

Cook, P., ed., *The Cinema Book* (London: BFI, 1985).

Corman, R. and J. Kerome, *How I Made a Hundred Movies in Hollywood and Never Lost a Dime* (London: Muller, 1990).

Creed, B., *The Monstrous-Feminine: Film, Feminism, Psychoanalysis* (London: Routledge, 1993).

Derry, C., *Dark Dreams: A Psychological History of the Horror Film* (New York: Barnes, 1977).

di Franco, P., ed., *The World of Roger Corman* (New York: Chelsea House, 1979).

Dillard, R. H., *Horror Films* (New York: Monarch, 1976).

Docherty, B., ed., *American Horror Fiction* (London: Macmillan, 1990).

Docherty, T., *Teenagers and Teenpics: The Juvenilization of American Movies in the 1950s* (Boston: Unwin Hyman, 1988).

Donald, J., ed., *Fantasy and the Cinema* (London: BFI, 1989).

Ehrenreich, B., *The Hearts of Men: American Dreams and the Flight from Commitment* (London: Pluto, 1983).

Everman, W., *Cult Horror Films: From 'Attack of the 50 Foot Woman' to 'Zombies of Mora Tau'* (New York: Citadel, 1993).

Ewen, S., *Captains of Consciousness: Advertising and the Roots of the Consumer Culture* (New York: McGraw-Hill, 1976).

Feyeraband, P., *Against Method* (London: New Left Books, 1976).

Feyeraband, P., *Science in a Free Society* (London: New Left Books, 1978).

Friedan, B., *The Feminine Mystique* (New York: Dell, 1963).

Galbraith, J. K., *The Affluent Society* (Boston: Houghton Mifflin, 1958).

Goodman, P., *Growing Up Absurd: Problems of Youth in the Organized Society* (New York: Vintage, 1956).

Grant, B. K., ed., *Planks of Reason: Essays on the Horror Film* (Metuchen: Scarecrow, 1984).

Grant, B. K., ed., *The Film Genre Reader* (Austin: University of Texas Press, 1986).

Greenberg, C., 'Avant-Garde and Kitsche', in B. Rosenberg and D. M. White, eds, *Mass Culture: The Popular Arts in America* (New York: Free Press, 1957).

Grey, R., *Nightmare of Ecstasy: The Life and Art of Edward D. Wood, Jr.* (Los Angeles: Fenal House, 1992).

Grixti, J., *The Terrors of Uncertainty: The Cultural Contexts of Horror Fiction* (London: Routledge, 1989).

Hardy, P., *The Encyclopedia of Science Fiction Movies* (London: Octopus, 1986).

Harvey, D., *The Condition of Postmodernity* (Oxford: Blackwell, 1989).

Herron, D., 'King: The Good, the Bad and the Academic', in T. Underwood and C. Miller, eds, *Kingdom of Fear: The World of Stephen King,* (London: New English Library, 1986).

Hollows, J. and M. Jancovich, *Approaches to Popular Film* (Manchester: Manchester University Press, 1995).

Jancovich, M., *Horror* (London: Batsford, 1992).

King, S., *Danse Macabre* (London: Futura, 1982).

Kuhn, T., *The Structure of Scientific Revolutions* (Chicago: University of

Chicago Press, 1962).

Lapsley, R. and M. Westlake, *Film Theory: An Introduction* (Manchester: Manchester University Press, 1988).

Lasch, C., *The Minimal Self: Psychic Survival in Troubled Times* (London: Picador, 1984).

Lucanio, P., *Them or Us: Archetypal Interpretations of Fifties Alien Invasion Narratives* (Bloomington: Indiana University Press, 1987).

Lukacs, G., *History and Class Consciousness* (London: Merlin, 1971).

MacDonald, D., *Against the American Grain* (London: Victor Gollancz, 1963).

McGee, M. T., *Roger Corman: The Best of the Cheap Acts* (Jefferson: McFarland and Co., 1988).

McRobbie, A., Settling Accounts with Subcultures: A Feminist Critique, in T. Bennett *et al.*, eds, *Culture, Ideology and Social Process: A Reader* (London: Batsford, 1981).

Mailer, N., 'The White Negro', in *Advertisements for Myself* (New York: G. P. Putnam's, 1959).

Marx, K., *Early Writings* (Harmondsworth: Penguin, 1975).

Marx, K., *Capital Vol. I* (Harmondsworth: Penguin, 1976).

McCarthy, J., *Movie Psychos and Madmen: Film Psychopaths from Jekyll and Hyde to Hannibal Lecter* (New York: Citadel, 1993).

Mills, C. W., *The Power Elite* (New York: Oxford University Press, 1956).

Mills, C. W., *The Causes of World War III* (New York: Simon & Schuster, 1958)

Mills, C. W., 'On the New Left', in Paul Jacobs and Saul Landau, eds, *The New Radicals* (Harmondsworth: Penguin, 1966).

Milne, T., ed., *The Time Out Film Guide* (London: Penguin, 1989).

Modleski, T., *The Woman Who Knew Too Much: Hitchcock and Feminist Theory* (New York: Methuen, 1988).

Modleski, T., ed., *Studies in Entertainment: Critical Approaches to Mass Culture* (Bloomington: Indiana University Press, 1986).

Mulvey, L., 'Visual Pleasure and Narrative Cinema', in Bill Nichols, ed., *Movies and Methods Vol. II* (Berkeley: University of California Press, 1985).

Naha, E., *The Films of Roger Corman: Brilliance on a Budget* (New York: Arco, 1982).

Neale, S., *Genre* (London: BFI, 1980).

Newman, K., The Roger Corman Alumni Association, in *The Monthly Film Bulletin*, 52:622, (Nov. 1985) and 52:623, (Dec. 1985).

Packard, V., *The Hidden Persuaders* (Harmondsworth: Penguin, 1960).

Pells, R., *The Liberal Mind in a Conservative Age: American Intellectuals in the 1940s and 1950s* (Middletown: Wesleyan University Press, 1989).

Penley, C., ed., *Feminism and Film Theory* (London: Routledge, 1988).

Poster, M., ed., *Jean Baudrillard: Selected Writings* (Cambridge: Polity, 1988).

Punter, D., *The Literature of Terror: A History of Gothic Fictions from 1765 to the Present Day* (London: Longman, 1980).

Rahv, P., *Literature and the Sixth Sense* (Boston: Houghton Mifflin, 1970).

Reisman, D., *The Lonely Crowd: A Study of the Changing America Character* (New Haven: Yale University Press, revised edition, 1970).

Rosenberg, H., 'The Herd of Independent Minds', *Commentary*, VI (Sept. 1948).

Ross, A., *No Respect: Intellectuals and Popular Culture* (London: Routledge, 1989).

Rutherford, J., ed., *Identity: Community, Culture, Difference* (London: Lawrence and Wishart, 1990).

Schatz, T., *The Genius of the System: Hollywood Film-making in the Studio Era* (New York: Simon and Schuster, 1989).

Skal, D. J., *The Monster Show: A Cultural History of Horror* (New York: Norton, 1993).

Sobchack, V., *Screening Space: The American Science Fiction Film* (New York: Ungar, 1987).

Sontag, S., 'The Imagination of Disaster', *Commentary* (Oct. 1965), pp. 42–8.

Sullivan, J., ed., *The Penguin Encyclopedia of Horror and the Supernatural* (New York: Viking, 1986).

Swados, H., 'Popular Taste and the Agonies of the Young', *Dissent*, V (Spring, 1958).

Tannen, D., 'Relative Focus on Involvement in Oral and Written Discourse', in David Olsen *et al.*, eds, *Literacy, Language and Learning: The Nature and Consequences of Reading and Writing* (Cambridge: Cambridge University Press, 1985).

Tasker, Y., *Spectacular Bodies: Gender, Genre and the Action Cinema* (London: Routledge, 1993).

Telotte, J. P., 'Science Fiction in Double Focus: *Forbidden Planet*', in *Film Criticism*, 13:3 (1989), pp. 25–36.

Tudor, A., *Monsters and Mad Scientists: A Cultural History of the Horror Movie* (Oxford: Blackwell, 1987).

Twitchell, J. B., *Dreadful Pleasures: An Anatomy of Modern Horror* (New York: Oxford University Press, 1985).

Vance, C. S., ed., *Pleasure and Danger: Exploring Female Sexuality* (Boston: Routledge, 1984).

Waller, G. A., ed., *American Horror: Essays on the Modern American Horror Film* (Urbana: University of Illinois Press, 1987).

Watson, N, and P. E. Schellinger, eds, *Twentieth Century Science-Fiction Writers* (Chicago: St James Press, 1991).

Welch, E., *Cult Horror Films: From 'Attack of the 50 Foot Woman' to 'Zombies of Mora Tau'* (New York: Citadel, 1993).

Whyte, W., *The Organization Man* (New York: Simon Schuster, 1956).

Will, D. and P. Willemen, eds, *Roger Corman: The Millenic Vision* (Edinburgh: Edinburgh Film Festival, 1970).

Willis, E., 'Sexual Politics', in I. Angus and S. Jhally, eds, *Cultural Politics in Contemporary America* (London: Routledge, 1989).

Wolf, L., *Horror: A Connoisseur's Guide to Literature and Film* (New York: Facts on File, 1989).

Wollen, P., *Signs and Meanings in the Cinema* (London: Secker and Warburg, 1972).

Wood, R., *Hollywood from Vietnam to Reagan* (New York: Columbia University Press, 1986).

Wood, R., *Hitchcock's Films Revisited* (New York: Columbia University Press, 1989).

Wylie, P., *A Generation of Vipers* (New York: Rinehart and Co., 1946).

Index